D1588593

# Certain People Of The Book

*By* MAURICE SAMUEL

CERTAIN PEOPLE OF THE BOOK (1955)

LEVEL SUNLIGHT (1953)

THE DEVIL THAT FAILED (1952)

THE GENTLEMAN AND THE JEW (1950)

PRINCE OF THE GHETTO (1948)

WEB OF LUCIFER (1947)

HARVEST IN THE DESERT (1944, 1945)

THE WORLD OF
SHOLOM ALEICHEM (1943)

THESE ARE *Borzoi Books*
PUBLISHED BY *Alfred A Knopf* IN NEW YORK

# Certain People of the Book

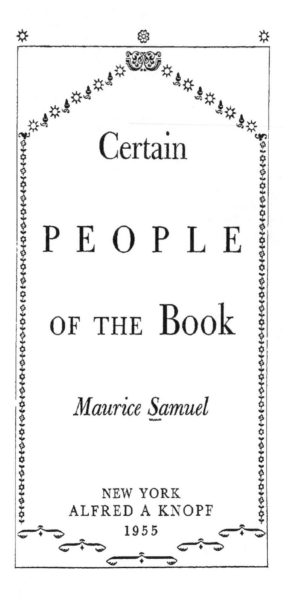

Certain

P E O P L E

OF THE Book

*Maurice Samuel*

NEW YORK
ALFRED A KNOPF
1955

L C catalog card number 55-8887

© Maurice Samuel, 1955

THIS IS A BORZOI BOOK,
PUBLISHED BY ALFRED A KNOPF, INC

PUBLISHED AUGUST 22, 1955
SECOND PRINTING, OCTOBER 1955

v

# Contents

Certain People of the Book

# The Source

❀

THE PEOPLE OF THE BOOK rise to me straight out of the Text. It seems to me that nothing about them is of my own invention. I read and reread the record, and there they are.

Some of them haunted my childhood before I could read, and they came to me then across an intervening medium of folklore. But though my early impressions are lively, they stand apart now. Even where the old phrases still fit, like Isaac the Sacrifice, and Balaam the Villain, and Ahasuerus the Fool, and Jacob the Tent-dweller, and Esau the Savage, and Esther the Queen, and Rebekah the Matriarch, it is in a different sense. This is not simply because I have grown older and see the world with different eyes. It is, rather, as though I had been listening to gossip about relatives in a faraway country until their images became fixed in my mind, and then had gone to live with them, and they weren't the same people at all.

Of the vast recorded folklore, the Tradition, accumulated in countless volumes of legend and commentary, I know very little. What I have to say about the People —how I feel about them, my surmises and reflections—

is born of prolonged personal contact. I am not taking anybody's word for anything. I shall quote the Tradition here and there by way of comparison, agreeing or disagreeing according to my lights; in my ignorance I shall no doubt reinvent some of it; I am concerned with my personal experience in direct contact with the Text —the source that is accessible to everyone. I am aware, of course, that there is no such thing as a completely independent judgment, but I have pursued that ideal while trying to guard against the love of independence for its own sake.

The Book, and the People, are so alive that many different pictures and many different opinions can be justified by the same Text. What is obvious and compulsory for me will strike others as fanciful. Some will be alarmed by my irreverence, some scandalized by my mysticism. A few may be impelled to go for the first time to the source. They are the only ones likely to derive any benefit from this book.

## CHAPTER I

## *The Comic as Fool*

✾

I MUST BEGIN by dispelling the popular notion that there is no humor in the Bible. I am not speaking of ironical passages here and there, or of figures held up for the complacent derision of the godly. I am speaking of sustained comic writing and of deliberately comic figures, of which there are many varieties: comics as fools, as dolts, as knaves, as grotesques, and even as beneficent gnomes. I shall present them in turn between the serious personalities; and I open with Ahasuerus the Emperor.

The humor of the Bible is deadpan. The narrative never abandons the stately rhythms that come through to us even in the translations, and an implacable solemnity seems to brood over individuals and incidents: let me say a suspiciously implacable solemnity, because it is inconceivable that the whole Biblical world should have lived its life in such a sustained severity of mood. Long ago I suspected that in many places the majestic façade only half concealed an invitation to mirth: a progressive mirth, developing from a startled and timid grin into a joyous chuckle, to explode at last into a convulsion of the diaphragm. And here I attempt the all but impossible task of infecting the reader with laughter at second hand, choosing the Book of Esther as material for the first experiment.

It opens with Ahasuerus, who is introduced in royal panoply: "This is Ahasuerus who reigned from India even unto Ethiopia, over a hundred and twenty-seven provinces. . . . And in the third year of his reign he made a feast unto all his princes and servants; the army of Persia and Media, the nobles of the provinces, being before him. He showed the riches of his glorious kingdom and the honour of his excellent majesty many days, even a hundred and fourscore." And after the great feast a smaller feast, for the residents of Shushan the capital, in the palace gardens. "There were hangings of white, fine cotton, and blue, bordered with cords of fine linen and purple, upon silver rods and pillars of marble; the couches were of gold and silver, upon a pavement of green, and white, and shell, and onyx marble. And they gave them drink in vessels of gold, the vessels being diverse from one another. . . ."

We have been lulled into dignity by the gravity of the style, awed into respect by the splendor of the setting. And we read:

"On the seventh day, when the heart of the king was merry with wine, he commanded Mehuman, Bizzetha, Harbonah, Bigtha, and Abagtha, Zethar, and Carcas, the seven chamberlains that ministered in the presence of Ahasuerus the king, to bring Vashti the queen before the king with the royal crown, to show the princes and peoples her royal beauty, for she was fair to look on."

4

It is time to put the Text down and to close our eyes. The narrator might have said simply that Ahasuerus commanded the queen to appear before him; or that he sent messengers; or that he himself went for her. No. Massively epic, the periods inform us that Ahasuerus appointed an Imperial Commission, and that it consisted of the seven chamberlains whose names are entered on the eternal scroll. Let us repeat them reverently: Mehuman, Bizzetha, Harbonah, Bigtha, and Abagtha, Zethar, and Carcas.

A wit has made a seasonal classification of fools: the Winter Fool and the Summer Fool. The winter fool enters concealed in parka, overcoat, earmuffs, galoshes, muffler, and gloves, a formidable figure of a man. He removes the wraps ceremoniously one by one, and what do we behold? A fool, an authentic and unmistakable fool, in unencumbered command of his inimitable talents, and already performing. The summer fool, on the other hand, rushes in bareheaded and in shorts, without defenses or pretenses, a fool at first sight. Ahasuerus is a winter fool.

Behold the seven Commissioners, befuddled, disconcerted, and conscious of high responsibility, in official procession from the king's banqueting hall to the queen's. There is no established protocol for their unprecedented assignment. Never before, to their knowledge, has a Persian consort been commanded to exhibit her imperial shapeliness at a state banquet. The Commissioners must improvise. Shall they enter in a body or select an envoy? What is the proper wording? His Imperial Majesty had said: "Go fetch the queen. I want the

5

boys to see her. And tell her to be sure to put the crown on." The language was irregular; where was the preamble, where were the distinguished guests, goodwill, innovation, Her Majesty's gracious co-operation? Mehuman, Bizzetha, Harbonah, Bigtha, and Abagtha, Zethar, and Carcas consult in the vestibule of the queen's banqueting hall. Time is short; action is imperative; minds are confused. "You go in, Bigtha." "No, Abagtha is the man." "Not I. What's the matter with Harbonah?" In a burst of confidence Mehuman squares off and exits.

We read: "But the queen Vashti refused to come at the king's commandment by the chamberlains."

Re-enter Mehuman, glassy-eyed and all but speechless. "Well?" "She won't come." "What do you mean, she won't come?" "She won't come. She threw me out. She practically insulted me." Incredulity followed by consternation among the seven chamberlains, Mehuman, Bizzetha, Harbonah, etc. Bigtha looks at Abagtha, Abagtha looks back at Bigtha, all seven look at each other. This is the Ahriman of a situation. "Let's try again. You go, Carcas." "The Ahriman I will! Go yourself!" "Who'll tell Ahasuerus?" "Not I." "Let's go home, maybe he'll forget, he's pretty high."

Meanwhile Ahasuerus, flushed and convivial, throws anticipatory glances at the door and knowing winks at the guests, and waits all unaware of the incredible turn of events. And the guests wait; and a whispering rises at the back. The seven Commissioners straggle in, distraction written on their faces, and there is an agonized interchange, *sotto voce*, on the dais. We are familiar with

6

the scene; we have all been at banquets where something has gone wrong, and the chairmen have gone into a panic of sibilation. But this is no ordinary banquet, and never was the miscarriage of a program fraught with more far-reaching consequences. The Commissioners stutter: "O King, live for ever—Her Imperial Majesty —that is, Queen Vashti—" "Speak up!" hisses the ruler of one hundred and twenty-seven provinces from India to Ethiopia. "What is it?" "Let not His Imperial Majesty be angry with his servants—the queen—unexpected —indisposed—" "Don't talk like an idiot. She was perfectly well this morning. You found her at the banquet, didn't you? Are you drunk, by any chance?" "No, Your Imperial Majesty, we are all sober, especially I—but the queen—I mean—indisposed to come—certain reasons —protocol—" The whispering at the back swells into a buzzing. Tittering is heard. The hearts of the guests are as merry with wine as the king's.

We read: "And the king was very wroth, and his anger burned in him. Then said the king to the wise men . . ." In brief, the wraps are off, and the performance is in full swing.

II

Always in the grand manner, without the flicker of an eyelash, the narrator now gives us the names of the seven Imperial Councilors whom Ahasuerus called into session in this hour of crisis: Carshena, Sethar, Admatha, Tarshish, Meres, Marsena, and Memucan. The single item on the agenda, we read, was formulated by the king

7

himself: "What shall we do unto the queen Vashti according to law, forasmuch as she hath not done the bidding of the king Ahasuerus by the chamberlains?" The narrator clearly hints at a rewording: "What shall we do that it be known unto all the Empire and unto all the generations that the king Ahasuerus did become exceeding drunk at the Imperial banquet?" For it was to this problem, whatever their other intentions, that the best brains of the Empire, the Seven Councilors, princes of Media and Persia, Carshena, Sethar, Admatha, Tarshish, Meres, Marsena, and Memucan, really addressed themselves, and with a success to which we are even now testifying.

Of the proceedings taken down by the Imperial speed-writers nothing has survived except the brilliant summation by Councilor Prince Memucan, which, standing alone, is an invaluable addition to our knowledge of classical Oriental statesmanship. Said Councilor Memucan: "Vashti the queen hath not done wrong to the king only, but also to all the princes, and to all the peoples, that are in the provinces of the king Ahasuerus. For this deed of the queen will come abroad unto all women, to make their husbands contemptible in their eyes, when it will be said: 'The king Ahasuerus commanded Vashti the queen to be brought before him, but she came not.' And this day will the princesses of Persia and Media who have heard of the deed of the queen say the like unto all of the king's princes. So there will arise enough contempt and wrath. If it please the king, let there go forth a royal commandment from him, and let it be written among the laws of the Persians and the Medes, that it be not altered, that Vashti come not before king Ahasuerus, and that the king give her royal estate unto another that is better than she. And when the king's decree which he shall make shall be published throughout all his kingdom, great though it be, all the wives will give to their husbands honour, both to great and small."

Memucan showed high skill in giving the question such wide moral and political perspectives. Admirable, too—at least on the surface—is his concern that not a single princess of Media of Persia shall remain ignorant of Ahasuerus's behavior at the banquet, and of what flowed from it. Ahasuerus liked the proposed measures; it is one of the advantages of being a fool of means that one need not languish in obscurity. His Council liked it, too. We read: "And the word pleased the king and the princes; and the king did according to the word of Memucan; for he sent letters into all the king's provinces, into every province according to the writing thereof, and to every people according to their language, that every man should bear rule in his own house, and speak according to the language of the people."

III

This Ahasuerus: he was not a man to be trifled with. He was stern—nay, inexorable—but just: majestic in anger, deliberate in chastisement. That was how he saw himself in the affair of the contumacious queen. But only for a time. We read: "After these things, when the wrath of the king Ahasuerus was assuaged, he remem-

9

bered Vashti, and what she had done, and what was decreed against her. Then said the king's servants that ministered unto him . . ."

What were they to say? He was remembering Vashti, but with wrath assuaged. He was remembering what she had done to him, but also what he had done to her. He had to remember, further, that he was inexorable, he was the personification of "the laws of the Medes and Persians," which do not change. It was depressing. Vashti had sinned, and she had been punished But perhaps she had had a change of heart; and "she was fair to look on." Clemency becomes a king. One is inexorable, certainly, but does one have to go to extremes? Can one not be inexorable within reason? If there were only some way—unfortunately all those letters had gone out, to all the provinces, each in its own language.

Ahasuerus brooded. Like all fools he had a new picture of himself for every need. He was always saying of himself, gaily or gloomily, impetuously or thoughtfully: "That's the kind of person I am, take it or leave it." Those of us who are not completely fools lapse into this practice only after a few drinks, and it is then that we utter the *cri de cœur:* "I've got to be myself, I've got to be honest with myself; I know it's not clever of me, but I can't help it." Ahasuerus, alas. added to his natural talents a weakness for the bottle. At the famous banquet, just before Vashti's ill-advised defiance, he had been old King Ahasuerus-Cole, democratic, hail-fellow-well-met. Immediately after it he had been outraged and inexorable majesty. The picture he now had of himself was of the tragic man-god-ruler, sacrificer and sacrifice, fated to

10

inexorability and yearning in the midst of his awful grandeur for the common human touch.

It was a tricky business, this of keeping pace with Ahasuerus's internal pictorial changes, and brief was the life of a councilor without an eye for art. Here, finally, is what his servants said to him:

"Let there be sought out for the king virgins fair to look on; and let the king appoint officers in all the provinces of his kingdom, that they may gather together all the fair young virgins unto Shushan the castle, to the house of the women; and let their ointments be given them; and let the maiden that pleaseth the king be queen instead of Vashti."

In effect, this was only a cleverly phrased reminder. Vashti had been deposed in accordance with the decree; but the decree also provided that "the king give her royal estate to another that is better than she." The delay was making it appear that the king despaired of finding a better queen than Vashti, and this, besides causing the king to eat his heart out, played into the hands of the subversives. We read that when his servants had spoken, "the thing pleased the king, and he did so." The servants were lucky that day; it pleased him only in the sense that he was lonely, and resigned to his duty. He showed no enthusiasm, and did nothing to hasten the leisurely proceedings. The officers had to be appointed; the candidates had to be chosen in one hundred and twenty-seven provinces and brought to Shushan. What with the local tryouts, the distances, and the travel conditions of those days, this cannot have taken less than several months. After they had been assembled, a whole

11

year was consumed by the preparations for the finals. "So were the days of their anointing accomplished, to wit, six months with oil of myrrh, and six months with sweet odours, and with other ointments of the women."

No committee presided at the awarding of the first prize. Ahasuerus was the sole judge, without appeal, and he must have anticipated the exercise of this untransferable royal prerogative with some uneasiness. For we read: "When the turn of every maiden was come, to go in to king Ahasuerus . . . in the evening she went, and on the morrow she returned to the house of the women. . . . She came in unto the king no more, except the king delighted in her, and she were called by name." There is no roster of unsuccessful candidates—a tactful piece of reticence. We can only guess at their number. It cannot have been less than two hundred and fifty-six —one winner for each of the one hundred and twenty-seven provinces and the capital, and for each one runner-up. The law was strict; Ahasuerus was not permitted to reject a candidate on sight, no matter how unfavorable his immediate impression. Like every other candidate she was entitled to her night in court. It therefore stands to reason that he could not arbitrarily suspend the competition at a point of his own choosing and declare himself satisfied. We read, in fact: "And the king loved Esther above all the women, and she obtained grace and favour in his sight more than all the virgins; so that he set the crown royal upon her head, and made her queen instead of Vashti." There were no omissions, and Ahasuerus probably got more of the common human touch than he had yearned for. It came to an end at last, and, whatever his criteria, we must assume that Ahasuerus found Esther not only better than all the other candidates, but, as prescribed by the decree, better than Vashti, too. In any case, the policy-makers had no grounds for complaint; Esther made a submissive and obedient queen; that was how she twisted Ahasuerus round her little finger.

Was he very much in love with her? We have only a comparative statement: "above all the women " She had great influence over him, and he thought highly of her —but love? We know that he would let weeks pass without sending for her, and since she was already queen the competition could no longer be blamed. If she came to him uninvited it was at the peril of her life. When her people was threatened with extermination by Haman, and her cousin Mordecai besought her to intervene personally with Ahasuerus, she had to return this message: "All the king's servants, and the people of the king's provinces, do know, that whosoever, man or woman, shall come unto the king in the inner court, there is one law for him, that he be put to death, except such to whom the king shall hold out the golden sceptre, that he may live; but I have not been called in unto the king these thirty days."

It was a general law, but that Esther was afraid to test it on herself reflects unfavorably on Ahasuerus as a lover. We cannot accuse her of undue mistrust, either, after he had ignored her for thirty days. And she was thoroughly afraid. Mordecai had to put strong pressure on her. He sent back word: "Think not with thyself that thou shalt escape in the king's house, more than all the Jews. For if thou altogether holdest thy peace at this time, then will relief and deliverance arise to the Jews from another place, but thou and thy father's house will perish; and who knoweth whether thou art not come to royal estate for such a time as this?" Esther made the decision in trembling, and sent this message to Mordecai: "Go, gather together all the Jews that are present in Shushan, and fast ye for me, and neither eat nor drink three days, night or day; I also and my maidens will fast in like manner; and so will I go in unto the king, which is not according to the law; and if I perish, I perish."

It appears that when the queen disobeyed the king he could do no more, according to the law, than depose her, whereas if she approached him unasked for and unwanted, the penalty might be death. Disobedience in a queen was a civic offense, nagging could be treated as a capital crime. The royal prerogatives in Persia were not uniformly onerous.

IV

We are told next how Haman asks Ahasuerus for permission to liquidate a sizable part of the population of the Empire.

Haman, Ahasuerus's current favorite, had been affronted publicly by Mordecai the Jew. The circumstances are not given, and Mordecai's disregard of the Jewish position, unexplained except by rumors in the Tradition, is hard to understand. We read: "When Haman saw that Mordecai bowed not down, nor prostrated himself before him, he was full of wrath. But it seemed contemptible in his eyes to lay hands on Mordecai alone. . . . Wherefore Haman sought to destroy all the Jews that were throughout the whole kingdom of Ahasuerus."

He went about it with the propaganda which, unchanged in any detail, has remained standard to this day. Like Memucan, he made his speech where it would do most good: in the ears of a fool; but unlike Memucan, privately, for the exclusive benefit of Ahasuerus: "There is a certain people scattered abroad among the peoples in all the provinces of thy kingdom; and their laws are diverse from those of every people; neither keep they the king's laws; therefore it profiteth not the king to suffer them. If it please the king, let it be written that they be destroyed; and I will pay ten thousand talents of silver into the hands of those that have charge of the king's business, to bring it into the king's treasuries."

Did King Ahasuerus ask for the name and identity of the people? He did not. Did he ask for the sources of Haman's information? He did not. When Vashti had disobeyed him he had called into session the Supreme Council of Seven to deliberate on the consequences to the welfare and morale of the Empire. Did he consult anyone as to the possible effects that the extermination of this unnamed people might produce on the economy of the Empire? Or want to know how long this had been going on, and why? He did not. Having listened to the speech, "the king took his ring from his hand, and gave it unto Haman, the son of Hammedatha the Agagite,

15

the Jews' enemy. And the king said unto Haman: 'The silver is given to thee, the people also, to do with them as seemeth good to thee.' "

And forthwith the secretaries were called in, and the couriers flew along the Imperial roads, "unto the king's satraps, and to the governors that were over every province; and to the province of every people; to every province according to the writing thereof, and to every people after their language. . . . The posts went forth by the king's commandment, and the decree was given out in Shushan the castle; and the king and Haman sat down to drink; but the city of Shushan was perplexed."

The last time the posts went out "to every province according to the writing thereof, and to every people after their language," it was to have them round up virgins for the king; this time it was to have them slaughter the Jews. It is an ingenious contrast, which teaches us something about the diverse uses of power in the hands of a fool.

In what terms did Ahasuerus dramatize himself to himself as he sat drinking with Haman after issuing the order for the extermination of the Jews? I may be wrong, and my career as adviser to Ahasuerus might have been a brief one, but I feel that they amounted to the Damn-decent-sort-even-if-I-am-an-inexorable-man-god-king picture, the sort who does a man a favor off-hand, without prying and hedging and stalling and acting the stuffed shirt with: "Don't you think one ought to consult the Council?" and: "Let me look into it and I'll let you know tomorrow." Perhaps there was also a hint of the and-they-say-I'm-incapable-of-a-simple-kindness-they'll-never-know theme. At any rate, he told Haman to keep his money: "The silver is given to thee, the people also, to do with them as seemeth good to thee." That was the kind of person he was.

Somewhat surprisingly he was still that kind of person —or was it again?—a few days later when, after her long fast, "Esther put on her royal apparel, and stood in the inner court of the king's house, over against the king's house; and the king sat upon his royal throne in the royal house."

He had not seen her for thirty days, and there she stood, uninvited, unexpected, and unannounced, that most acutely embarrassing of intruders, the neglected wife come to remind her husband of his conjugal obligations. It might have ended badly for her. Ahasuerus was, as we have seen, a busy man whose life was weighed down with cares of state. Women don't understand, they take such a personal and self-centered view of things, and many a husband would have sympathized with Ahasuerus if he had flown into a temper and put his scepter behind his back. Fortunately he was not that kind of person. We read: "And it was so, when the king saw Esther the queen standing in the court, that she obtained favour in his sight; and the king held out to Esther the golden sceptre that was in his hand. So Esther drew near, and touched the top of the sceptre. Then the king said unto her: 'What wilt thou, queen Esther? For whatever thy request, even to the half of the kingdom, it shall be given thee.' "

It was a generous offer. Kings have been known to give up the whole of a kingdom for love, but not to a

17

wife. And in those days kings had more to give up. How proud Ahasuerus must have been when Esther made her reply: "If it seem good to the king, let the king and Haman come this day unto the banquet that I have prepared for him"! He had reason to be proud. How wisely and with what masterly insight he had picked her out from among the hundreds of contestants with nothing more than a single night's acquaintanceship to go on! How different she was from Vashti! Not a hint of reproach for his prolonged abstinence. It was of him alone that she was thinking. How adoring the woman was, how humble, how good-looking! And if he had only known, how hungry!

"Then the king said: 'Cause Haman to make haste, that it may be done as Esther hath said.' " In his excitement he forgot to give the queen her title. No matter; he was not the kind of man to stand on ceremony. The order to Haman was, we may be sure, superfluous. Haman had no idea that Esther was a Jewess. Neither had Ahasuerus. She had kept it secret on the advice of Mordecai, her cousin, and adoptive father, and general counselor. But it would have made no difference. In every generation, from Berenice to Magda, there have been Jews and Jewesses to whom Jew-haters could say in all sincerity: "If only the others were like you!" Not that Ahasuerus was a Jew-hater; he was merely the kind of person who votes a Haman into office and then says: "Buchenwald? I never heard of the place." Also, in the more familiar phrase: "Why, one of my dearest friends is a Jew"—or "a Jewess."

Haman was there on time; so was Ahasuerus, who,

whatever else he was, was never late at a banquet, especially when it was prepared by his Esther, on whom he could rely for the right menu. We too may rely on her to be more attentive to her husband's thirst than to her own hunger. So we read: "And the king said unto Esther at the banquet of wine: 'Whatever thy petition, it shall be granted thee; and whatever thy request, even to the half of my kingdom, it shall be performed.' Then answered Esther and said: 'My petition and my request is—if I have found favour in the eyes of the king, and if it please the king to grant my petition, and to perform my request—let the king and Haman come to the banquet that I shall prepare for them, and I will do tomorrow as the king hath said.' "

Have I done Ahasuerus an injustice? It does seem from the above that he was not entirely taken in by Esther's loving solicitude, and that he suspected her of having something up her brocaded sleeve. If this is so, if he was not merely talking court language, I am glad to apologize. But let me add that after years of intimacy with the man and his record I have found just this one flaw in Ahasuerus's fatuity. Nevertheless my apology is wholehearted. I shall not be evasive; I shall not resort to the subterfuge so beloved of Bible scholars, and say: "This passage is an obvious interpolation." When I am wrong I am always ready to admit it. For better or for worse, I happen to be that kind of person.

But by no stretch of the imagination can we discover in Haman even a glimmering of suspicion. We are now treated to a marvelous portrayal of blissful self-complacency poisoned by a single frustration: "Then went

19

Haman forth that day joyful and glad of heart; but when Haman saw Mordecai in the king's gate, that he stood not up nor moved for him, Haman was filled with wrath against Mordecai. Nevertheless Haman refrained himself, and went home; and he sent and fetched his friends and Zeresh his wife. And Haman recounted to them the glory of his riches, and the multitude of his children and everything as to how the king had promoted him, and how he had advanced him above the princes and servants of the king. Haman said moreover: 'Yea, Esther the queen did let no man come in with the king unto the banquet that she had prepared but myself; and tomorrow also am I invited by her together with the king. Yet all this availeth me nothing so long as I see Mordecai the Jew sitting at the king's gate.' "

We could profitably spend more time on Haman as a sub-type; for if Ahasuerus is the Pure or Blithering Fool, Haman is the Masterful or Self-Destroying Fool. He had everything to make him happy except Mordecai's homage, and that was his undoing. "All this availeth me nothing, as long as I see Mordecai the Jew sitting at the king's gate." But our subject is Ahasuerus and the other characters, as well as the rest of the story—the plot to destroy the Jews, the foiling of it by Mordecai and Esther, the downfall of Haman—must be subordinated to it. It must suffice here to mention that Zeresh and the friends of the family offered Haman the following gratifying advice: "Let a gallows be made of fifty cubits high, and in the morning speak thou to the king that Mordecai may be hanged thereon; then go thou in merrily with the king unto the banquet." The

20

"thing" pleased Haman; and he caused the gallows to be made. Not a moment was lost, for we read that they were ready by the next morning.

Nor shall we linger over Haman's humiliation before his execution, except in so far as it sheds additional light on our main subject. A rare thing happened to Ahasuerus between the two banquets: he passed a sleepless night. "And he commanded to bring the book of records of the chronicles. And it was found written, that Mordecai had told of Bigthana and Teresh, two of the king's chamberlains, of those that kept the door, who had sought to lay hands on the king Ahasuerus. And the king said: 'What honour and dignity hath been done to Mordecai for this?' Then said the king's servants that ministered unto him: 'There is nothing done for him.' "

I cannot account for the directness of the reply and the forbearance of the king. It would have been no more than right if he had hanged a few officials for such criminal negligence. Here a man had saved the king's life by uncovering a palace conspiracy, and some months later the king's servants blandly reveal that no reward had been made, no distinction conferred, nothing, but nothing, done about it. Did they expect him to think of everything? And suppose he had not happened to pass a sleepless night, or had not asked for the chronicles, or they had picked on another passage—was he to assume that the incident would have been buried forever, and he would be made to appear, before his contemporaries and posterity, a monster of ingratitude?

But Ahasuerus did not make a scene. He was perhaps too tired, and too disgusted. Besides, what was the use?

He was now the man with a thousand servants who, when he wants a thing done, has to do it himself. Tired as he was, he acted promptly. "And the king said 'Who is in the court?' Now Haman was come into the outer court of the king's house, to speak unto the king to hang Mordecai on the gallows he had prepared for him." Well, there at least was a servant who would not let him down. And he called Haman in, and put the question to him: "What shall be done to the man whom the king delighteth to honour?"

As we know, or ought to know, and would expect by now if we did not know, Haman took the question as applying to himself. In his state of mind it was perfectly natural. Whom else would the king want to honor first thing in the morning? They must have told Haman, too, that Ahasuerus had hardly slept that night—such tidings spread swiftly through a palace—and it was a profoundly moving thought that what had kept the emperor awake was his anxiety to heap fresh honors on his favorite and his inability to hit on something appropriate. Indeed, Haman was so moved that he forgot to ask for permission to hang Mordecai. That is a pity. I have often wondered what Ahasuerus would have said under the special circumstances, and what personality he would have assumed for the occasion.

He was spared the effort. In a transport of joy Haman cried: "For the man whom the king delighteth to honour, let royal apparel be brought which the king useth to wear, and the horse that the king rideth upon, and on whose head a royal crown is set; and let the apparel and the horse be delivered into the hand of one of the king's

22

most noble princes, that they may array the man there-with whom the king delighteth to honour, and cause him to ride on horseback through the streets of the city, and proclaim before him. 'Thus shall it be done unto the man whom the king delighteth to honour.' "

Good man! It was a solid, detailed answer such as Ahasuerus expected from a competent adviser. He said: "Make haste, and take the apparel and the horse, as thou hast said, and do even so to Mordecai the Jew, that sit-teth at the king's gate; let nothing fail of all that thou hast spoken."

At this moment we can be quite sure of Ahasuerus's projection of himself. He had shown once more that he knew how to pick his advisers; he had discharged a debt of honor; he had made good an outrageous administra-tive oversight. Let the world now look on the king who never forgot a service. He was, if possible, more than usually satisfied with himself as he watched Haman de-part on his mission, and it is altogether unlikely that he noticed the peculiar green tinge that had crept over Haman's face.

I permit myself another brief digression. Haman's feelings on this occasion are indicated in the record. After he had performed the ghastly ceremony, he "has-tened to his house, mourning and having his head cov-ered." Nothing is said about the way Mordecai took the extraordinary episode. But he cannot have been any happier than Haman. Here he was, dressed in the king's robes, riding the king's caparisoned and crowned horse, being led through the city by his inveterate and despised enemy, who croaked at irregular intervals: "Thus shall

23

it be done unto the man whom the king delighteth to honour." And all the time he was sick with worry over the impending massacre of the Jews. It was mad.

v

We are at the high point of suspense in our story, and we must stop for a moment to take stock. I have just said that to Mordecai the whole thing was mad. But none of the principals, except Ahasuerus, can have felt sure that day of the sanity of things. For that matter, the uncertainty must have extended to the entire population of Shushan, the capital, as it stood on the sidewalks and stared, more perplexed than ever, at the astounding spectacle. Orders were out for a St. Bartholomew's Night, a Sicilian Vespers, a November Burning of the Synagogues—there are unfortunately synonyms enough for what was awaiting the Jews of Persia—and here the leading member of the Jewish community was being accorded the highest honors by the man responsible for the orders. To add to the confusion, everyone knew that it was Mordecai's noble dignity, or reckless insolence— the description depended on one's point of view—that had set off Haman's hatred.

One could not make sense of it. What had happened? Had Haman suddenly been cured of his anti-Semitic complex? Had a reconcilation taken place? Then why did Haman look as if he had been dead for several days? And if he was doing it against his will, and the orders for the massacre had been canceled, why had not the city been told, and why did Mordecai look even worse

24

than Haman? We can better imagine than reproduce the debates which rent the air that day in the homes and saloons of Shushan, and on the street corners. At the center of it all Ahasuerus, and he alone, moved serenely about his business, if we may so put it, never doubting the essential sanity of a world that his intelligence directed.

On the day of the denouement Ahasuerus's business, after his exacting labors on behalf of Mordecai, was to prepare for the evening. "So the king and Haman came to the banquet of Esther the queen. And the king said again unto Esther on the second day at the banquet of wine: 'Whatever thy petition, queen Esther, it shall be granted thee; and whatever thy request, even to the half of the kingdom, it shall be performed.' "

Honor where honor is due. In this matter Ahasuerus was a gentleman. Drunk or sober he remembered his promise to his wife, and he did not, as some husbands will, take advantage of the delay to whittle it down. He had said: "half the kingdom." He did not now say: "three eighths of the kingdom," or "a third, things haven't been going too well this week." Always assuming, of course, that it was not merely an Oriental court formula. And now Esther made her request, and we are about to view one of the world's greatest paintings: "Fool Getting a Jolt."

"Then Esther the queen answered and said. 'If I have found favour in thy sight, O king, and if it please the king, let my life be given me at my petition, and my people at my request; for we are sold, I and my people, to be destroyed, to be slain, and to perish. But if we had

25

been sold for bondmen and bondwomen, I had held my
peace, for the adversary is not worthy that the king be
endamaged ' "

I have more than once met the suggestion that the
famous Esther was just a pretty puppet manipulated by
the brilliant Mordecai; it was her body and his brains,
her voice and his inspiration—the original Trilby-
Svengali combination. The view owes more to mascu-
line vanity than to common sense. We need not under-
rate Mordecai's part in the affair, or deny that he had
much to do with formulating the general policy. He may
even have suggested the foregoing speech. But to deliver
it at the right moment with an air of spontaneity, to balance it so neatly, to know exactly when to stop and on
what note, was beyond the capacity of a puppet. If ever
the reader finds himself under the necessity of pleading
for his life with an Ahasuerus, let him study Esther's
diplomatic technique. In the absence of her physical advantages I cannot guarantee success, but it is impossible
to improve on the psychological approach.

The real purpose of the speech, gathered into its
climax, is to protect the king's good health. Nothing but
the threat of death—her own and that of her people—
could have induced Esther to endanger it. Everlasting
bondage was preferable to such a crime. As for Haman,
he did not count at all. Nobody counted but Ahasuerus.
There was even a certain presumption in trying to save
one's life, and prevent a general massacre, at the cost of
the king's peace of mind. But the flesh is weak—he
would understand and forgive.

"Then spoke the king and said unto Esther: 'Who is

he, and where is he, that durst presume in his heart to do so?' And Esther said: 'An adversary and an enemy, even this wicked Haman.' Then Haman was terrified before the king and queen. And the king arose in his wrath from the banquet of wine and went into the palace garden."

We have come full circle and are back at the beginning! Ahasuerus is at a banquet; he has been drinking; he has been affronted; he is angry. There it was Vashti; here it is Haman. The difference is immaterial. Let happen what will in the outside world, Ahasuerus's interior life follows its own cycle. This time he is angrier, perhaps drunker; words fail him, and he must go into the garden to cool off and think things over. We know him well enough by now to be sure that, with him, thinking things over will not lead back to any such question as: "Who was it gave Haman permission to exterminate an entire people without so much as asking for its name, and then sat down to have a drink on it?" The nearest he will come to it, and even this is unlikely, will be: "Why didn't the scoundrel, the snake-in-the-grass, the traitor, tell me it was the queen's people?" What his mind is busy with is the choice of the personality he ought to put on. In what capacity shall he face the situation? Who is he? The betrayed monarch? The brilliant uncoverer of another conspiracy? The knight errant of justice? The merciful father of his people? The disappointed friend? There is such a wide range of selves, and he looks among them frantically, unable to decide, and this makes him angrier and angrier. What ingratitude, to put him in such a quandary without a

27

moment's warning! And he must act without delay, to show his queen—tears of pride mingle with tears of rage as he thinks of her—who he is. No time to call the Imperial Council into session. She is waiting for him, his Esther, his chosen one, to show her and that villain who he is. Yes, but who is he?

He is still undecided when he rushes into the banqueting hall, and there, Ormuzd be thanked, he finds that the solution has been prepared for him.

Haman had remained "to make request of his life to Esther the queen; for he saw that there was evil determined against him by the king. Then the king returned out of the palace garden into the place of the banquet of wine; and Haman was fallen upon the couch where Esther was."

It comes to Ahasuerus like a flash of lightning. We read: "Then the king said: 'Will he even force the queen before me in the house?'" But of course! How obvious! How natural! The problem is solved, the crisis is over. He is the outraged husband.

"As the word went out of the king's mouth, they covered Haman's face. Then said Harbonah, one of the chamberlains that was before the king: 'Behold also, the gallows fifty cubits high, which Haman hath made for Mordecai, who spoke good for the king, standeth in the house of Haman.' And the king said: 'Hang him thereon.'" That was magnificent. He was the man of lightning-like decisions. "So they hanged Haman on the gallows he had prepared for Mordecai, and the king's wrath was assuaged."

As for the rest of the story, how the king handed over

the house of Haman to Esther, and how he exalted Mordecai in Haman's place, and how he sent out orders to the Jews in the provinces to defend themselves against their enemies, and how the Jews slaughtered those who attacked them, and how they did the same in Shushan the capital, and how Haman's ten sons were hanged—behold, is it not written in the chronicles of the Book of Esther?

What is not written there is what happened to the marriage in later years, and whether the king ever regretted his choice, and how long he reigned. But we can be certain that there were many banquets, and Ahasuerus was never sober for long, and his wrath was often roused and assuaged, and, whatever happened, he was that kind of person and he proclaimed it to the world. For it is written the dead will rise, and be alive, and black will become white, and the crooked shall be made straight, but the fool will remain a fool.

# CHAPTER II

## *Perverted Genius*

❀

To the world at large, Balaam is the owner of a talking ass; to the better-informed, the prophet who was asked to curse and had to bless; to me, who know him well, a fool, like Ahasuerus. But unlike Ahasuerus he does not move me to hilarity. There is nothing funny about him. He is a sinister and frightening fool. He fascinates me; I think about him a great deal, and always with disgust.

But first: Balaam a prophet? Yes, and judging by what remains of his utterances, a prophet of stature. The Tradition goes so far as to rank him with Moses, his contemporary; but this is a ridiculous exaggeration.

Balaam's is an involved story, which begins very simply. The time is shortly after the Exodus. Balak son of Zippor, king of Moab, alarmed by the advance of the liberated Israelites toward the borders of the Promised Land, sends messengers with gifts to Balaam son of Beor in Pethor on the Euphrates, saying: "Behold, there is a people come out of Egypt; behold, they cover the face of the earth, and they abide over against me. Come now therefore, curse me this people: for they are too mighty for me; peradventure I shall prevail, that we may smite them, and that I may drive them out of the land; for I know that he whom thou blessest is blessed, and he whom thou cursest is cursed."

Who is this Balaam son of Beor? We do not know. There is no previous mention of him, and he is not introduced circumstantially, like Ahasuerus. We must gather our knowledge as we go along. The distance of the call, a seventeen-day journey across the desert, and the importance of Balak's delegation, which is made up of elders and princes of Moab and Midian, testify to Balaam's immense reputation. The wording of the message, however, points to a serious misunderstanding. Balak looks on Balaam as a magician able to bless and curse at will. Actually Balaam is an ordained prophet of the One God, and his function is to reveal divine decisions; he blesses here below those who have already been blessed above, he curses those who have already been cursed. He has obviously been pursuing his high calling for many years, to be so widely and favorably known. But in Balak's mind to reveal and to bring about are the same thing, a superstition frequent among primitive peoples.

Balaam himself publicly disclaims independent or magical powers. To Balak's delegation he says at once: "Lodge here this night, and I will bring you back word, as the Lord may speak to me." Quietly, tacitly, he indicates that he has free access to the Presence, and the Text proceeds to show that it is not an empty boast. Let us take in the full force of this remarkable fact. Balaam does not belong to the chosen people. He is not in the line of Abraham, Isaac, and Jacob, the God-seekers. He belongs to the pagan or idolatrous world, or at least lives entirely within it. Yet he can consult God at will— the only human being of his generation so privileged except Moses; and this helps to explain why the Tradition speaks of him with awe.

But Balaam, who can consult God—and who, if he had remained faithful, might have risen to a higher function—knows, when we meet him, that this is his limitation. He cannot compel; his disclaimer of independent powers is clear, and he will repeat it over and over again: "As the Lord may speak to me." Whether he remains content to do so, whether he continues to repeat the words willingly, whether he is reconciled to his function as God's mouthpiece, is another matter.

The consultation with God took place that same night, as Balaam had promised. "And God came to Balaam, and said: 'What are these men with thee?' And Balaam said unto God . . ." thus and thus, repeating Balak's message to him. "And God said unto Balaam: 'Thou shalt not go with the men; thou shalt not curse the people; for they are blessed.' "

There are difficulties in our story which I shall not ignore, though I cannot resolve them to the satisfaction of every reader. This matter of God's question to Balaam, for instance. Did God have to ask him who his visitors were? I take it that the report of an experience of the Presence is very different from the experience itself. I take it that God did not ask for information. The form of the report is based on the reader's need, not God's; it is intended to refresh his memory or emphasize the issue; and we must either accommodate ourselves to

32

the method and terminology of the narrative or forego its values. It is enough for our present purpose to understand that God gave Balaam explicit instructions, announcing at the same time the dispositions He had taken concerning the Israelites. "Thou shalt not go with the men; thou shalt not curse the people; for they are blessed."

Balaam heard, and he obeyed without questioning. Such is our first impression. We read: "And Balaam rose up in the morning, and said to the princes of Balak: 'Get you into your land, for the Lord refuseth me leave to go with you.'"

It is an abrupt and categoric answer. The Moabites, worshippers of Chemosh and other gods, cannot have known who Balaam's "the Lord" was. Throughout the story Balak and Balaam will be using the word "Lord" to denote different powers. They will also talk of "the blessing" and mean two different things. But whatever power they may have had in mind, the Moabite delegates were turned back with a resounding "No." Or so it seems until we re-examine Balaam's answer. On second thought it occurs to us to ask why he failed to add that the Israelites were already blessed, and that there was nothing to be done about it. At any rate, why did he not express himself in such wise as to end the business there and then?

It will be argued that he would have been wasting his breath, for the delegates did not take back an honest report anyhow. According to the Text, all they said to Balak on their return to Moab was: "Balaam refuseth to come with us." Nothing about a prohibition from

33

"the Lord," whoever He was to them. It may not have been dishonesty. They undoubtedly shared Balak's belief that in his dealing with the powers the great magician of Mesopotamia did not take orders; he issued them. So they may have misheard him; that is, they heard the words clearly enough, but interpreted them as Balaam's decision, not "the Lord's " And that is how they would have interpreted any answer, however worded. And even if they had reported Balaam's reply verbatim, Balak would have put the same interpretation on it.

Reasonable as all this is, I cannot accept it. Balaam's prestige being what it was, and his powers of expression what they were, he could have found a way of slamming the door on further importunity.

He did not want to, that is the top and bottom of it. He was fishing for a renewal of the offer, and he got it. We read: "Balak sent yet again princes, more, and more honourable than they. And they came to Balaam and said: 'Thus saith Balak the son of Zippor: "Let nothing, I pray thee, hinder thee from coming to me. For I will promote thee to very great honour, and whatsoever thou sayest to me, I will do; Come therefore, I pray thee, curse me this people." ' "

Balaam's reception of the second delegation dispels any doubt we may have had as to his deviousness. He begins with a great show of vehemence: "If Balak were to give me his house full of gold and silver, I cannot go beyond the word of the Lord my God, to do anything great or small." And now, if he adds anything, it should be to the effect that the Israelites are already blessed, irrevocably, and that Balak must stop pestering him with

34

impossible requests. Whether or not the Moabites understand what it means, he is a prophet of God, an appointed proclaimer of the divine will, not a professional hexer or voodoo man; and let them begone. What he adds, however, is this: "Now therefore, I pray you, tarry ye here also this night, that I may know what the Lord will speak to me more."

This is very queer statement. We who have overheard the first interview in the night, and know that God has already revealed His will, are driven to the disturbing conclusion that Balaam is hoping for a retraction. Perhaps God will have thought it over in the last few weeks; perhaps Balaam can persuade Him to change His mind at the second interview. The Moabite delegates, however, who know nothing about God, or His decision, are bound on the other hand to conclude that Balaam is, in colloquial terms, putting it on, playing hard to get. And here the riddle of Balaam's character, motives, and beliefs begins to unfold.

Why should he want to curse the Israelites? Obviously, to earn Balak's fee. It had cost him an effort to dismiss the first delegation, and he had done it cagily, with a fine show of forthrightness, so that God could have no grounds for complaint. Here, as he had hoped, was a second delegation, and it was more numerous, more distinguished, more urgent than the first. He might never again have such an opportunity. We note with amusement, also with some respect, that while Balak talks of honors and high influence at court, Balaam specifies gold and silver. The honors at the disposal of a Moabite king, the prospect of commanding a Moabite king's obedience, have little appeal to Balaam. He wants money. Here, we would say, are no riddles; it is as straightforward as can be.

Unfortunately "straightforward" is the last word to apply to Balaam, and the Tradition properly considers his transactions with Balak so complicated that it has coined to a folk phrase: "I will teach him Balak," meaning: "I will give him a nut to crack on which he will break his teeth." We may suppose that Balaam was interested in money, and even that he was slightly money-mad. But that was not his ruling passion. Such is not the nature of the great artist, however mercenary he may be. And if we think that the Balaam story merely tells how a peddler of prophecies was frustrated in a big sale, we shall miss both its point and the spirit of Biblical narrative. We shall wonder at the space accorded to Balaam, and at the impression he left on later generations—not to mention his sustained intimacy with God. Above all, it is impossible to square so banal a conception of Balaam with the quality of his utterances, prophetic in the most exalted sense. If the reader cannot agree with me at this point, I ask him to wait until we have looked at some of the utterances; also until the last unexpected fragment of the record is in. We have to do here with an extraordinary man.

We continue: "And God came to Balaam at night, and said to him: 'If the men are come to call thee, rise up, go with them; but only the word which I speak, that shalt thou do.' And Balaam arose in the morning, and saddled his ass. And God's anger was kindled against him because he went; and the angel of the Lord placed himself in the way for an adversary against him."

We are pulled up once more. How could God tell Balaam to go with the men and then be angry with him for going, especially after He had Himself changed His mind? The same general question troubles us in other places. God hardens Pharaoh's heart, and then punishes him for his hardheartedness. Is this just? Are we to understand that God issues orders and then comes down on His creatures for obeying them? Or, rather, compels them to be bad and then punishes them for it? I shall not pretend to settle this ancient problem. But I cannot help pointing out how fiercely—and successfully—a man resists being made good, and how readily he acquiesces in being made bad. When he is bad on order, he blames God's omnipotence; when he is bad against orders, he blames God's impotence. That is not just either. One thing is sure: if we look on man as an automaton, in either religious or other terms, the concept of justice disappears. We have to assume a certain mysterious leeway, whether we talk of God's omnipotence or the inevitable procession of cause and effect; without that our lives are literally unthinkable. And leeway means responsibility. God told Balaam to go, and Balaam went with alacrity. He could have offered up a prayer against the command. He could have disobeyed God's command, as men often do, and waited for the consequences. No: he saddled his ass and went.

As for the "change of mind," is that an accurate description? This particular change is beside the issue, which is the blessing and cursing of the Israelites. If at first God forbids Balaam to go with the messengers, it is because there is no sense in undertaking the journey. Balaam obeys, and dismisses the messengers—and does it in such a way as to invite a second call. In other words, he is pestering for permission to go. Very well, comes the answer, go; it makes no difference to the issue, you can still say nothing but what I tell you to say. God orders him to go, but disapproves.

One way or another Balaam is acting very queerly. Has he ever done this before? Has he ever tried to break out of his destiny as God's messenger and become God's adviser? That is, has he ever tried to substitute his will for God's? It is unlikely. One cannot retain in one's employ a messenger who argues about the contents of one's messages. Something is happening to Balaam. If he has not tried before, he is certainly doing it now. His going to Moab has no other conceivable purpose. He has set his heart on cursing the Israelites, and as he rides westward to Moab he is dreaming of the steps by which he will force God's approval.

II

His dreams are interrupted by the grim but ludicrous incident of the speaking ass.

"Balaam was riding on his ass, and his two servants were with him. And the ass saw the angel of the Lord standing in the way, with his sword drawn in his hand; and the ass turned aside out of the way, and went into the field; and Balaam smote the ass to turn her into the way. Then the angel of the Lord stood in a hollow way between the vineyards, a fence being on this side, and a fence on that side. And the ass saw the angel of the Lord, and she thrust herself unto the wall, and crushed Balaam's foot against the wall; and he smote her again. And the angel of the Lord went further, and stood in a narrow place, where there was no way to turn either to the right or to the left. And the ass saw the angel of the Lord, and she lay down under Balaam; and Balaam's anger was kindled, and he smote the ass with his staff. And the Lord opened the mouth of the ass, and she said unto Balaam: 'What have I done unto thee, that thou hast smitten me these three times?' And Balaam said unto the ass: 'Because thou hast mocked me; I would there were a sword in my hand, for now I had killed thee.' And the ass said unto Balaam: 'Am I not thine ass, upon which thou hast ridden all thy life long unto this day? Was I ever wont to do so unto thee?' And he answered: 'Nay.' "

This is the end of the famous colloquy which, not without some justice, has made of Balaam's name a prefix to an ass. The strange animal disappears from the story, to haunt the ages and excite our speculation. The Tradition says that she was specially created for her role. I should like to think otherwise. It would be more appropriate that an ordinary ass should have been provoked to the most extraordinary behavior by Balaam's growing insanity "Have I ever done so to thee before?" she asks, and Balaam is stopped short in the midst of his murderous fury. "Nay!" he says And the moment he makes the admission—that is, the moment he comes out of his madness—he understands. "Then the Lord opened the eyes of Balaam, and he saw the angel of the Lord standing in the way, with his sword drawn in his hand; and he bowed his head and fell on his face. And the angel of the Lord said: 'Wherefore hast thou smitten thine ass these three times? Behold, I am come forth for an adversary, because thy way is contrary unto me; and the ass saw me, and turned aside before me these three times; unless she had turned aside from me, surely now I had even slain thee, and saved her alive.' "

Balaam's temporary blindness was real, but it was purposive and obsessional. He knew perfectly what it was that he could not see and what the ass saw. Hence his towering rage. "Thou hast mocked me three times!" he yells. There was a churning in his mind, and his nerves were giving way. He should not have been on this journey, even, or especially, after God's command or permission. The angel said: "I am come forth for an adversary, because thy way is contrary unto me." "Thy way" did not refer just to the journey. It referred to his thoughts, his purpose, his hopes, his self-deception. The whole business was wrong, and Balaam knew it, and when the poor ass sided with his struggling conscience, he went wild and was ready to kill.

He was on the journey to Balak because he had a cunning notion that he was circumventing God. It was his first attempt, and it was going quite well. He had got round the prohibition to accept Balak's invitation; he would get round the prohibition to curse the Israelities. He had managed to put God in an embarrassing position; he had obtained one concession; it was impos-

40

sible for God to withhold the second, which flowed logically from the first. So, step by step, God would be driven to reverse Himself, to curse what He had blessed. These were the dreams that the ass had disturbed and the angel dispelled. But only momentarily. For if we look at Balaam's reply to the threatening angel, we are plunged once more into disquietude and chagrin.

"I have sinned," he says; "for I knew not that thou stoodest in the way against me; now therefore, if it displease thee, I will get me back " It is a deliberately distorting reply. He did not know that he was sinning until he saw the angel! Whom does he think he is deceiving with that hypocritical statement? Worse than that, if possible, is: "If it displease thee, I will get me back." This is such a disingenuous falsification that to hear it without losing one's temper one must indeed have the patience of an angel. Balaam knows that the angel knows that he has God's command or permission for the journey; and he has taken good care to get himself into such a situation that to go back is extremely difficult. We must see this literally and physically as well as psychologically and politically. There he is on his ass, his two servants behind him; he has maneuvered himself into "a narrow place where there was no way to turn to the right hand or the left." He, and his servants, would have to back up all the way, and in the midst of it, sweating and cursing, he would have burst out with: "Why did you tell me to go in the first place?"

He was not given the opportunity. The angel simply repeated: "Go with the men; but only the word that I shall speak to thee, that shalt thou speak."

41

III

"And when Balak heard that Balaam was come, he went out to meet him unto Ir Moab, which is on the border of Arnon, which is the utmost part of the border. And Balak said unto Balaam: 'Did I not earnestly send unto thee to call thee? Am I not able indeed to promote thee to honour?' and Balaam said: 'Lo, I am come unto thee; have I now any power to speak anything? That *which God putteth in my mouth, that shall I speak.*' "

This is the first time that Balak hears of the strict limitations of Balaam's functions, and he hears it from Balaam himself. And what does he say to it? Nothing. Nothing at all. He ignores it. It is as if he had not heard. And now the reader will surely interpose: "You see, I was right. No message that Balaam could have sent back with the first delegation would have convinced Balak." I still cannot agree. The situation is now radically different. Balaam has come to Moab, thereby implying that he has the power to help Balak. Otherwise Balak might challenge him with: "Why did you come in the first place?"—something like the words that Balaam intended to fling at the angel if he had been bidden to return. Balaam is now tangled in the net of his lies.

"Nevertheless," the reader insists, "he does tell Balak the truth: 'That which God putteth in my mouth, that shall I speak.' " Yes, it is the truth; but it has been turned into a lie by the context. The word "God" does not mean the same to Balak as it does to Balaam. The two concepts have nothing in common; they are, in fact, mutually exclusive. Balak has always known that a magician has to speak the words "God" puts into his mouth. That does not trouble him in the least. He merely shrugged silently when Balaam referred to this well-known fact. For, as Balak sees it, the magician is the one who first chooses the words which "God" will put in his mouth. If the magician cannot do that, he is no magician.

Balaam understands perfectly what Balak is thinking; as an appointed prophet he knows it to be sheer primitive supersition; and yet he plays up to it. That is the lie.

But within that lie there is, horribly enough, a contradictory lie, because Balaam *is* hoping to impose his will on God. Where, when, and how such a hope first occurred to him is beside the point. We only know it is there. And so, in an exasperating way, Balaam has himself become a victim of superstition; and to that extent his deception of Balak is shaded by a certain degree of self-deception. There is no point in struggling further into the undergrowths of his mind; it is everywhere just as black, and tangled, and incomprehensible.

Let us go on with the story.

Balak has ignored Balaam's disclaimer of independent powers. The record immediately passes on to action: "Balaam went with Balak, and they came to Kiriath-huzoth. And Balak sacrificed sheep and oxen, and sent to Balaam and to the princes that were with him. And it came to pass in the morning that Balak took Balaam, and brought him up unto Bamoth-baal, and he saw from thence the utmost parts of the people. And Balaam said unto Balak: 'Build me here seven altars, and prepare me

43

here seven bullocks and seven rams.' And Balak did as Balaam had spoken; and Balak and Balaam offered on every altar a bullock and a ram. And Balaam said unto Balak: 'Stand by thy burnt offering, and I will go; peradventure the Lord will come to meet me; and whatsoever He showeth me I will tell thee.' "

I call attention to the elaborateness of the proceedings. We remember that when the delegations came to Balaam in Mesopotamia he had entered or summoned the Presence by simple request and he had at once received a communication. Here, on the heights of Bamoth-baal, in the presence of the assembled princes of Moab, he prefaces the request with a highly complicated ritual of sacrifices. He is no longer seeking a revelation of God's will; he is trying to influence it.

Was this really such an outrageous ambition? We have often heard of good men petitioning God to reconsider a decision. Balaam the Mesopotamian must have known the history of his fellow countryman Abraham, the father of these very Israelites, how he had begged God to rescind the edict of destruction against Sodom and Gomorrah. Abraham had even bargained with God, and, far from expressing disapproval, God had been willing to come to terms. He was ready to accept conditions which Abraham himself proposed but unfortunately could not fulfill, so that the edict stood and the cities were destroyed. And more recently, in Balaam's own day, and most assuredly to Balaam's knowledge, Moses had pleaded with God not to carry out His announced intention to destroy the Israelites—the people of the blessing!—for their worship of the golden calf. And he

44

had been successful! Nor can it be said that this divine
change of mind was "beside the issue." It was the issue
itself.

Surely, then, Balaam had precedent and warrant for
his hope; the more so as in wanting God to withdraw the
blessing from the Israelites he was not, in a sense, asking
for anything new. He only wanted God to revert to the
decision that Moses had persuaded Him to recall.

All this would be relevant if Balaam were pleading
or praying; if, like Abraham and Moses on those two
occasions, he had begged in humbleness of heart and in
the knowledge of his own insignificance, and if his petition had like theirs been born of goodwill and love.
Then, though he might not have succeeded, he would
have been free from blame. But there was no goodwill
in his heart, and he was not praying; he was compelling,
he was exerting illicit pressure. He was plotting. First
he thought he had outmaneuvered God in getting the
permit or order to travel to Moab, and now he was re-
sorting to compulsive magic.

One feature of the preparations is particularly suspicious. Animal sacrifices were not necessarily idolatrous. It depended on the direction. But Balaam, as we
have seen, associated to himself in the mystical ritual
Balak the idolater, whose thoughts could not have been
addressed in the same direction as Balaam's—that is, if
Balaam himself was rightly directed. For we have to do,
now, with a schizophrenic condition. Balaam was addressing himself to the One God, the Only God, the God
of the universe, whose mouthpiece he was. But to use
the shaman's compulsions on the God of the universe is

45

nonsense. Therefore Balaam was addressing a not-God, and was being helped by Balak; that was the meaning of Balak's participation; which also makes nonsense. Again I refuse to go farther into the labyrinth. I retreat while the entrance is still within sight; and I only wish to remark that in addition to the above-mentioned sacrifices Balaam also performed certain undescribed magical rites, which are mentioned later in the Text; so there cannot be the slightest doubt that he was appealing to outside powers while he was negotiating with God. This is all we need to know for our purpose.

## IV

And yet we shall see in a moment that in spite of these paralyzing confusions and corruptions Balaam is still capable of the utmost clarity of vision, and when the spirit comes upon him he speaks a language of pure prophetic quality. He cannot help it. He is then under God's compulsion, and "only the word that I shall speak unto thee, that shalt thou speak." Once more let us beware of arguing that this makes an automaton of Balaam. God's compulsions are not applied at random; they are connected with a man's will. Balaam's rebellion was a folly precisely because he had the capacity to co-operate with God's compulsion, and the will to exercise his capacity. We sometimes say of a man: "He is a great artist in spite of himself." We mean that when the moment of inspiration comes, all his mercenary calculations, all his knavish plans to gull an ignorant public with his second best, or third best, are carried away by an irresistible flood of integrity.

And now Balaam has offered sevenfold double sacrifice, with the participation of Balak the idolater, and with his own admixture of magic, and with various unfathomable reservations and childishly crafty calculations. "And he went to a bare height. And God met Balaam; and he said to Him: 'I have prepared the seven altars, and I have offered up a bullock and a ram on every altar.' "

We must be most attentive here to the exact wording of the record. It might again be objected that Balaam did not have to tell God what he had just done; God knew it. The reader knows it, too. But what the reader does not know, unless he has been very attentive indeed, is that Balaam is telling a lie. "*I* have prepared the seven altars, and *I* have offered up," is the crudest misrepresentation. It should be "we"; Balak the idolater was, with the deepest purpose, made an equal partner in the preparations, and in fact did most of the work. And so we must again observe that information repeated in an interview with God is for our benefit. Here we learn that up to the last moment of free choice, and in the very Presence, Balaam is scheming and contriving. He is muttering: "I have prepared the altars, I have offered the sacrifices, Thou hast received Thy due." He is "repressing" Balak's participation, which is an appeal to the other powers, or a flank attack on God, or something not really definable; only we know its purpose, which is to impose his worldly designs on the Unworldly. Then comes the seizure of artistic integrity and undoes all his driveling calculations:

"And the Lord put a word in Balaam's mouth, and said: 'Return unto Balak, and thus thou shalt speak.' And he returned to him, and, lo, he stood by his burnt offering, and all the princes of Moab, and he took up his parable. . . ."

It is the moment. Balak and the assembly stand silent in the sunlight on the heights beside the smoking altars, waiting for the Great Anathema. Here is what comes pouring out of Balaam's mouth:

*"From Aram Balak bringeth me,*
*The king of Moab from the mountains of the East:*
*'Come, curse me Jacob,*
*And come, execrate Israel.'*
*How shall I curse whom God hath not cursed?*
*And how shall I execrate whom the Lord hath not*
*    execrated?*
*For from the top of the rocks I see him,*
*And from the hills I behold him.*
*Lo, it is a people that shall dwell alone,*
*And shall not be reckoned among the nations.*
*Who hath counted the dust of Jacob,*
*Or numbered the stock of Israel?*
*Let me die the death of the righteous,*
*And let mine end be like his!"*

The strange, powerful verse rings out across the assembly on the heights and across the ages. This is prophecy, or revelation, and there is no mistaking it. The vibrations have their source in a primal power. But we cannot, for the moment, speak of a blessing. All that Balaam has done, so far, is refrain from cursing the people. He has characterized it in two mysterious phrases, and he has promised it great increase of numbers; and he has closed with an apparently irrelevant personal interjection.

We read: "And Balak said unto Balaam: 'What hast thou done to me? I took thee to curse mine enemies, and, behold, thou hast blessed them altogether.' And he answered and said: 'Must I not take heed to speak that which the Lord putteth in my mouth?' "

Something is wrong here. We understand Balak's disappointment and frustration, and his angry cry: 'Thou hast altogether blessed them." In his rage he exaggerates wildly, but that is natural. It is Balaam who puzzles us. All he seems to have given the Israelites is the one blessing of numbers, and there is no mention of conquest, territory, empire, wealth, and all the other goods without which numbers are an affliction. Why does he sullenly endorse Balak's protest, by saying: "Must I not take heed to speak that which the Lord putteth in my mouth?" He could very well have said: "That wasn't a bad beginning. I could have done much worse."

We must now look more closely at the relationship of these two men.

We have seen how Balaam and Balak use the word "Lord" with different, and in fact opposed, meanings. It is inevitable that they should also have different and opposed concepts of a "blessing" from the "Lord."

We have been thinking of "blessing" and "curse" in Balak's terms. When the blessing of Israel was uttered we missed it, because it is in Israel's terms. But Balaam

49

did not. He knew at once the significance of those strange phrases:

*"Lo, it is a people that shall dwell alone,*
*And shall not be numbered among the nations."*

It is the very essence of *the* blessing. This people, we are told, is set apart; it is not on the roster of history and is not subject to the laws of history. It is subject to God's law. The uniqueness of its status is wrapped up in the uniqueness of the blessing, which is imposed rather than conferred upon it: a people unlike all other peoples, and a blessing unlike all other blessings.

Does Balak understand this? How can he, if he does not understand what Balaam means by "the Lord"? The terms of the blessing of Israel are not revealed to him If they were, if he knew of the responsibilities and agonies to which the blessing is tied, he would start away in horror, he would exclaim: "Do you call that a blessing? That is a curse! Keep it!" And he would send Balaam home quickly before he spoiled anything. The Tradition, to make this point clear, has a legend which hints that Balak did know something about the terms of the blessing They had been explained to him, and to all other rulers and peoples, and he had rejected them with a shudder. So had everyone but the Israelites. They were given the blessing, the Law, at Sinai, and not so much because they were really willing, but because they were the least reluctant. The legend must be believed for its lesson only; it teaches us that Balak would under no circumstances have accepted the blessing, *the* blessing which fell to the Israelites.

50

We must believe it for another reason. The Israelites had to accept the blessing, and they were the least reluctant, because it had been given to Abraham, Isaac, and Jacob, and it was the irrevocable blessing. Sinai was in a sense a confirmation, a massive reminder. And the Tradition goes on subtly to say, in this sense, that all the unborn descendants of the Israelites then present were also in attendance, and accepted for all the generations to come.

All this Balaam understood perfectly. He understood also that Israel's blessing was irrevocable because it was conferred on the spirit at the expense of the flesh, while other blessings, ordinary blessings, which have to do with material values, are provisional. They too come from God, as everything does, but they are subject to revision and recall; not, of course, at a magician's command, but by their very nature under God's direction. Only a primitive barbarian could regard a guaranteed eternity of dominion and prosperity as the highest purpose of life, and that was why he would call it the "blessing."

We know, I think, what Balak wants, and Balaam knows it, too. Balak wants an ordinary curse against the Israelites; he wants the ordinary blessing, in so far as they have it now, withdrawn from them, so that he can drive them off, or destroy them. But what has Balaam in mind?

I shall perhaps be laughed at, but only by those who have never become acquainted with the lunacies of the artist. Balaam wants primarily to be an independent power, controlling a part of the universe. He does not

51

care a goat's bleat about Moab, or about Israel, about who defeats whom, and who is destroyed. He wants a share of the omnipotence and he thinks, God help us, that he has found a way of turning the trick. He will compel God to have him say what *he* wants, not what God wants. He is not interested now in the distinction between ordinary blessings and *the* blessing, because it is impossible to compel God in either area. If he can only prevent God from overmastering him at the crucial moment, and turn the tables on Him, precisely at the moment of communion, he will have won. And he remembers with especial self-loathing and God-loathing how, in the first attempt, he was so carried away by submission and honesty that he wailed:

*"Let me die the death of the righteous,*
*And let mine end be like his"*—

and meant it, meant it to the depths of his tormented soul.

They stand looking at each other, the king and the defecting prophet. They recover slowly from the shock, and consider. What's to be done now? Widely divergent as their views and motives are, they agree on one point: the situation is unacceptable.

To Balaam it is unacceptable that he is doomed forever to be God's public crier, without a role of his own in the ordering of world affairs. To Balak it is unacceptable that the "Lord" has got out of control and refuses to yield to magic pressures. Whether this "Lord" be Chemosh or another, such a thing is unheard of, and one must be an atheist to believe it. There had undoubtedly been a mistake in the procedure, he suggests, and Balaam agrees with him. And so we read:

"And Balak said unto Balaam: 'Come, I pray thee, with me unto another place, from whence thou mayest see them; thou shalt see but the utmost part of them, and shalt not see them at all: and curse me them from thence.' "

It sounded reasonable. The sight of the Israelite encampment had had a diversionary effect, it had concentrated the protective forces of God against Balaam. They will choose a spot from which the encampment is barely visible, or not at all.

And so Balaam goes with Balak to the top of Pisgah—of all places!—and repeats the performance from beginning to end: the seven altars, and the seven bullocks, and the seven rams, with Balak participating as before, and all the rest of the ritual, not excluding Balaam's private bit of hocus-pocus. He is ready again. And again we read:

"And he said unto Balak: 'Stand here by thy offering, while I go toward a meeting yonder.' "

The result? A demonstration of God's measureless patience. We might have expected that He would now withdraw completely. He manifests Himself again. "And the Lord met Balaam and put a word in his mouth, and said: 'Return unto Balak, and thus shalt thou speak.' And he came to him, and, lo, he stood by his burnt offering, and the princes of Moab with him. And Balak said unto him: 'What hath the Lord spoken?' "

We have made some progress. Balak actually puts the emphasis on "the Lord."

53

"Arise, Balak, and hear," answers Balaam from between clenched teeth.

*"Give ear unto me, thou son of Zippor;*
*God is not a man, that He should lie;*
*Neither the son of man, that He should repent.*
*When He hath said, will He not do it?*
*Or when He hath spoken, will He not make it*
   *good?"*

How so? How so? And what of God repenting after the Flood? And what of His decision to destroy the Israelites after the incident of the golden calf, and His retraction under pressure from Moses? Yes, particularly this incident, inasmuch as it had to do with the blessing, *the* blessing, which is not subject to earthly vicissitudes, but once accepted must endure forever? What of that? But Balaam knows what he is saying "God is not a man. . . ." God's changes, where there are such, are His own decisions. He is not led by the nose, like human beings, or like the local gods, upon whom magicians force changes, so that they all, men and gods alike, must invent lies to account for the changes. For in Balaam's day they used the word "lies" for what we now call rationalizations. When God accepts a human suggestion, it is one that He planted there as participant in man's upward struggle, and He will plant such suggestions where the changes are an unfolding of the original and unchanged intention.

And Balaam continues, to the horror of the princes of Moab, and to his own horror, for he is alert in the midst of his seizure:

54

*"Behold, I am bidden to bless;*
*And when He hath blessed I cannot call it back.*
*None hath beheld iniquity in Jacob,*
*Neither hath one seen perverseness in Israel."*

What is he talking about? We are told a hundred times in the record that there is iniquity in Jacob and perverseness in Israel, and backsliding, and whoring after false gods, and punishment therefor. And still Balaam knows what he is saying. It is not for Balak and the Moabites to judge, and not for Pharaoh and the Egyptians. They who refuse the Law cannot reproach Israel with breaking it; indeed, they cannot understand wherein Israel has broken it, they cannot behold iniquity in Jacob and perverseness in Israel. If we are told of it a hundred times, it is by Israel's own recorded confession.

And now Balaam's voice rises; he screams into the sunlight;

*"The Lord his God is with him,*
*And the shouting for the King is among them.*
*God who brought them forth out of Egypt*
*Is for them like the lofty horns of the wild-ox.*
*For there is no enchantment with Jacob,*
*Neither is there any divination with Israel."*

He is screaming at God, at the Moabites, at himself: "There is no enchantment with Israel!" Magic is useless, compelling God is a delusion, divination cannot replace revelation.

*"Now is it said of Israel:*
*'What hath God wrought!'"*

55

God alone is master and source and explanation and inspiration. And still the words pour from Balaam's distended throat:

> *"Behold a people that riseth up as a lioness,*
> *And as a lion doth he lift himself up;*
> *He shall not lie down until he eat of the prey,*
> *And drink the blood of the slain."*

The vision, increasingly ecstatic, has begun to clothe itself in gorgeous imagery. Let us not take the words secularly, thereby falling into Moabite error. "He shall not lie down until he eat of the prey" has the same force as the parallel phrase in Balaam's next utterance: "He shall eat up the nations that are his adversaries"— namely, he shall outlive them, he shall swallow them into his history, he shall make them a part of his record, the booty of his time-span, until he himself lie down, until history passes away, and man is in the post-historic stage. Much that Balaam says as his spirit lifts itself higher and higher in successive utterances must be reinterpreted, for the symbolism is pitched here and there to the mental idiom of the Moabites. They, under any circumstances, must have found the second utterance more devastating than the first. And when the voice ceases to ring, when Balaam comes out of his seizure, the Moabite king is not only in despair; his mind has begun to wander.

He says to Balaam: "Neither bless them nor curse them at all," which sounds as if he is asking Balaam to hold his peace, to shut up, and that would be an intelligible if not an intelligent request. But he means something else: if Balaam cannot induce the Power to reverse the blessing, let him at least obtain a declaration of neutrality, that is, if he cannot get all the moon for Balak, let him just get half. And Balaam, exhausted by his second flight, is not much better. He can only repeat parrotlike: "Told I not thee, saying: All that the Lord speaketh, I must do?" And then Balak bethinks himself; what will he do with half a moon? And anyhow, one should try three times. The day is waning, another attempt must positively be made. "Come now," he babbles, "I will take thee unto another place; peradventure it will please God that thou mayest curse the people." Balak is losing his simplicity without becoming wiser; he is, instead, acquiring some of Balaam's confusions. He has begun, vaguely, to recognize "the Lord's" supremacy, and Balaam's helplessness, and still he goes on with the magic rites.

Now Balaam has given up hope, but he has not the strength to refuse Balak's request; all the mummery with Balak is repeated, and then follows a significant admission. We read: "When Balaam saw that it pleased the Lord to bless Israel, he went not, as at the other times, to meet with enchantments, but set his face toward the wilderness." This is really staggering. Balaam the prophet sees at last that "it pleased God to bless Israel"! He is finally convinced that his enchantments, his bag of tricks, can do nothing for him. Finally convinced? He was convinced all along; and he is not convinced now. It is a temporary and conditional conviction, like a drug addict's resolution; it is less an establishment of truth than a lull of cynicism. And so he

57

does not go to meet God, he only sets his face toward the wilderness.

"And Balaam lifted up his eyes, and he saw Israel dwelling tribe by tribe; and the spirit of God came upon him. And he took up his parable. . . ."

This is the third and most magnificent of his utterances. It is also the most moving, because it begins with a confession that is repeated at the beginning of the fourth and last utterance:

*"The saying of Balaam the son of Beor,*
*And the saying of the man whose eye is opened;*
*The saying of him who heareth the word of God,*
*Who seeth the vision of the Almighty,*
*Fallen down, yet with opened eyes."*

Pitiful, pitiful and horrible, the more so as the words have two opposite meanings, both simultaneously valid. "Fallen down, yet with opened eyes." He played the fool with God, he fell down from his position of trust, and his eyes were open. He knew all along what he was doing. And on the other hand: he has failed in his blasphemous ambition, he has fallen and been defeated, but God is not fooling him, his eyes are open. Surrender and defiance, worship and mockery, high wisdom and low cunning, all in one.

He breaks off, to continue on a note of tenderness and vain-longing and envy:

*"How goodly are thy tents, O Jacob,*
*Thy dwellings, O Israel!*
*As valleys stretched out,*
*As gardens by the river-side;*

58

*As aloes planted of the Lord,*
*As cedars beside the waters;*
*Water shall flow from his branches,*
*And his seed shall be in many waters;*
*And his king shall be higher than Agag,*
*And his kingdom shall be exalted."*

Then the mood changes again, the note of frenzy returns, the furious imagery of the primitive world bursts open again:

*"God, who brought him forth out of Egypt,*
*Is for him like the lofty horns of the wild-ox;*
*He shall eat up the nations that are his adversaries,*
*And shall break their bones in pieces,*
*And pierce them through with his arrows.*
*He couched, he lay down as a lion,*
*And as a lioness; who shall rouse him up?"*

Once again he breaks off, and to make sure that Balak and the princes of Moab will understand, ends on their level:

*"Blessed be every one that blesseth thee,*
*And cursed be every one that curseth thee."*

He has at last delivered the message, and the effect is tremendous. "And Balak's anger was kindled against Balaam, and he smote his hands together; and Balak said unto Balaam: 'I called thee to curse mine enemies, and, behold, thou hast altogether blessed them these three times. Therefore now flee thou to thy place; I thought to promote thee to great honour; but, lo, the Lord hath kept thee back from honour.' "

One does not expect gratitude from kings, but com-

59

mon courtesy should have protected Balaam from public insult. He had done his best for Balak, not the less for his private motives. Did it not occur to the thick-witted Moabite that if the words he had just listened to were a dagger in his heart, to Balaam, who had been compelled to utter them, they were gall and wormwood? What is his reward? "Flee thou to thy place!" That is: "Begone, before I forget myself." Kings have been known to liquidate prophets for not obtaining the right answers. The threat is accompanied by a sneer. When Balak in his terror of the Israelites sent his first delegation to Balaam he wrote respectfully: "I know he whom thou blessest is blessed, and he whom thou cursest is cursed." Balaam was to him the controller of the power. And now it turns out that Balaam is nothing but a messenger boy; and the fact that he is the messenger boy of the power means nothing to Balak. "I thought to promote thee to great honour; but, lo, the Lord hath kept thee back from honour." In other words: "Where is your boasted influence? Where did you get your reputation? Your 'Lord,' whoever he is, does not want you to be promoted; he wants you to know your place. And now that I know it too, get out!"

The long day is ending. Twilight is creeping up across the desert that separates Balaam from the homeland, and he must travel back empty-handed and consider himself lucky that he has escaped with his life. He must travel for seventeen days reflecting on his damaged reputation and the possible loss of the divine privilege, for the man who sets out to corrupt himself will always succeed in the end; even genius can stand so much abuse and no more. But for the moment Balaam too is bursting with anger He is going, and before he goes he will show the king *his* place, and let him do what he will. He gathers his last energies.

"And Balaam said unto Balak: 'Spoke I not also to thy messengers that thou didst send unto me, saying· "If Balak would give me his house full of silver and gold, I cannot go beyond the word of the Lord, to do either good or bad of mine own mind; what the Lord speaketh, that will I speak"? And now, behold, I go unto my people; come, and I will announce to thee what this people shall do to thy people in the end of days.' "

And this time without preparations and sacrifices and enchantments, without consultation, spurred only by rage, he launches on his fourth utterance:

> *"The saying of Balaam the son of Beor,*
> *The saying of the man whose eye is opened;*
> *The saying of him who heareth the word of God,*
> *And knoweth the knowledge of the Most High,*
> *Who seeth the vision of the Almighty,*
> *Fallen down, yet with opened eyes:*
> *I see him, but not now;*
> *I behold him, but not nigh;*
> *There shall step forth a star out of Jacob,*
> *And a sceptre shall rise out of Israel,*
> *And shall smite through the corners of Moab,*
> *And break down all the sons of Seth.*
> *And Edom shall be a possession,*
> *Seir also, even his enemies, shall be a possession,*
> *While Israel doth valiantly. . . ."*

61

This is Balaam's parting shot. The king and the princes listen, petrified, in the gathering darkness

"And Balaam rose up, and went and returned to his place; and Balak also went his way."

## V

We seem to be at the end of the story, and even careful Bible-readers usually think we are. Balaam is riding back to Mesopotamia, Balak has left the heights; they, and we, have much to ponder on. But if this were all, I should not have asked the reader to withhold judgment until "the last unexpected fragment of the record is in," nor would I have started out with the confession that I find Balaam disgusting. Tragic, reprehensible, perplexing, and if you like amusing in a wry way, but so far not disgusting.

The record now returns to the general history of the people of Moses, the people of the blessing, to tell of iniquity in Jacob and perverseness in Israel.

"And Israel abode in Shittim, and the people began to commit harlotry with the daughters of Moab. And they called the people unto the sacrifices of their gods; and the people did eat, and bowed down to their gods. And Israel joined himself to the Baal of Peor. And the anger of the Lord was kindled against Israel And the Lord said unto Moses: 'Take all the chiefs of the people, and hang them up unto the Lord in the face of the sun, that the fierce anger of the Lord may turn away from Israel.' And Moses said unto the judges of Israel: 'Slay ye every one his men that have joined themselves unto the Baal

of Peor.' And, behold, one of the children of Israel came
and brought unto his brethren a Midianitish woman in
the sight of Moses, and in the sight of all the congregation of the children of Israel, while they were weeping
at the door of the tent of meeting. And when Phinehas,
the son of Eleazar, the son of Aaron the priest, saw it,
he rose up from the midst of the congregation of Israel,
and took a spear in his hand. And he went after the man
of Israel in the chamber, and thrust both of them
through, the man of Israel, and the woman through her
belly. So the plague was stayed from the children of
Israel. And those that died by the plague were twenty
and four thousand."

This does not make pleasant reading, and is not sup-
posed to. But while some will murmur, appalled: "It is
true; a hundred times they offended, and a hundred
times they were disciplined, before the obstinacy of
backsliding was turned into the obstinacy of fidelity;
though we are sickened we must not skip these passages
which teach how long and bitter is the road to self-realization"; while these murmur, others will be muttering
under their breath: "Horrible stuff! If we read it at all—
but let us keep it away from the children—it is to remember how far we have come from that primitive and
insanely jealous God of the desert, and from His murderous revenges. We protest against this talk of 'iniquity' and 'perverseness,' and against this one-sided
writing. Who knows whether the Baal of Peor was not
just as good as the God of—God save the mark—the
blessing? As a practical matter it adds up to this: a
rapprochement was taking place between Israel and

Moab; the danger of bloody conflict was being diminished, and whatever diminishes mutual killing between human beings should be welcomed, irrespective of particular sexual codes and religious affiliations. We simply have to admit that the temple prostitutes of Moab and Midian were doing a good work, and we who have so long acquiesced in the revolting spectacle of war should not be so squeamish about methods of promoting peace."

And sometimes this muttering rises to a screaming, and I see round me the glaring eyes, and distorted faces, and clenched fists of fathers and mothers, and I hear: "We want peace! We want peace! Blood, oceans of blood since life began, fangs, bludgeons, bows and arrows, arquebuses, cannon, gunpowder, TNT, atom bombs, hydrogen bombs . . . Let them do anything, let them fornicate their way into peace, we want to live, we want our children to live, we want them at least to have a chance to straighten things out. Damn you and your mystical blather about blessings. . . ."

Wait, please, I want to explain. I understand you; sometimes I am just as hysterical as you about it all. The thing isn't as you think it is. And don't prejudge me. I'm not going to fob you off here with comparisons between the god of Moab and the God of the blessing. I shan't plead: "We don't know what the god of the Moabites wanted, but we do know what the God of Israel was driving at—the long purification that would lead toward the dream of Micah, who said: 'It hath been told thee, O man, what is good, and what the Lord doth require of thee: only to do justly, and to love

64

mercy, and to walk humbly with thy God.' " And I shall
not offer the words of both Isaiah and Micah to show
what pacifists they were and I am: "Nation shall not
lift up sword against nation, neither shall they learn
any more war," because we are talking of an immediate
practical question, peace in our time, peace in the time
of the Moabites and Israelites, and not of dreams of the
millennial future.

And I know I must find an answer, if there is one, in
the record itself, and it must deal with this incident at
Peor, not with another. We don't want analogies and
interpretations. We want to know why this particular
peace move at Peor was repressed with such brutality,
if it wasn't just for the sake of tribal mores and dogmas
and mystical twaddle about blessings. Will you listen,
then, just for a little while?

We read on, subdued, or trembling with indignation,
according to our point of view, and we find ourselves
involved in a long detour on civic and religious enactments. We forget what we are looking for, some of us
the more readily because we are sure it does not exist;
so that when it stares us in the face we pass it by. But
it is there—that "last unexpected fragment." We have
arrived at an account of war—of course!—between the
Israelites and the Midianites, and we are told that the
Israelites had taken captive the women of Midian and
their little ones. Then: "Moses was wroth with the
officers of the host, the captains of thousands and the captains of hundreds, who came from the service of the
war. And Moses said unto them: 'Have ye saved all the

65

women alive? Behold, these caused the children of Israel, through the counsel of Balaam, to revolt so as to break faith with the Lord in the matter of Peor."

So that was it! "Through the counsel of Balaam." The Moabite-Midianite peace move was a trap. Its purpose was not to disminish the bloodshed between the two peoples, but to make it one-sided and annihilative; the Israelites were to be demoralized and softened up for the slaughter. Otherwise we must assume that Balak, accepting Balaam's counsel, planned to absorb them peacefully into the faith and nation; and we who have seen his dread of them will throw the assumption out as fantastic.

And so from the strictly practical and humanitarian point of view we are now discussing, "iniquity" and "perverseness" are the correct words. Whatever the Israelite converts in the sacred red-light district of Chemosh may have thought they were doing, they were in effect delivering themselves to certain death; and if this was their "privilege," we have to bear in mind the weakened majority that they left exposed. And even if it was the privilege of the entire people to deliver itself up to slaughter, let us not talk about peace moves.

I shall be challenged. We have only the word of Moses that Balaam had anything to do with it. But we either argue on the record as it stands or forget about the whole business. There are no grounds for doubting the word of Moses here if we accept it elsewhere.

I am not asking anyone to like what God and Moses and Phinehas did at Peor. I am only asking that we see the incident for what it was. The pacifist intentions on

66

the Moabite-Midianite side, such as they were, were
confined to the proselytizing prostitutes of Chemosh—
and to Balaam. He at least would have preferred to see
the Israelites peacefully absorbed in this fashion. It was
an immensely attractive picture, even though it meant
a stronger Moab. His contempt for Balak and his bar-
barians was overridden now by his loathing for the people of the blessing, and that too was secondary to his
rancor against the God who had been his inspiration and
had become his nemesis. How delicious, after he had
been compelled to cry before the assembled Moabites:

> *"How goodly are thy tents, O Jacob,*
> *Thy dwellings, O Israel!"*—

how delicious to see tent and dwelling permanently
abandoned for the groves and altars of Chemosh, and to
think of the yet unborn Moabite-Israelite generations
as a continuing mockery of the blessing, if not in the
fleeting memory of man, then in the reliable memory
of God.

Such were his "intentions," and he harbored them,
after his fashion, though he knew them to be impossible,
for he can have had no doubt that when the Israelites
had come over to Moab they would be put to the sword.
There were other prospects almost as gratifying—and
quite as impossible. God might intervene to spoil that
first and happiest of climaxes, and in His fury go back to
the decision Moses had averted. Well then, Balaam
would be satisfied with second best. But he knew this to
be impossible too, amounting as it did to that reversal
of the blessing which he had been unable to force on

God. And the fact that all these things were impossible, the fact that he was denied a share in the omnipotence, goaded him on to the effort. "He returned to his place" after his humiliation on the heights, and he could not rest. He remembered the preliminary success of his first attempt, when God had after all commanded him to go with Balak's messengers. There must be some way, there must be some way, magical or non-magical, by assault or by ambush. . . . And he went westward again, uninvited, bringing new counsel to the king who had kicked him out.

And once more he could delude himself with a preliminary success. Come what might later, he was for the time being filled with the drunkenness of victory, and with an obscene *Schadenfreude*. He was satisfying his visceral itch to desecrate the highest with the lowest, and while the revels in the groves lasted he tasted the bliss of anticipated omnipotence.

The Balaam story sank deep into the folk memory. In the later summary we read: "An Ammonite or a Moabite shall not enter into the assembly of the Lord for ever; because they met you not with bread and water in the way, when ye came forth from Egypt; and because they hired against thee Balaam the son of Beor from Pethor of Aram-naharayim, to curse thee. . . ." Joshua during the wars of conquest reminds the Israelites of the conspiracy Many centuries later the prophet Micah refers to it: "O my people, remember now what Balak king of Moab devised, and what Balaam the son of Beor answered him." And hundreds of years after that, when Judea had been destroyed and the Jews—they were

68

Jews now, not Israelites—were rebuilding it, they are reminded how the Moabites "hired Balaam against the Israelites, to curse them."

The prohibitions against the Ammonites and the Moabites were so far relaxed that long before the time of Micah Ruth the Moabitess entered "the assembly" overnight, as it were; and her great-grandson David became the most famous king in Israel, the prototype of good kingship, and the channel to the Messiah. Balaam remains ever unforgiven. Whence the obstinate grudge? I think the reason lies in the man as such more than in the incident. If the great majority of Bible-readers— apart from the greater popular majority that does not read the Bible, and catches only at phrases—is not sufficiently attentive to the record, a few in every generation are, and they keep alive the disgust which a closer knowledge of the man inspires. The rabbis, as I have mentioned, have put it into the Tradition that Balaam was among the greatest prophets, a rival to Moses, "whose like has not arisen in Israel." At the same time the Tradition hints that Balaam was in the habit of committing sodomy with his ass! One cannot imagine a more striking symbol of the ghastly ambivalence of the man.

These same rabbis, to whom the Tradition was almost as sacred as the record, have selected from the utterances of Balaam the words which have opened the morning prayers of practically all Jews for centuries, and do so until this day:

*"How goodly are thy tents, O Jacob,*
*Thy dwellings, O Israel!"*

# CHAPTER III

# The Supporting Cast

❀

Y FEELING about some of the People of the Book
is purely subjective. I cannot explain it to myself, and
must assume it springs from unconscious associations.
Other Bible-lovers conjure up the same outward picture
from the Text, and their feelings are altogether different.

There is, for instance, a man called Paltiel, or Palti,
son of Laish, for whom I have a frankly unreasoning dislike, though nothing like my aversion for Balaam son of
Beor, which I regard as justified. This Paltiel flits in and
out of the David epic; he appears and disappears without speaking a word, and he leaves a vivid impression—
or, rather, variety of impressions.

He belongs to the days when David was an outlaw,
hunted by Saul. We are told how David was helped by
his wife Michal, Saul's daughter, to escape from a trap
laid by her father, while she remained behind; and how
the years passed and David, after sundry adventures,
took to himself two other wives, Abigail and Ahinoam.
Suddenly we read: "Now Saul had given Michal his
daughter, David's wife, to Palti son of Laish, who was

of Gallim." That is all, it seems. The David epic is resumed, and we do not expect to hear of Palti again.
More years pass, filled with stirring events. Saul dies on
Gilboa, fighting the Philistines, and David becomes king,
reigning in Hebron. Then Abner, Saul's former general,
sends a message to David: "Make thy league with me,
and, behold, my hand shall be with thee, to bring over
all Israel unto thee"; and David sends back word: "Well;
I will make a league with thee; but one thing I require
of thee, that is, thou shalt not see my face except thou
first bring Michal Saul's daughter, when thou comest
to see my face." Then we read: "And David sent messengers to Ishbosheth Saul's son, saying: 'Deliver me my
wife Michal, whom I betrothed to me for a hundred
foreskins of the Philistines.' And Ishbosheth sent, and
took her from her husband, even from Paltiel the son of
Laish. And her husband went with her, weeping as he
went, and followed her to Bahurim. Then said Abner
unto him: 'Go, return'; and he returned."

Exit Paltiel son of Laish, from Bahurim and from the
record.

What kind of man was he? I do not ask truculently,
like one spoiling for a fight, or egging others on. I ask
quite simply: What kind of man was he? What kind of
love did he have for Michal, the king's daughter? Abner
the general said to him: "Scram!" and he scrammed. No
anger on the one side, no resistance or protest on the
other. A fly was brushed off.

What was he doing among those demonic personalities, those makers of history, those generals and kings,
and sons and daughters of kings? What did Michal think

71

of him, she who was so energetic of spirit and bitter of tongue? What did the others think, if they thought about him at all?

I see him as the pushing little fellow who hankers for the company of the prominent, the man—often it is a woman—who is forever saying: "I want to be in the swim. I want to go places and do things. I want to talk with big executives, and distinguished scientists, and famous statesmen," though what entitles him to such privileges, and what he has to offer in exchange, neither he nor another can tell. Quite often he gets there, and hangs on a long time, sometimes by persistence, sometimes by accident. We meet him in the memoirs of the great, flitting in and out of their pages like Paltiel in and out of the Text. Paltiel's persistence was moderate. He followed Michal, weeping, all the way to Bahurim, but when he was told to go, he went quietly. He must have got there by accident. Saul had given him Michal his daughter, and Michal had let herself be given. He was permitted to hang on until somebody stamped on his foot. That is how I see him, and I dislike little people who pander to the egotisms of big people.

I cannot defend my impression, it is just there, inescapably. Others take a different view; I listen respectfully, with much interest, and retain my own. The others do the same. When I discussed this case publicly with Mark Van Doren we made no effort to convince each other. To Van Doren Paltiel son of Laish is a sad and likable figure, who loves Michal the proud with a hopeless and helpless love. He is not a fighter. He is the everlasting type of the innocent bystander, the pushed-

around, the unresisting victim of the powerful and ruthless.

The Tradition takes still another view. There Paltiel
is neither an intrusive toady, as I would have it, nor Van
Doren's gentle *schnuckel,* but a hero of the spirit, a saint,
a paragon of chastity and self-discipline. The Tradition
says that he would not claim his marital rights, seeing
that Michal had been David's wife, or still was, legally.
When they slept together, it continues, he put a sword
between them, to be used on the one who tried to cross
it with unchaste intentions.

I have tried now and then to imagine Paltiel as a
heroic saint or a quiet, unassuming soul, and have had
no success. Least of all can I imagine him using a sword
on Michal under the prescribed circumstances; I see
him, instead, paralyzed with fright.


II


Sometimes argument is unavoidable even when it is
fruitless.

I once heard a man who had taken a dislike to Abel
the son of Adam maintain that though Cain was the
killer, the guilt was Abel's. In the youth of the world,
he said, when God was still inexperienced in the ways of
mankind, one could do things with Him that have since
become impossible. Why did Cain kill Abel? The record
tells us: "In process of time it came to pass, that Cain
brought from the fruit of the ground an offering to the
Lord. And Abel, he also, brought of the firstlings of his
flock and of the fat thereof. And the Lord had respect

73

unto Abel and his offering; but unto Cain and his offering He had not respect. And Cain was very wroth and his countenance fell." Why did God reject Cain's offering? The record tells us again: "And the Lord said unto Cain: 'Why art thou wroth, and why is thy countenance fallen? If thou dost well, shall it not be lifted up? And if thou dost not well, sin coucheth at the door; and unto thee is its desire, but thou mayest rule over it.' "

That is the whole of the indictment. From God's act of discrimination flowed the most famous crime in history, and perhaps the greatest—the killing off of a quarter of the world's population. Are we not entitled to a bill of particulars, however short? What had Cain done? Nothing we know of. Sin couched at his door and tempted him; there is neither direct statement nor indirect evidence that he had yielded; there is on the other hand evidence that Cain was a reasonable man. We read that after he had listened to God's explanation "Cain spoke unto his brother Abel." He wanted his explanation, too. He got none. And then: "It came to pass, when they were in the field, that Cain rose up against his brother Abel, and slew him."

The defender of Cain was acquainted with the Tradition, and with the legends and discussions surrounding the first murder, and with the purported conversations between Cain and Abel; but his principle, like mine, was to stand by the Text, agreeing or disagreeing with the Tradition according to his own lights. He would not let me plead that the Text was corrupt, and I had no intention of doing so; that way madness lies. To him it was clear from the accepted Text that Abel had poisoned

74

God's mind against his older brother, and God's vague, unspecifying statement had all the earmarks of unverified slander. What was Cain to do, in the absence of an organized society and with the one recognized Authority duped?

My answer was that the man who invented murder must have been inherently wicked. Thereupon my opponent said that Cain did not invent murder, he stumbled on it. This time he was quoting the Tradition, in which Cain is allowed to enter the defense that, never having seen a dead man, he could not have known what death was; he therefore had no idea that if he bashed his brother's head in with a stone, the thing we now call death would ensue. To which I said this "stumbling" on great inventions and discoveries is a popular delusion. Archimedes "stumbled" on the law of liquid displacement in the bath, and Galileo on the isochronism of the pendulum in the Cathedral of Pisa, and Newton on the law of gravitation in the garden, when he saw an apple fall. But was it not odd that these men happened to be Archimedes, and Galileo, and Newton, who brooded all their lives on such problems, and had a gift for finding answers? "Sin coucheth at the door," said God; it lurked expectantly on the threshold of Cain's mind. Far from being a tyro at handling his unpredictable creature, man, God's understanding of him was, as this sentence proves, perfect from the beginning.

The argument went on a long time, with no result other than a possible sharpening of the wits. Finally my opponent said that I was literal-minded, while he was reading between the lines. I said I was doing the same,

75

the difference being that I did it in a receptive spirit, waiting there for the pictures to rise from the Text, whereas he did it in a spirit of contrariness, looking for trouble. Having become personal, we stopped.

Sometimes argument and an exchange of views are both impossible.

I read once a vindication of Jezebel, the murderess of Naboth and the prophets, according to which she was not the hellcat of the record, but a woman of high character who devoted her life to religious reform; only it happened that her god was Phœnician, like her father's, and she did her work among her husband Ahab's people, the Hebrews, whose God was the God of Abraham. "She failed," ran the vindication, "and the chauvinistic Hebrew chroniclers revenged themselves by making of her a byword for wickedness. Except for the few foregoing facts the whole account must be thrown out." This man too claimed to be "reading between the lines," but how can you read between lines that you have thrown out? There is no account of Jezebel anywhere else. She does not exist except in the Bible, and there, the writer maintains, she is ninety-nine per cent a figment of the Hebrew imagination. In exchange he offers, as historic truth, a one-hundred-per-cent figment of *his* imagination. But he has the logic of his purpose; he is exploiting Jezebel's name and reputation in the hope of establishing his own, and offering to take behind the Bible those who have never been through it. We can neither argue nor exchange views with him because on any assumption we shall not be talking about the same thing.

I have long had a frustrated affection for a little servant girl in the Second Book of Kings. She, like Paltiel
son of Laish, appears suddenly and as suddenly disappears in the midst of the mighty, but in how different
a spirit! I would not cross the street to find out what
happened to Paltiel after he left Bahurim weeping; I
would go a long way for knowledge of what the years
did to the nameless Israelite servant girl in the household of Naaman the Syrian general. She is like a benediction uttered by a humble stranger who passes us in a
crowded palace courtyard. A quiet assurance issues from
her brief presence, adding a permanent note of goodness to the world's consciousness.

She had a hand in a famous affair; she was, we might
say, its indispensable instrument. Hers were the few
words that led to the meeting of her master with the
prophet Elisha, concerning which I hope to say more
some day, in another place and in a different connection.
Because of my special feeling for her I single her out
here, to make sure that she will not be lost in the tumult
of the events she set in motion.

We read: "Now Naaman, captain of the host of the
king of Aram, was a great man with his master, and held
in esteem, because by him the Lord had given victory
unto Aram; he was also a mighty man of valour, but he
was a leper. And the Arameans had gone out in bands,
and had brought away captive out of the land of Israel
a little maid; and she waited on Naaman's wife. And she

77

said unto her mistress· 'Would that my lord were with the prophet that is in Samaria! then would he recover him of his leprosy.' "

Had the record broken off here, were we dealing with a fragment, I should already have found it arresting. It already has an unusual ring. A little girl is carried off from Israel by a band of marauders. Because of some special quality about her, she is reserved for, or ultimately finds her way into, the household of the country's commanding general, and becomes his wife's personal maid. An unhappy wife in a stricken household, an alien slave child in enemy hands—it augurs badly: the mistress embittered, the servant brutalized; at the best gloom, repression, and silence. It is unimaginable that the servant shall dare to make reference before her mistress to her master's hideous disease, and if one day she does so because she believes in the prophet Elisha, and because she dreams wildly that she may thus regain her freedom and her home, it is unimaginable that the mistress shall regard it as anything but boundless impudence.

Yet even if the record went no farther our impression would be quite different. The wording bespeaks a kindly relationship. The advice comes from the heart, a spontaneous, untimorous exclamation of pity and faith. What follows more than confirms the impression, and we are thrown into a contemplative mood, wondering what there was about the Israelite slave child that so affected her captors. For her simple conviction met with no resistance. The next sentences read: "And he went in, and told his lord, saying: 'Thus and thus said the maid that

78

is of the land of Israel.' And the king of Aram said: 'Go now, and I will send a letter to the king of Israel.' "

Thus her words carried into the highest places, and their weight was imparted to them by her alone. I have often brooded on the original Text, and I am sorry to note that some translators, while they admit that the king of Aram said to Naaman: "Go now, and I will send a letter to the king of Israel," cannot bring themselves to see that the slave child was known at court. "Thus and thus said the maid that is of the land of Israel," they insist, could not have been said by Naaman to the king. So they make it appear that it was said to Naaman by some manservant in the house. "One went in and told his lord . . ." they translate, and then, without transition: "The king of Aram said to Naaman. . . ."

I am reluctant to draw the reader into this kind of discussion, and I will do it as seldom as possible, but here I cannot help myself. Nothing in the grammar justifies the rendering: "One went in" as preferable to: "He went in." Everything in the spirit speaks against it. We are asked to believe that it was not Naaman's wife who repeated the advice to her husband, but some manservant who had overheard it. Or else that the little girl went about pleading with the servants, and one of them spoke to the master. Why should we do this violence to a clear picture of decent relationships? Only that we may be led from one improbability into another? We have been told that Naaman "was a great man with his master, and held in esteem." We have just seen how promptly the king responded with an offer of a letter to the king of Israel. The relationship between the king

79

and the general was a human one, too. It is a thousand to one that Naaman had told his lord about the captive from Israel, not merely by way of a report, but because of the unforeseen good she had brought into the house. It all comes naturally to me, this conversation between Naaman and the king: "You know that little girl from Israel I was telling you about. . . ."

However it fell out, the king was certainly told of her when Naaman made his request, and no one denies that one way or another she was a factor in the lives of the mighty. At this point her formal role ends, she withdraws from the record, but not from my imagination and concern. Concern? That is perhaps presumptuous. We need not fear for her. Whatever harm may befall her, she will not take the kind of hurt which disfigures most of us. There is hypocrisy in our protective attitude toward our moral superiors. We want to play the benefactor when we can only be beneficiaries. Let me therefore speak only of my affection and of my frustrated longing to know more about her.

But the Text is silent and cannot be forced. I do not want to daydream about her, and convince myself that when Naaman came back cured he sent her home to her parents, or that such a bond was created between her and the husband and wife that she remained with them as their daughter. The Text has given me much, I will not spoil it by pretending it has given me more.

IV

I have a warm and grateful liking of quite another kind
for the two midwives of Egypt, who are somewhat better
known than the slave child of Syria, but far from well
enough. Their names are recorded: Shiphrah and Puah,
and, to get over the shock at once, I see them as two
lovable and heart-warming comics.

Disrespectful? Not a bit of it. The moral person as
comic, as sly, beneficent gnome, who makes a huge joke
of foiling evil in the midst of danger, and makes the
villain look ridiculous, wants us to laugh with him. He is
puzzled and offended by the long face and the moral ex-
hortation, and the only wrong I shall be doing these
ladies is in explaining the joke so solemnly.

I begin with the setting. A few generations had passed
since the original band of Hebrews had been brought
into Egypt by Joseph, the savior of the country. We read
that they "were fruitful, and increased abundantly, and
multiplied, and waxed exceeding mighty; and the land
was filled with them"—that is, they were everywhere.
The description is borne out by the statistics. They
counted seventy souls on their arrival, they were some
six hundred thousand at the time of the Exodus. They
averaged a doubling of their numbers every fifteen years.

"Now there arose a king over Egypt, who knew not
Joseph. And he said unto his people: 'Behold, the people of the children of Israel are too mighty for us; come,
let us deal wisely with them, lest they multiply, and it
come to pass, that, when there befalleth any war, they

also join themselves unto our enemies, and fight against us, and get them up out of the land.' "

This statement of policy when analyzed is as rewarding in its way as Memucan's. It is history and comedy in one, and if you like, it is the essential tragicomedy of history. The Israelites were no longer a free people—they wanted to leave Egypt and could not. Still, they were already "too mighty" for the Egyptians—that is, for the comfort of the Egyptians—and they were multiplying rapidly. Unchecked they would soon become so mighty that in the event of a war they would be able to fight their way out of the country, after having lent their assistance to the enemy. Then, in heaven's name, why not let them go without waiting for a war? Ah no, that would be to act unhistorically. Never, says Pharaoh, and he calls upon the Egyptians to bestir themselves, to "deal wisely" with the Israelites, and to grapple with the national danger before it slips out of their fingers perhaps to be lost forever.

But this was just talk, and Pharaoh must have known what he was doing. He was a realist, the Israelites were a valuable property; they had to be kept, and that was feasible if they were kept down. And so, with statesman-like realism, Pharaoh created for himself the fatal dilemma presented by all slave populations, which may be formulated thus; the energies that make them valuable make them dangerous; the supineness that makes them safe makes them unprofitable. And either way their masters are demoralized.

"Therefore they did set over them taskmasters to afflict them with their burdens. And they built for

82

Pharaoh store-cities, Pithom and Raamses." As we have seen, and as the Tradition pointed out long ago, it was done by degrees. "But the more they afflicted them, the more they multiplied and the more they spread abroad. And they were adread because of the children of Israel."

They were adread! How insane can people get? We are beginning to feel like the Bedouins of Transjordan when they saw their first movie, a Western, and screamed to the stupid hero to watch out. We can hardly suppress the scream· "Idiot, let go!" The idiot could not let go because he was an actor in the continuous movie called history  Our grandchildren who will see on the screen the installment we are enacting today will also want to scream. Is it any wonder that we long for a Messiah to lead us into the post-historic stage?

The Pharaoh we are looking at is setting the pattern for the later Pharaoh who will have trouble with Moses, not midwives—the one who got ten chances, and bungled them, and they had to drown him before he would let go. For the moment we are perhaps a century before the Exodus, and three generations of practice will go into the ultimate Egyptian suicide. Meanwhile history hardens Pharaoh's arteries.

"And they made their lives bitter with hard service, in mortar and in brick, and in all manner of service in the field; in all their service, wherein they made them serve with rigour "

The Israelites kept multiplying. And now enter our two characters. Population-control by excessive enforced labor having failed, "the king of Egypt spoke to the Hebrew midwives, of whom the name of the one was

83

Shiphrah, and the name of the other Puah; and he said: 'When ye do the office of a midwife to the Hebrew women, ye shall look upon the birthstool; if it be a son, then ye shall kill him; but if it be a daughter, then she shall live.' "

It was an ingenious idea. Before long there would be only female Hebrews, laborers but noncombatants— diminished value, but increased safety. Thereafter the begetting would have to be done by Egyptians, with safeguards against emotional entanglements, especially between father and son. The male offspring could perhaps be siphoned off.

What did Shiphrah and Puah answer the king of Egypt? Those who would have liked a heroic rebuke, a "far-be-it-from-us-O-king" oration followed by a martyrdom, will be disappointed. Shiphrah and Puah answered never a word. We only read: "But the midwives feared God, and did not as the king commanded them, but saved the men children alive."

And now let us get our bearings. I repeat: Pharaoh must have known what he was doing. These two Hebrew agents must have come to him with the highest recommendations. It is inadmissible that he would entrust the execution of this fateful policy to relatives of its victims without the assurance that they were cowardly and corrupt. Shall we assume that the God-fearing Shiphrah and Puah had cunningly cultivated such a reputation among the Egyptians? Or did they bribe their way into the strategic position? A little of both; dissimulation and bribery go hand in hand; and when it is for the defeat of villainy, comedy is in the air. In any case our mid-

84

wives dissimulated before Pharaoh, and in no case do they emerge as epic heroines or as pious simpletons. The data so far reveal them as moral comics; more follow.

The deception could not go on indefinitely. Unbribed Egyptians were bound to smuggle through to Pharaoh the disturbing intelligence that new male children were appearing among the Hebrews. We read: "And the king of Egypt called for the midwives, and said unto them: 'Why have ye done this thing, and have saved the men children alive?' And the midwives said unto Pharaoh: 'Because the Hebrew women are not as the Egyptian women; for they are lively, and are delivered ere the midwife come unto them.' "

This is one of the cheekiest cock-and-bull stories ever handed to a baffled government by a professional saboteur, and it proves that the successful big lie is not a monopoly of the wicked. Pharaoh was completely taken in. He did not even punish the midwives for inefficiency. They remained in office. We read: "And God dealt well with the midwives; and the people multiplied, and waxed very mighty. And it came to pass, because the midwives feared God, that He made them houses."

How did the thing work? There was collusion by bribery, and there was undoubtedly collusion from moral protest. There were Egyptians—Pharaoh's daughter was one of them—who "had compassion" on a Hebrew child. There were not enough of them, and there was not enough moral revulsion, for an uprising. But life does not stand still, and the situation had to get better or worse. It got worse before it got better. For we read: "And Pharaoh charged all his people, saying:

'Every son that is born ye shall cast into the river, and every daughter ye shall save alive.' " That is, he finally took the matter out of the hands of the midwives, who had done their sorry best, and transferred it to the reliable assassins called people's courts.

The game was over, but while it lasted we may be sure that Shiphrah and Puah were the heart and soul of it. We may wish they had acted like Elijah before Ahab, or Daniel before Nebuchadnezzar, or Hannah of the Seven Sons before Antiochus; we may also wish that the dissidents among the common people had staged a revolt, however hopeless. But let us not despise the decency of the timid; prophecy is for the prophet and heroism for the hero; for the rest of us there is a halfway morality between martyrdom and damnation. This morality does not defy; it tries to subvert by evasive disobedience, which after all implies a certain degree of goodwill and courage. It may be described as the little man's contribution to collective salvation. When it is widespread the hero comes into his own; when it shrinks he is helpless. But while it is small, it needs the Shiphrahs and Puahs, who feed it with laughter and do not demand of it what it cannot give. And when they go, it goes with them, as we learn from our story.

## V

I am ill at ease in the presence of the wise woman of Abel, and of Jael, the wife of Heber the Kenite. The first saved a city from destruction, the second put an end to a tyranny. I feel I ought to be more friendly, but

86

whenever I meet them, as I am compelled to now and then in spite of myself, I am conscious of my equivocal attitude, and get away as soon as I decently can.

The wise woman of Abel has no other name; she is a representative figure, for it appears that her city had been famous for wisdom. She is none the less strikingly individual, and if I find her confusing, it is not for lack of definition. To be honest, I see her only too well.

She emerges, shouting, in the midst of a battle. Sheba, the son of Bichri, "a base fellow," had stirred up the northern tribes against King David, who sent an expedition against him. Sheba threw himself into the city of Abel, and Joab the general besieged it, and it looked like a long and bloody affair; for the division between the northern and the southern tribes, the ten and the two, was deep-rooted, reaching back to the beginnings of the people. David had united them, but after the death of his son Solomon they broke apart again, forever. So the siege went on, and Joab's men "cast up a mound against the city, and it stood in the moat; and all the people that were with Joab battered the wall, to throw it down."

Then, above the din, a voice rises from the city wall. It is the wise woman of Abel. "Hear, hear!" Her appearance must have been as formidable as her voice, for they suspended operations and listened. "Say, I pray you, unto Joab: come near hither, that I may speak with thee." Joab is brought to her, the battering rams are motionless, the besiegers stand in the moat, the defenders on the wall, the two voices are heard in the sudden silence.

"And the woman said: 'Art thou Joab?' And he an-

87

swered: 'I am.' Then she said unto him: 'Hear the words of thy handmaid.' And he answered: 'I do hear.' Then she spoke, saying: 'They were wont to speak in old time, saying: "They shall surely ask counsel at Abel"; and so they ended the matter. We are of them that are peaceable and faithful in Israel; seekest thou to destroy a city and a mother in Israel? why wilt thou swallow up the inheritance of the Lord?' And Joab answered and said: 'Far be it, far be it from me, that I should swallow up or destroy.' "

It is a subtle conversation. The woman spoke for the peace party in the city, and she knew that she was addressing a notorious man of blood. Joab had just murdered a rival general, Amasa, in the most treacherous fashion; and it was he who had arranged for the murder of Uriah the Hittite at the command of David. Her rhetoric forced a double protestation from him: "Far be it, far be it from me that I should swallow up or destroy." And he plunged on: "The matter is not so"; he is not a killer: "But a man of the hill-country of Ephraim, Sheba the son of Bichri by name, hath lifted up his hand against the king, even against David; deliver him only and I will depart from the city."

What the wise woman says next makes me shudder: "Behold, his head shall be thrown to thee over the wall." She foresees that Sheba will not let himself be delivered to execution while a chance remains of fighting it out in the city. Nevertheless, I say, it is not her business to promise that he shall be killed. If he is to be executed— on the not too remote assumption that he can be taken alive—it should be by the rightful authorities. This is not sentimentality; it is morality and law. And then the additional flourish, that the head shall be thrown over the wall, making proper burial impossible—what is that for? We must suppose that the wise woman of Abel, knowing what kind of man she is addressing, has found the phrase and gesture that will produce the best effect.

We read: "Then the woman went unto all the people in her wisdom. And they cut off the head of Sheba the son of Bichri, and threw it out to Joab."

"She went unto all the people." I sometimes think of her as the woman with the voice: yelling above the thunder of the battering rams, piercing into the ears of Joab, whispering, pleading, exhorting, arguing in the streets and homes of Abel, unto all the people: "Cut his head off, cut his head off, there'll be no peace otherwise, I've promised it to Joab, cut his head off."

Her wisdom prevailed, and Joab "blew the horn, and they were dispersed from the city, every man to his tent, and Joab returned to Jerusalem unto the king."

I will put my personal prejudices aside and forget that like King Lear I think a low voice an excellent thing in a woman. I am troubled less by what the wise woman of Abel is than by what she did; and the Tradition is similarly troubled, without sharing my prejudice. We will also forget the details of her action, and with the Tradition ask, irrespective of the merits of the rebellion, whether a besieged city has the right to save itself by surrendering a designated person to the enemy. The question occurs a million times in history, and it takes diverse forms, like preventive arrest, and forehanded liquidation. We met it in the Balaam story, where thou-

sands of Israelites were put to death that the rest might
be saved. There, as everywhere else, the action can be
justified on a statistical view of morality, and even then
we daringly take it for granted that the calculation is
correct. Can it be justified on any other view?

I have no absolute answer, and after years of thinking
not even a clue. I am not indifferent to numbers, or to
lives that are anonymous. I see the unreason of letting a
hundred perish blindly from reluctance to do an injustice to one. All the same, there is a hammering at the
back of my mind: morality is not statistical. I have to
know what the hundred are living for. If they say:
"Whatever we are living for, it is automatically moral to
kill one person 'unjustly' if thereby we save a hundred—
or fifty, or twenty, or two—equally innocent persons,"
then I must answer: for me that takes away the meaning of living. The key-words here are "automatically,"
and "whatever we are living for."

Every case must be judged on its merits, and the dread-
ful decision must be referred to something that is not
just numerical. I bowed miserably to the ruling at Peor
because it was a question of saving "the blessing." I stand
undecided before the case of Sheba son of Bichri, and I
am speechless when I meet the woman of Abel. I accept
the statements that Sheba son of Bichri was base and she
was wise. It is not enough. The text does not supply the
data for a moral judgment, and probably what distresses
me most is the woman's furious and strident certainty.
When I get down to it I discover that my distaste for her
loud voice has some connection with the purpose she
used it for. I am sure that if a woman in the record

screamed for a whole year in an effort to save a life, my heart would still go out to her.

The question is posed more sharply by Jael, the wife of Heber the Kenite. Her contribution to peace and security was much greater than the wise woman's, and her picture is proportionately more terrifying. She, as some will remember, is the woman who gave refuge to Sisera, King Jabin's general, and murdered him in his sleep. Of her I think as the woman with the tent-peg.

To appreciate the extent of her service we must rehearse briefly the circumstances in which it was rendered.

In the long and cruel inner struggle which the blessing had imposed on them, the Israelites, at that time only part masters of the Promised Land, had again "done that which was evil in the sight of the Lord . . . and the Lord gave them over into the hand of Jabin, king of Canaan, that reigned in Hazor; the captain of whose host was Sisera, who dwelt in Harosheth-goyim. And the children of Israel cried unto the Lord; for he had nine hundred chariots of iron; and twenty years he mightily oppressed the children of Israel."

Then arose Deborah, the wife of Lappidoth, a prophetess, and a judge, and she inspired Barak the son of Abinoam to rise against Jabin; and in a battle near Mount Tabor the Canaanite army was destroyed to a man, with the exception of Sisera, who fled from the field on foot toward Kedesh.

We read that "Heber the Kenite had severed himself from the Kenites, even from the children of Hobab, the father-in-law of Moses, and had pitched his tent as far

91

as Elon-bezaanannim, which is by Kedesh." When Sisera appeared before the tent, Jael was alone, and he approached hesitantly, though "there was peace between Jabin the king of Hazor and the house of Heber the Kenite." He may not have known whose tent it was. She saw him from the distance and went out to meet him, and spoke to him, and her voice was not at all like the wise woman of Abel's; it was gentle and inviting and solicitous. "She said unto him: 'Turn in, my lord, turn in to me; fear not.' And he turned in unto her into the tent, and she covered him with a rug. And he said unto her: 'Give me, I pray thee, a little water to drink; for I am thirsty.' And she opened a bottle of milk, and gave him drink, and covered him."

These grisly details were remembered afterwards by the Israelites, who gloated over them, and incorporated them gleefully in the wild Song of Deborah:

> *Blessed above women shall Jael be,*
> *The wife of Heber the Kenite.*
> *Water he asked, milk she gave him;*
> *In a lordly bowl she brought him curd.*

Then she covered him again. "And he said unto her: 'Stand in the door of the tent, and it shall be, when any man doth come and inquire of thee, and say: "Is there any man here?" that thou shalt say: "No." ' Then Jael Heber's wife took a tent-pin, and took a hammer in her hand, and went softly unto him, and smote the pin into his temples, and it pierced through into the ground; for he was in a deep sleep; so he swooned and died."

Over this, too, the Israelites roared with laughter:

*Her hand she put to the tent pin,*
*And her right hand to the workman's hammer;*
*And with the hammer she smote Sisera, she smote*
  *through his head,*
*Yea, she pierced and struck through his temples.*
*At her feet he sunk, he fell, he lay;*
*At her feet he sunk, he fell;*
*Where he sunk, there he fell down dead.*

Relief from twenty years of oppression howls in these verses. Pity? How much pity did we feel when we read and reread the details of Mussolini's horrible death, and of Hitler's? And yet the killing of Sisera brought happier years than we in our generation have known. For we read: "And the land had rest for forty years."

And lest we should be tempted to quibble that the death of one man could not have affected the outcome, the record makes the contrary clear. From that time on, with the great Canaanite general removed, the Israelites went from victory to victory. "And the hand of the children of Israel prevailed more and more against Jabin the king of Canaan, until they had destroyed Jabin king of Canaan."

What am I to say now? Forty years of peace and tranquillity against the killing of one man. I shall be told: "The man had to be killed. Does it matter how? It is childish, and morbid, to dwell on the details. Forget about them." But if we ought to forget about them, why does the record insist on them, and so vividly? It could have read: "And Sisera fled to the tent of Jael the wife of Heber the Kenite, and she slew him in his sleep."

The record wants us to know, and to remember, and to consider, and the generations have pondered the problem.

I have tried to forget, and though I cannot quite shake myself free of her, I linger in her company as little as possible. I ought to thank her and all I can do is stare. I keep wondering what she felt like when she wheedled the exhausted man into her tent; and at what precise moment she determined on the deed; and what she was thinking when she rummaged about for the implements, and when she knelt down and lifted the hammer. She was a strong woman with a steady hand to have been able to drive the peg through from temple to temple at a single blow, as she must have done. There was little blood, or else we would have read: "And she arose and washed herself." We only read: "And, behold, as Barak pursued Sisera, Jael came out to meet him, and said unto him: 'Come, and I will show thee the man whom thou seekest.'" She was calm, as well as strong, the woman with the tent-peg.

VI

They rise to me straight out of the Text, the People of the Book. I see them with my own eyes, and nothing that I see is of my own invention or by anyone else's suggestion. Many of them are given only a few lines, and yet their presence can be as solid as that of the principals. They are like great actors with short roles; they are there for a few moments, but they are mightily there. I have called these obscure ones the supporting cast only out of

94

deference to their standing with the general public. As human beings they are nearly all major to me.

Sometimes one is disheartened by the irresponsibility and even the frivolity of the public reaction. Sir Thomas Browne complains that the iniquity of oblivion blindly scattereth her poppy; fame is not discriminating, either. Everyone knows Methuselah, not one in a thousand the servant girl of Naaman. And Methuselah is not a person; he is a few numbers between "begats." Even the numbers—his longevity—are not impressive, when examined in context. He died at nine hundred and sixty-nine; his grandfather Jared, whom nobody so much as mentions, was only seven years younger when he died, and Adam lived to the age of nine hundred and thirty.

I can understand that Cain should be better known than Abel. He is the more vivid figure. Abel is, as it happens, one of the few People of the Book who do not linger with us. He is killed without ever having come to life. He says nothing, whereas most of the words spoken by and about Cain are unforgettable: "Am I my brother's keeper?" and: "A fugitive and a wanderer in the earth" and: "My punishment is greater than I can bear" and: "Thy brother's blood crieth to Me from the earth" and: "The mark of Cain." But why should Jezebel, that prototype of wickedness, be famous mostly in the phrase "a painted Jezebel"? She happened to paint her face one day—she was well on in years, and it was the day of her violent death—and that is what the public chiefly remembers against her, so that for millions she passes as the symbol of wantonness, though the record never once reflects on her continence.

95

But the aptest of catchwords destroys the individual, and with him the type is also destroyed. This is inevitable, because despite our vague belief to the contrary, the more individual a man is, the more he is a type. The French are right when they say of an original character: *"C'est un type!"* Thus "Jezebel that prototype of wickedness" is merely less misleading than "a painted Jezebel."

We lose person and therefore type because a catchword takes hold of a feature to the exclusion of the totality that gives it force. Such is, for instance, the case with Goliath. We think of: "Giant Killed by Boy," or, better: "Brute Force Overcome by Spirit," and these will do as headlines or filing references, but as nothing more. Their biggest drawback, incidentally, is that they make Goliath, like Abel, famous for what was done to him rather than for what he was. I grant that if David had not killed him he might never have been heard of, but the meaning of the encounter—even when we understand that it represents Brute Force versus the Spirit —comes home to us only if we know the fighters as persons, and Goliath as "Giant" or "Brute Force" is not a person. We must take a good look at him.

Notice first that though he is a giant he is not impossible. His height is given as "six cubits and a span," or ten feet, which is just a few inches more than Machnow the Russian Giant, who was exhibited throughout the world when I was a boy. Other measurements correspond. His coat of mail weighed "five thousand shekels of brass," or about eighty pounds, according to one authority. "The shaft of his spear was like a weaver's beam,

96

and his spear's head weighed six hundred shekels of iron."

This huge but not impossible creature parades before the army of Israel day after day, roaring: "Why do ye come to set your battle in array? Am I not a Philistine, and ye servants to Saul? Choose you a man for you, and let him come down to fight with me. If he be able to fight with me, and kill me, then will we be your servants; but if I prevail against him, then shall ye be our servants, and serve us." And again: "I do taunt the armies of Israel this day; give me a man, that we may fight together."

Notice, further, how he introduces himself. "Am I not a Philistine?" The word is taken up. It is a most curious circumstance that in the detailed account of the great duel Goliath is mentioned by name only three or four times, but he is referred to as "the Philistine" dozens of times. It is "this Philistine," "this uncircumcised Philistine," "the Philistine looked about him," "the Philistine cursed," "the Philistine arose," David took a stone from his bag and slung it, "and smote the Philistine in his forehead," and "David took the head of the Philistine." The chronicler is enormously impressed with Goliath's typicality, his representative character, his Philistinism, which he himself stressed in his opening words.

A third point has always held my attention. Offer to decide a battle by single combat is nothing new; but here it seems, because of the second point, to carry a special meaning. We are dealing with an issue that individuals must fight out; an intensely personal matter. What is the nature of the issue?

On the surface it is, in agreement with the accepted headline, "Brute Force versus the Spirit." We get it from a quick reading of the encounter and of the speeches exchanged. David comes out against Goliath unaccoutered, and unarmed but for his staff and his sling. "And the Philistine came nearer and nearer unto David; and the man that bore the shield went before him. And when the Philistine looked about, and saw David, he disdained him; for he was but a youth, and ruddy, and withal of fair countenance. And the Philistine said unto David: 'Come to me, and I will give thy flesh unto the fowls of the air, and to the beasts of the field.' Then said David to the Philistine: 'Thou comest to me with a sword, and with a spear; but I come to thee in the name of the Lord of hosts, the God of the armies of Israel, whom thou hast taunted. This day will the Lord deliver thee into my hand; and I will smite thee, and take thy head from off thee; and I will give the fowls of the air, and to the wild beasts of the earth . . . carcasses of the host of the Philistines this day unto the that all this assembly may know that the Lord saveth not with the sword and the spear; for the battle is the Lord's. . . .' "

The speeches at once confirm the headline: "Brute Force versus the Spirit." But as we reread them an odd little matter of phrasing obtrudes itself. Goliath shouts: "I will give thy flesh to . . . *the beasts of the field,*" and David answers: "I will give the carcasses of the host of the Philistines . . . *to the wild beasts of the earth.*" The wild beasts of the earth are carnivorous, but the beasts of the field, which means cattle, are grass-eaters; they would not touch David's flesh.

"Oh, come now," says the reader, "that was just a slip of the tongue on Goliath's part." So it was—and a very significant one; it is the clue to the Philistinism that Goliath represented, and to the peculiarly individual or personal nature of the combat here described.

And now I must repeat an apology and make a short digression. I must once more refer to the Hebrew Text, and to the self-evident fact that no translation can produce all the original effects. Although "beasts of the field" and "wild beasts of the earth" are excellent renderings, they do not quite reproduce the contrast between *behemat ha-sadeh*—cattle—and *hayat ha-aretz*—wild beasts of the earth—which startles the Hebrew-reader.

One brilliant Hebrew commentator who pauses over this significant difference between *behemat ha-sadeh* and *hayat ha-aretz* tells us that the moment David heard Goliath say *behemat ha-sadeh* he said exultantly to himself: "The man's mad! He's mine!" And as he advanced to the kill he corrected the Philistine: *"Hayat ha-aretz—*the wild beasts of the earth."

Goliath is mad, stark, raving mad. He is shouting: "I will throw your carcass to the sheep and horses and cows to devour." He towers before us, not the primitive we took him for at first, but man reverting to the brute, man stripped of his intelligence and controls. He is, in our new phraseology, the Id, the furious idiot impulse, the blind, blundering hunger, the "I want! I want!" of

99

sheer appetitional propulsion. He is Heidelberg Man erupting in contemporaneous life hundreds of centuries after his time.

It was a fine and subtle notion to assign the killing of Goliath to David, the comely youth who watched his flock under the stars, and from them drew the inspiration of the harpist and psalmodist. Equally subtle is the individualization of the battle in this place, and there is more than the obvious meaning in the challenge: "Choose you a man for you, and let him come down to fight with me. If he be able to fight with me, and kill me, then will we be your servants; but if I prevail against him, then shall ye be our servants, and serve us."

All this gathers force, becomes more palpable, if we consider Goliath as a person. It may startle the reader to learn that Goliath had a brother, whose name was Lahmi. He too was a giant, and the staff of his spear, too, was like a weaver's beam. He was slain by Elhana the son of Jair. One wonders if they were similar in other respects, and who was the older, and by how much; and whether as youngsters they played happily together. One of them, says the record, had a giant son with six fingers on each hand and six toes on each foot, and he was slain by Jonathan—not *the* Jonathan, but a nephew of David's.

The Text does not make gigantism synonymous with brutishness, or malice. It gives us at least one giant—I always associate him with Goliath by contrast—who is a comic—namely, Og. Whereas we meet Goliath armed and roaring on the hillside, we meet Og in bed, almost literally; he is introduced as king of the Amorites in

Bashan, and: "Behold, his bedstead was a bedstead of iron; is it not in Rabbah of the children of Ammon? Nine cubits was the length thereof, and four cubits the breadth of it." Goliath is abnormal, Og legendary. He is given a height of over thirteen feet—a structural impossibility for a human being. He is a third as tall again as Goliath, and the famous oak of Bashan is not strong enough to support his weight. For if he is of proportionate girth, as the record indicates, he weighs nearly a ton. He contrasts with Goliath, too, in being not a throwback but a genuine primitive—"of the remnant of the Rephaim"—the giants of old, offspring of the sons of God and the daughters of men. He was therefore born in the pre-Flood age. Unnoticed, he escaped drowning, and lived through the patriarchal age and the centuries of the Egyptian slavery. He was a contemporary of Noah, Abraham, Isaac, Jacob, Joseph, and finally of Moses, who killed him. He makes Methuselah's much touted longevity look silly.

Unlike Goliath he nowhere appears in an extended description; but he is mentioned more frequently, and almost always in one breath with Sihon, king of the Amorites in Heshbon; he is in the First Book of Kings, and in the Psalms, and in the Book of Nehemiah, and by repetition he becomes as familiar as Goliath. Of Sihon there is no description at all, but we are told of his churlishness; when Moses begged permission to pass through the land—"thou shalt sell me meat for money, that I may eat; and give me water for money, that I may drink"—he refused, being a pro-Canaanite noninterventionist. There are no derogatory marks against Og, and we are not asked to remember him with resentment; we are, instead, invited to visit Rabbah, in Ammon, and measure his bed. By his side Sihon was of course a dwarf, apparently a malicious dwarf, tagging along and providing the ideas.

The Tradition makes merry with Og, and surrounds him with tremendous and uproarious legends for which I can find not the slightest warrant in the Text. The Bible certainly indicates a rollicking, Paul Bunyanesque figure, but the stories about him in the Tradition, besides ignoring the specific measurements we are given, and expanding him into meaningless dimensions, contain much incongruous moralizing about him.

With all his preposterous jollity, he has his touch of pathos. He must have been lonely after the Flood, and as the past receded, and his memory of the grand old times and of the companionship of his fellow giants became rather dim, he no doubt told many tall stories of the people he had known and the things he had done. These are perhaps the basis of some of the legends; but apart from the fact that the memory of such an old man cannot be trusted, the legends are not even transmitted in his name. In any case, we have nothing against Og, and I, for one, regret that he had to be swept out of the way, though in all probability he himself felt that he had had about enough and was not too sorry to go.

## CHAPTER IV

## *An Idyl of Old Age*

❀

I SMELL goodness when Naomi approaches. She is Naaman's little servant girl grown old, and as she draws near we realize that the years have dealt cruelly with her. I think of them together, the widow of Bethlehem and the slave child of Syria. But it is easier to write about Naomi—for two reasons. We have a full-length portrait and a happy ending.

The Book of Ruth—which should be called the Book of Naomi—begins like an epilogue. On a day late in the summer three widows stand arguing and weeping on the road that leads from a Moabite village to the Jordan and the land of Israel. The oldest is trying to persuade the other two, who are her daughters-in-law, to let her go on alone, to let her return, bereft as she is of husband and sons, to the town of Bethlehem in Judah, the place of her birth. For the years of famine which had driven her and her husband and her two sons from Judea to Moab are over at last; and over, too, are the years of her happiness and fruitfulness. She will stay no longer; and the two younger widows, Moabitesses both, plead with her to take them with her.

"And Naomi said unto her daughters-in-law: 'Go, return each of you to her mother's house; the Lord deal kindly with you, as ye have dealt with the dead, and with me. The Lord grant you that ye may find rest, each of you in the house of her husband.' Then she kissed them; and they lifted up their voice, and wept. And they said unto her: 'Nay, but we will return with thee unto thy people.' And Naomi said. 'Turn back, my daughters; why will ye go with me? Have I yet sons in my womb, that they may be your husbands? Turn back, my daughters, go your way; for I am too old to have a husband. If I should say: I have hope, should I even have a husband tonight, and also bear sons; would ye tarry for them till they were grown? would ye shut yourselves off for them and have no husbands? nay, my daughters, for it grieveth me much for your sakes, for the hand of the Lord is gone forth against me.' And they lifted up their voice and wept again. And Orpah kissed her mother-in-law; but Ruth cleaved unto her. And she said: 'Behold, thy sister-in-law is gone back unto her people and unto her god; return thou after thy sister-in-law.' And Ruth said: 'Entreat me not to leave thee, and to return from following after thee; for whither thou goest I will go; and where thou lodgest I will lodge; thy people shall be my people, and thy God my God; where thou diest, will I die, and there will I be buried; the Lord do so to me, and more also, if aught but death part thee and me.' And when she saw that she was steadfastly minded to go with her, she left off speaking unto her. So they two went until they came to Bethlehem."

We listen, awed, across the interval of three thousand

years; and through the mist of our own tears we see the
one that returned, and the two that went on. And when
they have vanished we remain standing there, and ask:
what was there about Naomi of Bethlehem, the mother
of the dead Mahlon and Chilion, that wrought so on the
two Moabite girls? And why was it that they did not say
a single word to hold her back in Moab, though they
for their part were prepared to follow her into an alien
land, and only one of them was finally dissuaded? And
why was she, with whom they had dealt so kindly—with
her, as with the dead—so insistent on returning?

I shall not try to answer the first question. The mys-
tery of Naomi's being, the source of the love she inspired, is outside my reach. I can only turn over in my
mind the simpler questions, and to these my answers are
tentative.

I cannot believe that she was anxious about her old
age, and afraid of becoming a dependent on strangers in
a strange land; by strangers I mean, of course, only the
families into which her daughters-in-law might remarry.
Was she, then, suffering from the childhood regression of
the old and unhappy? No, she was not the kind to withdraw selfishly from the love of the living into the memory of the dead. Did she want to die among her own, and
be buried with them? These Moabite women had become her own, and she would die among them; and she
would be buried with her own, her husband and her
two sons. What, then, made her so resolute, and what
gave her resolution such an edge that her daughters-in-
law made no effort to change it?

I read and reread these words: "It grieveth me for

your sakes, for the hand of the Lord is gone forth against me." For their sakes she would leave them, lest they should continue to be involved in her unhappy destiny. It cannot be denied that Naomi's mood was one of despair. She had lost faith in life—in her own life, that is; she was not to be granted that which could make her happy—namely, the sight of the happiness of those she loved. It was best, then, for her to remove herself from them; they might yet find happiness if she did not seek to share it. And so by the roadside she tried to take an everlasting farewell of these beloved links with the beloved dead.

It is difficult to think of Naomi as the victim of despair: this is the kind of hurt from which we thought her immune. It is also discouraging. If her character does not give her a safe-conduct through the years and disaster, whose will? Should we say resignation instead of despair? Thus far in the Text it is still possible, but not a few lines farther on: "And it came to pass, when they were come to Bethlehem, that all the city was astir concerning them, and the women said: 'Is this Naomi?' And she said unto them: 'Call me not Naomi (that is, pleasant), call me Marah (that is, bitter) ; for the Almighty hath dealt very bitterly with me. I went out full, and the Lord hath brought me back home empty; why call ye me Naomi, seeing that the Lord hath testified against me and the Lord hath afflicted me?' "

It is despair, and the chapter is an epilogue in which a life's tragedy is reviewed, and softened, and made bearable, by the hint that not everything has been lost;

something remains, the return for Naomi's goodness, a love as strong as her own. We may reasonably hope that the lesson—for an epilogue is a lesson—points to a better time, when we shall be able to speak of resignation. And when we come to the end of the first chapter, and see that there is a second, and turning the pages we see that there are a third and a fourth, we begin to hope that the epilogue is also a prologue, and that we will not be left to resign ourselves to Naomi's resignation.

II

That epilogue-prologue, with its supreme utterance of human love, towers above the rest of the book—and yet the story does not suffer thereby if rightly understood. Those who are looking for the sources of Naomi's influence will be expecting a whole series of spectacular situations accompanied by immortal phrases. Instead they will only be told how Naomi acted in a commonplace world from commonplace day to commonplace day. They will see her planning and arranging things in a setting of small-town interests. They will place her, at first, among the Managerial Women; they will call her a schemer, and I agree that she was the subtlest and most loving schemer of them all, and if she is not, somewhere in the world, the patron saint of matchmakers, there is no justice in hagiology. But what is the secret of her grace? Gradually it dawns on us that the small-town interests veiled big-world meanings. The levels below the mountain of the prologue have their own fascination.

107

The quiet, undramatic substance of Naomi's daily life is the expression of her extraordinary spirit. We become more and more attentive.

And now we move into the workaday and practical. How were the two women to live? Naomi had a tiny property, left her by her husband, Elimelech, but it brought in nothing. She also had relatives by marriage. One of them, Boaz, was a leading citizen, "a mighty man of valour"; that is, a rich and important man. Another, unnamed, was at least well enough off to be able to buy her out. I am ashamed to say that neither of them so much as called on her or inquired after her welfare, and the contrast with the kindness she had met among the Moabites is as painful as it is striking. It is no use looking for excuses. They knew of her return: "all the city was astir concerning them." They simply ignored her, and the two widows were thrown on the social-security system of ancient Judea, which provided that at harvest time the corners of fields and stray ears of grain had to be left for the poor.

"And Ruth the Moabitess said unto Naomi: 'Let me now go to the field, and glean among the ears of corn after him in whose sight I shall find favour.' And she said unto her: 'Go, my daughter.' "

Naomi could have said: "Go to Boaz's field; it is the largest; besides, he is a relative." Out of delicacy she did not mention him or the other well-to-do relative who had not inquired after her, or, for that matter, any of her relatives, since the right of gleaning was the law, applying everywhere. Nor did she warn Ruth against any particular field; this would have been an excess of

108

delicacy, amounting to a reflection. She simply said: "Go, my daughter."

We read· "And she went, and came and gleaned in the field after the reapers; and her hap was to light on the portion of the field belonging unto Boaz, who was of the family of Elimelech. And, behold, Boaz came from Bethlehem, and said unto the reapers: 'The Lord be with you.' And they answered him: 'The Lord bless thee.' Then said Boaz unto his servant that was set over the reapers: 'Whose damsel is this?' And the servant that was set over the reapers answered and said. 'It is a Moabitish damsel that came back with Naomi out of the field of Moab; and she said: "Let me glean, I pray you, and gather after the reapers among the sheaves"; so she came, and hath continued even from the morning until now, save that she tarried a little in the house.' "

What a long-winded and wandering reply! What is the foreman gabbling about? What are all these self-evident details for? Well—he is miserably embarrassed. "A Moabitish damsel that came back with Naomi," he begins, and does not know which way to look. He can't say: "*The* Moabitish damsel who came back with Naomi"—it would sound like a reproach. And yet "*A* Moabitish damsel" sounds absurd, implying that Boaz does not know what all the town is talking about. So he gulps on apologetically and eagerly, hardly knowing what he is saying: You see, she came early in the morning, and she asked permission to glean, and I gave it of course, naturally, why not? and she's been at it all day, but she did take a little rest in the house, why shouldn't she? . . . I am embarrassed, too.

109

And then, to his relief and mine, the following conversation develops between Boaz and Ruth:

Boaz: "Hearest thou not, my daughter? Go not to glean in another field, neither pass from hence, but abide fast here by my maidens. Let thine eyes be on the field that they do reap and go thou after them; have I not charged the young men that they shall not touch thee? And when thou art athirst, go unto the vessels, and drink of that which the young men have drawn."

Ruth (bowing to the ground): "Why should I have found favour in thy sight, that thou shouldst take cognizance of me, seeing I am a foreigner?"

Boaz: "It hath been fully told me, all that thou hast done unto thy mother-in-law since the death of thy husband; and how thou hast left thy father and thy mother, and the land of thy nativity, and art come unto a people that thou knewest not heretofore. The Lord recompense thy work, and be thy reward complete from the Lord, the God of Israel, under whose wings thou art come to take shelter."

And this long-windedness of Boaz's, too. Of course he knows all about her. Also, he had, as a matter of fact, seen the stranger from afar, as he drew near his field, and had found who she was before he put the question to the foreman; and he has already warned the young men not to molest her. What is it, then? I think he is almost as embarrassed as the two of us, the foreman and I. And looking at her, and hearing her voice, he wants to know angrily: "Why did nobody tell me?" He cannot take his eyes off her, or stop talking. He goes away, and he returns. For we read:

"And Boaz said unto her at meal-time: 'Come hither and eat of the bread, and dip thy morsel in the vinegar.' And she sat beside the reapers; and they reached her parched corn, and she did eat, and was satisfied, and left thereof. And when she was risen up to glean, Boaz commanded his young men, saying: 'Let her glean even among the sheaves, and put her not to shame. And also pull out some for her of purpose from the bundles, and leave it, and let her glean, and rebuke her not.' "

Yes, he is making up for his neglect, somewhat precipitately; and later that night he may reflect on it with some uneasiness, and wonder whether he has not let himself be carried away a little too obviously in the presence of the foreman and the young men and the maidens; whether, in fact, he has not been overprecipitate, considering who he is. And if I seem to be carping, let me say that I have my reasons.

Meanwhile Ruth finishes her gleaning and returns to Naomi in the evening with a whole ephah of barley: "And her mother-in-law said unto her: 'Where hast thou gleaned today? and where wroughtest thou? Blessed be he that did take knowledge of thee.' And she told her mother-in-law with whom she had wrought, and said: 'The man's name with whom I wrought today is Boaz.' "

Boaz: it is just a name to Ruth, she has not heard it before, she has no idea that he is of her husband's family. I read this passage once with a friend, and he smiled at my naïveté. He said: "That is not the way to read it. Put a dash before the last word: 'The man's name is—Boaz.' Ruth is being coy. Is it likely that no one dropped a word to her all day long? Be sure that she not only knew, but that she also repeated a good many of the things that Boaz said to her."

I will not have it. Certainly Ruth repeated some of the warm words, leaving out Boaz's praise of her goodness. We are told so. But it was not in character for her to act coyly with her mother-in-law, or anyone else. Besides, what follows contradicts my friend's reading: "And Naomi said unto her: 'The man is nigh of kin unto us, one of our near kinsmen.' And Ruth the Moabitess said: 'Yea, he said unto me: "Thou shalt keep fast by my young men, until they have ended all my harvest." ' "

### III

We are at the turning-point of the story, and of the lives of Naomi and Ruth; and I would include Boaz, if he mattered very much, or rather if it had mattered very much to him at the time. It would be easy to say here that so far what I have called Naomi's managerial genius has not been much in evidence. So far luck, or God's will, has played into her hand, and Ruth's. I could not disagree more vigorously. How many of us spoil our luck by anticipating it, and make God change His schedule by haste! At least one half of the managerial gift consists in not doing anything when nothing ought to be done.

One might urge, with a greater appearance of reason, that in any case "skill" and "managerial" do not belong here. They are invidious words in the field of human relations. We don't want to be managed, however skillfully. We don't want anyone to scheme for us, even lovingly. We want unaffected and true relationships. Our trouble, it seems to me, is with words. "Art" is a noble word, but it has no acceptable adjectives: "artistic" is suspect when it is not neutral, "arty" is offensive, and "artful" is reprehensible. "Craft" in the sense of workmanship has no adjective, "crafty" being derived from "craft" in the sense of "guile." "Managerial skill" and "scheming" applied to human beings are unfortunate; and they have not their innocent analogues in language. But the innocent realities exist. Naomi, being good, did that which was right, and it turned out to be what we have to call the right thing.

She was unaffected and true, and she never blundered. She was aware, that first evening, of what was afoot. She said to Ruth: "It is good, my daughter, that thou go out with his maidens, and that thou be not met in any other field." For a moment we take it to be a smiling correction. Ruth had repeated Boaz's invitation: "Thou shalt keep fast by my young men," and Naomi answered: "Go out with his maidens." That is not the meaning. The young men were the reapers, and they had been instructed to drop ears of corn deliberately and specially for Ruth; Naomi cautioned her against letting unfriendliness develop between her and the young women. Also, since she had not sought out Boaz's field, and he had said· "Go not to glean in another field," she ought not to snub him. Naomi had something else in mind too, which will shortly become apparent.

The thing that was afoot was of course the prospect of marriage. That Ruth should have chanced, the first day she went out, on Boaz's field was not a very extraordinary

113

coincidence; but it was enough of one to tell Naomi what she had been waiting for. When her kinsmen had ignored her she had said nothing, which is the equivalent of not saying: "So this is how matters stand." And when Ruth came home with her ephah of barley and the account of Boaz's friendliness and talkativeness, it was again: "So this is how matters stand " And after that the weeks went by, and the reapers reaped, and the gleaners gleaned, and every evening Ruth brought home her gleanings, and not a word more from or about Boaz. We read· "So she kept fast by the maidens of Boaz to glean unto the end of barley harvest and of wheat harvest; and she dwelt with her mother-in-law." An exciting start, big with promise—and no sign of a follow-up. He had said: "It hath been fully told me, all that thou hast done unto thy mother-in-law since the death of thy husband. . . . The Lord recompense thy work. . . ." And he had talked and talked, and had shown such friendliness on that first day. And now silence. "So this is how matters stand. . . ."

IV

I said that Naomi had something more in mind when she cautioned Ruth against looking for other fields to glean in. I am dealing clumsily with exquisitely delicate matters: Naomi's sense of timing—which had as little to do with shrewdness and calculation as did the little servant girl's advice to Naaman's wife—and her natural feeling for the fitness of things, which also had its seat in the heart rather than in the mind.

The second relative who has been mentioned, the unnamed one, stood closer than Boaz to Naomi and Ruth. The degrees of relationship are not recorded, but they were close enough to come under some provision of the law of Halitzah, which meant the following: If there had been living a brother of Ruth's dead husband, Mahlon, it would have been his duty to marry Ruth and "raise up seed" to Mahlon. The duty was moral only. It could be repudiated. But the defaulter was then under the legal obligation to issue a statement of repudiation on request, and the widow could not remarry until she had obtained such a statement. It appears from the Text that neither the unnamed relative nor Boaz was a brother of Mahlon—that would have made them sons of Naomi; they merely stood within the application of the law. The nearer kinsman could come forward with the first claim on her hand; and he was the one whose relinquishment of the claim would leave Ruth free to marry anyone, relative or no relative. Far from coming forward with his claim, he did not evince the slightest interest in her, any more than Boaz did until he saw her gleaning in his field.

This relative or kinsman of unspecified degree has an important part in the story, and I wish I had his name, so that I could refer to him less awkwardly. But it is not supplied, and I cannot just invent one for him. I marvel at the boldness or offhandedness of writers who tell us out of their heads what Potiphar's wife was called, or Noah's, or Pharaoh's daughter, and invariably I quarrel with their inventions: like the heads supplied to the Winged Victory, or the arms to the Venus of Milo, they

115

never seem to fit. It was probably not intended that the unnamed should be named; and in the case of this kinsman of Ruth's the text goes pointedly out of its way to avoid naming him, and on one occasion refers to him as "such a one," which under the circumstances is practically the same as a "so-and-so."

He did not come forward of his own free will at any time, to offer marriage or assistance, and now that Ruth had received such encouragement from Boaz it would have been most unfitting for her to go gleaning elsewhere, perhaps to light, again by chance, on the other kinsman's field. Not that she knew of *his* existence until Boaz told her about him, any more than she had known of Boaz's until she met him, or of the kinship until Naomi told her about it. It is extremely unlikely that she would have looked for another field even if Naomi had not advised her against it; the words are put in Naomi's mouth because she was the one who knew all the facts.

What looked like a quick cooling off on Boaz's part could have been uneasiness about the intentions of the unnamed kinsman. Boaz could very well have bethought himself, the evening of the encounter with Ruth, that brothers-in-law and other near kinsmen of widows had been known to abuse their rights; themselves unwilling or unable to take up the claim, they could by delay exploit its nuisance value. The kinsman knew, as certainly as Boaz had known, Ruth's history; he knew also that she was gleaning in Boaz's field, and that Boaz had showered her with attention on the first day, this was the little town of Bethlehem, filled with small-town talk. He

still kept out of the way; for he was not obliged to
linquish his privilege before he was challenged  Supp
he were to make difficulties. Hint at a "gift." And si
pose he asked to speak to Ruth first, and on meeting l
should decide to ask for her hand. Her charms would
no means be diminished for him by the probability tl
the wealthy and distinguished Boaz had wanted her fi

Such a view of the situation reflects the minimum
discredit on Boaz's sudden and prolonged reserve.
must therefore have been Naomi's view. Which does i
mean that she had a bad opinion of the unnamed ki
man, who had not come to see her and had not inquii
after her. She understood Boaz's suspiciousness withc
giving it that name and without sharing it; and s
would not act until Boaz had had the opportunity
straighten himself out, to take heart and to put the iss
to the test on his own initiative; but when the mome
came for decisive action, she knew her course and f
lowed it unerringly.

The harvest days were ending. After them Boaz wou
hardly ever see Ruth, if at all  He was not her last chan
but in Naomi's judgment this was the marriage i
Ruth, and I bow to her judgment.

So we read: "And Naomi her mother-in-law said ur
her: 'My daughter, shall I not seek rest for thee, that
may be well with thee? And now is there not Boaz c
kinsman, with whose maidens thou hast been? Beho
he winnoweth barley tonight in the threshing-flo
Wash thyself, therefore, and anoint thee, and put t
raiment on thee, and get thee down to the threshii
floor; but make thyself not known unto the man, un

he shall have done eating and drinking. And it shall be, when he lieth down, that thou shalt mark the place where he shall lie, and thou shalt go in and uncover his feet, and lay thee down; and he will tell thee what thou shalt do ' And she said unto her: 'All that thou sayest unto me I will do.' "

We know so little about the customs of those days that we cannot determine how much boldness there was in Naomi's counsel and how much convention. We rule out at once any suggestion of impropriety. We cannot decide from the brief account—it was written, after all, by and for those to whom the customs were self-understood—whether women were present at the winnowing, which was accompanied by evening meals of a better kind, or whether Ruth was to steal down there alone and unobserved, to mark the place where Boaz would lie down for the night. If women were present and Ruth came openly, they must all have gone in their Sabbath best. And then the "make thyself not known to the man" would mean that she was not to approach him, or seek to attract his attention. These questions are interesting, but the answers do not affect the story, nor do they reflect on Naomi's wisdom, which displayed itself in the perfection of her timing.

We read further: "And she went down unto the threshing-floor, and did according to all that her mother-in-law bade her. And when Boaz had eaten and drunk, and his heart was merry, he went to lie down at the end of the heap of corn; and she came softly, and uncovered his feet, and laid her down. And it came to pass at midnight, that the man was startled, and turned himself;

and, behold, a woman lay at his feet. And he said: 'Who art thou?' And she answered: 'I am Ruth thy handmaid; spread therefore thy skirt over thy handmaid; for thou art a near kinsman.' "

There is an unconscionable amount of drinking done in the Bible, begining with Noah, the discoverer of the vine, and going on through Lot, and Boaz, and Nabal, and Uriah, and Ahasuerus, to mention only people I touch on in this book. But let us note that of Boaz it is told that "his heart was merry," and not that "it was merry with wine." Noah and Lot got very drunk indeed, so that they did not know what was happening to them; Ahasuerus's heart was "merry with wine," and Nabal was "very drunken"; but Boaz drank decently, with dignity, and in moderation. The moment he was awakened by Ruth he was himself, and he talked in his normal manner. The fact is that after Ruth had identified herself she did not get a word in. It is all monologue, almost soliloquy, a man talking more or less to himself, thinking things out, reviewing the pros and cons of an important transaction, going over the whole ground and sensibly reaching a provisional conclusion. I quote his speech verbatim, partly because it is so in character, and partly to show again how the Bible, with its extreme economy, can suggest loquaciousness without falling into it.

"And he said: 'Blessed be thou of the Lord, my daughter; thou hast shown more kindness in the end than at the beginning, inasmuch as thou didst not follow the young men, whether poor or rich. And now, my daughter, fear not; I will do all that thou sayest; for all the men in the gate of my people do know that thou art a virtuous woman.' "

I simply must interrupt here, before I forget. He was going to do everything that Ruth had said; but she had not said a word; she did not get a chance. What Boaz heard was, as on the day of their first meeting, his conscience. It was a bit fatuous of him to say that Ruth had shown more kindness to him than to Naomi, whom she had followed into a strange land, or have we here a touch of modesty? On the other hand that "fear not" of his was less than tactful. And what exactly did he mean by: "For all the men in the gate of my people do know that thou art a virtuous woman"? That was something of a comedown from his impetuous tribute at their first meeting. Is it possible that he had been collecting opinions on her? Or overhearing them while he was trying to make up his mind? That is what his condescension hints: "You won't have wasted your time. It was not a mistake to have waited for me. I know all about you now, and I am prepared to do the right thing by you."

He continues: "And now it is true that I am a near kinsman; howbeit there is a kinsman nearer than I. Tarry this night, and it shall be in the morning, that if he will perform unto thee the part of kinsman, well; let him do the kinsman's part; but if he be not willing to do the part of a kinsman to thee, then will I do the part of a kinsman to thee, as the Lord liveth; lie down until the morning."

I have come across warmer proposals, even from men no longer in the first flush of youth. A display of passion would have been improper under the circumstances, but surely he was carrying respectful restraint to extremes. He did not have to contemplate the possible loss of Ruth with this excess of manly fortitude. He puts queer ideas into our head—he might have been waiting all these weeks for the unnamed kinsman to take Ruth off his hands.

And Ruth, how did she feel about it? The Text is a blank. We know only of her immeasurable devotion to Naomi. We also know that there are persons for whom love is part of a setting, a rounding out of a life in which others than the chosen one also play essential parts, and such love can be as true as direct and unconditional passion. It can be more enduring, too. Ruth was fulfilling Naomi—and in Naomi herself. Let not romantics put such love outside the pale because it sometimes dispenses—as it did in this case—with the standard responses. The beginning may be cautious esteem; the end, with many purposes achieved, may climb to unanticipated levels.

Now we read: "And she lay at his feet until the morning; and she rose up before one could discern another. For he said: 'Let it not be known that the woman came to the threshing-floor.'"

We are again at a loss for the details. That there was nothing of the brazen in Ruth's nocturnal intrusion is now absolutely clear; she had done nothing of which Boaz, or public opinion, would have disapproved. We must conclude that if Boaz did not want her to be seen, it was because he was ashamed of having driven her, by his shilly-shallying, to appeal to custom. And still this does not quite fit in with what follows: "And he said:

'Bring the mantle that is upon thee, and hold it'; and he measured six measures of barley, and laid it on her. . . ." It was an incautious thing to do, for she might be seen entering the city with her load. This part of the narrative leaves me somewhat confused, but again it does not affect the essence of the story, which from now on returns to its usual clarity.

"And when she came to her mother-in-law, she said: 'Who art thou, my daughter?' And she told her all that the man had done to her. And she said: 'These six measures of barley gave he me; for he said to me: "Go not empty unto thy mother-in-law." ' Then she said: 'Sit still, my daughter, until thou know how the matter will fall; for the man will not rest, until he have finished the thing this day.' "

Many wonderful things spring to the mind from that startled and startling question of Naomi's: "Who art thou?"—the very question Boaz had addressed to her in the darkness. The Traditionalist will answer for Ruth, that she was now the Affianced One, and the light of the Messiah, who was to issue from her line, surrounded her with a glory that made her almost unrecognizable; and with or without the Tradition we know that she came back another person. But the talk thereafter was work-aday; and once more it was a question of waiting, but not for long, as Naomi at once understood. Boaz was determined to put an end to the uncertainty before sundown that day.

V

"Now Boaz went up to the gate, and sat him down there; and, behold, the near kinsman of whom Boaz had spoken came by; unto whom he said: 'Ho, such a one! turn aside, sit down here.' And he turned aside and sat down."

"Such a one" was definitely not Boaz's manner of speech. It is the Text itself that thus introduces the man. It gives us the names of Naomi's husband, and of Naomi's sons, who have only off-stage parts in the story; but the kinsman becomes "such a one."

"And he took ten men of the elders of the city, and said: 'Sit ye down here.' And they sat down. And he said unto the kinsman: 'Naomi, that is come back out of the field of Moab, selleth the parcel of land which was our brother Elimelech's; and I thought to disclose it unto thee, saying: 'Buy it before them that sit here, and before the elders of my people. If thou wilt redeem it, redeem it; but if it will not be redeemed, then tell me, that I may know; for there is none to redeem beside thee; and I am after thee.' "

"Brother" is figurative here. The unnamed kinsman was willing enough to buy the parcel. "I will redeem it," he said. "Then said Boaz: 'What day thou buyest the field of the hand of Naomi—hast thou also bought of Ruth the Moabitess, the wife of the dead, to raise up the name of the dead upon his inheritance?' " In other words, not so fast, Such-a-one, there is the matter of Ruth, the widow. The property is indivisible, and she has a share in it, and her share goes together with her

123

hand. And Such-a-one, who seems to have overlooked this complication, at once backs down. "And the near kinsman said: 'I cannot redeem it for myself, lest I mar mine own inheritance; take thou my right of redemption on thee, for I cannot redeem it.' " And so the near kinsman now has to perform in public the humiliating shoe-ceremony which custom prescribes, and which among Traditionalists has survived until this day, and has become, in the Hebrew language, the general figure of speech for a man's bankruptcy. I shall take my leave of him without reluctance, but not before I have had my say. He is a paltry creature—and worse. Up to this point one could make allowances for him. He did not bother about his poor relatives—well, there may have been old family quarrels. Certainly his reluctance to marry Ruth would not discredit him in our eyes—unless he was such a rigid fundamentalist that he frowned on marriage with a Moabitess even though she had accepted the faith. The family quarrel, too, could have hinged on some such narrowness, for Naomi's sons had both married Moabitesses. But even this fundamentalism, which is a slap in the face to the decency and kindliness of the community, can be swallowed. What cannot be swallowed, and what perhaps lies behind the text's contemptuous "such-a-one," is his prompt offer to buy the parcel, without a thought for Ruth. It was of his kind that the prophet was to cry: "Woe to those that join house to house, that lay field to field."

Let him go, he is spoiling the story. For now it rises to a glorious choral climax, in which Boaz too is caught up, and we feel him taking the first steps in the ascent which his marriage will mean for him. "And Boaz said unto the elders, and unto all the people: 'Ye are witnesses this day, that I have bought all that was Elimelech's, and all that was Chilion's and Mahlon's, of the hand of Naomi. Moreover, Ruth the Moabitess, the wife of Mahlon, have I acquired to be my wife, to raise up the name of the dead upon his inheritance, that the name of the dead be not cut off from among his brethren, and from the gate of his place, ye are witnesses this day.' And all the people that were in the gate, and the elders, said: 'We are witnesses. The Lord make the woman that is to come into thy house like Rachel and like Leah, which two did build the house of Israel; and do thou worthily in Ephrath, and be famous in Bethlehem; and let thy house be like the house of Perez, whom Tamar bore unto Judah, of the seed which the Lord shall give thee of this young woman.' "

He has taken it upon himself, this Boaz, to be the surrogate of the dead man, and to be known forever, therefore, as the husband of Ruth the Moabitess. His very lineage seems to be renounced in the act, for though his father's name occurs in the genealogical table, never once do we read of "Boaz the son of Salmon," as befits a person of importance. He is only the consort of Ruth, but he is a progenitor of the Messiah. In the declaration of acceptance he speaks with a new dignity and grace, and we recognize in it an intimation, almost a prophecy.

And now, in what is really a second epilogue, though there is no break in the Text, we are confronted with a strange shift of attention:

" So Boaz took Ruth, and she became his wife; and

he went in unto her, and the Lord gave her conception, and she bore a son. And the women said unto Naomi: 'Blessed be the Lord, who hath not left thee this day without a near kinsman, and let his name be famous in Israel. And he shall be unto thee a restorer of life, and a nourisher of thine old age; for thy daughter-in-law, who loveth thee, who is better to thee than seven sons, hath borne him.' And Naomi took the child, and laid it in her bosom, and became nurse unto it. And the women her neighbours gave it a name, saying: 'There is a son born to Naomi'; and they called his name Obed; he is the father of Jesse, the father of David."

And so the scroll closes, except for a genealogical appendix.

How extraordinary! Is not this the Book of Ruth, and does it not celebrate primarily her sweetness and devotion? Naomi, the chief beneficiary, rightly plays an important part, but how can the book end so strangely, with Naomi in the center of the epilogue and Ruth somewhere at the side: so much so, that the women even say: "There is a son born to Naomi"—as though the great-grandmother of King David were Naomi, not Ruth?

Have we fallen into an error only because the Book should have been called the Book of Naomi, in which case we would not be taken aback by the epilogue? That is what I have suggested. Nevertheless I have the feeling that the recorder originally thought of Ruth, the more obviously dramatic of the two women, as the heroine, and that is how he tried to write it; and certainly Ruth is one of the loveliest and most moving beings known to us; and it is not a question here of comparing her with Naomi but of finding out with what closing impression the recorder wanted to leave us. I feel sure that he chose Ruth and her fate as focus and climax before he began the writing; but as he went along, Naomi, with whom the story opens, drew him more and more, even as she had drawn her daughters-in-law, and he was not quite aware of it, and by the time he ended he had forgotten what he started out to say.

### SUB-EPILOGUE

We are told that the story of Ruth and Naomi was written as a protest against Jewish chauvinism. Someone recalled it, or thought it up at a late period, in the days of Ezra the Scribe, when he was compelling the Jews of his time to divorce their foreign and idolatrous wives. I do not accept this view, but I honor it and gladly acknowledge the points in its favor. It is pleasant to observe how often the text insists on the phrase "Ruth the Moabitess." There is no glossing over of her origins. There is no attempt to turn Naomi into a proselytizer, and if Ruth accepts the faith there is no reflection on that of her people. Naomi found great kindness among the Moabites, into whose midst she and her husband and sons, and no doubt many others, came from a famine-stricken country. We are a long way from the Balak-Balaam incident and passion. Ruth the Moabitess has the right to glean in the fields of Israel and her case comes under Israel's Halitzah law, though of course we must remember she was the widow of an Israelite. She was nevertheless a foreigner, and she stressed it when Boaz was kind to her. But the chorus of the people and the elders at the gate welcomes her spontaneously into the blessing the moment Boaz declares his intentions. Moreover the recorder makes her the great-grandmother of King David, whence the Tradition makes her, in turn, the ancestress of the Messiah.

If, with all this in its favor, I still reject the theory of a propaganda piece, it is simply because I do not believe that such writing can be born of a public-relations assignment; which is not to deny that the circumstances at the time of the writing had much to do with the inspiration. The story came up, and the time may have been the propagandist, but not the writer. At most he was the conscious propagandist when he tacked on the genealogical table leading to David. Nor did he intend to preach, even to the extent of producing a study in goodness. He set out to tell a marvelous story, and toward the end he lost his way, and did better than he planned.

And now that we are at the end, I should like to ask: what ever became of Orpah? Who? asks the reader, Orpah, don't you remember? Naomi's other daughter-in-law, who let herself be persuaded to go back to her people and her god. What became of her? We do not know. She disappears, as so many of the People have a disconcerting habit of doing. But I am sorry to say that the Tradition has perpetuated all sorts of miserable and scurrilous stories about her. They have absolutely no foundation in the Text; they are—like some other legends, favorable and unfavorable—out of the whole cloth. I will not repeat them; I think they are uncalled for, and in violent contradiction with the spirit of the story. For my part, I just wonder. Did Orpah learn of Ruth's and Naomi's good fortune? Did they ever hear from each other again? Was there ever a visit? Moab and Judea are not far from each other, but simple people did not travel much in those days even in peaceful times, and most of them could not write, and though there was always the village letter-writer, there was no reliable postal system. However it all fell out, whether or not Orpah remarried, and whomever she may have married, she can never have forgotten her former sister-in-law or the extraordinary woman of Bethlehem-Judah for whose sake she had almost left her people and her god.

```
CHAPTER V

The Manager

        ❀
```

"M̲ANAGERIAL," too, is the best over-all word for Rebekah, the wife of Isaac; and after it "intuitive," "unerring," "competent," all with a touch of greatness. I am dazzled by her masterly grasp of things, and by her executive dash. If I had a problem in human relations it is Rebekah I would want to consult. What, not Naomi, whom I have just called the subtlest and most loving schemer of them all? No, not Naomi, who, I suspect, would solve my problem by making me into the kind of person who doesn't have that kind of problem.

We remember Rebekah chiefly as the principal in the *cause célèbre* of the embezzled blessing. She is the woman who hoodwinked her blind old husband into deeding to their son Jacob the family legacy that should have gone to Jacob's older twin brother, Esau. Thousands of monographs, and stories, and plays, and poems, have been written round the rights and wrongs of the affair. My stand in the immemorial controversy will become apparent in due course, but by way of preface I have this to say: whatever the formal rights and wrongs, the character of the legacy was such that to have loaded it onto Esau would have been fantastically cruel—assuming that the fantastically impossible could have happened—namely, that Esau could have received it.

Certainly Rebekah's handling of that involved and explosive situation, in which murder was latent, is the climax of her career, and it is proper to think of it first when her name is mentioned. But please note: the climax of her career; not an isolated incident, not one of those sudden, breath-taking displays of will and skill which make us gape at the performer and exclaim: "The devil! Who would have thought he had it in him!" On the contrary, anyone who has studied Rebekah and her life with Isaac would expect and even demand it of her. She was born for it, she prepared for it, and she alone could have carried it off.

It amuses me to compare the image I formed of Rebekah in my childhood with my present evocation of her. I was influenced then—as I still am, though how differently!—by her entry into the story, by her meeting with Eliezer, the wife-seeking emissary, for which she is remembered almost as often as for her deception of Isaac. As a pictorial subject "Rebekah at the Well" is one of those compulsive insipidities which are standard equipment for Bible illustrators. All of us have seen hundreds of Rebekahs with a sweet and earnest simper proffering water to the weary, wayworn wanderer and his camels. The pious Rebbi whose life I helped to shorten aided and abetted the artists by his discourses on Rebekah's moral perfections. And I am amused because my present image is so dissimilar in the midst of so much similarity.

Let us go to the Text.

Eliezer, the old and trusted servant of Abraham, has come from Canaan, all the way across the desert that Balaam traversed, to seek a wife for Isaac, his master's son. He stands by the well outside the city of Nahor, perplexed. His instructions, clear in some respects, are in others obscure. Here is what his master said to him before he started out: "Put, I pray thee, thy hand under my thigh. And I will make thee swear by the Lord, the God of heaven and the God of the earth, that thou shalt not take a wife for my son of the daughters of the Canaanites, among whom I dwell. But thou shalt go unto my country, and to my kindred, and take a wife for my son, even for Isaac."

These are already strange terms of reference. The choosing of a wife for Isaac is henceforth Eliezer's exclusive responsibility, and Isaac's acquiescence in the choice is taken for granted, while Eliezer assumes the responsibility as a matter of course. We read only that he foresaw a possible obstacle: "Peradventure the woman will not be willing to follow me unto this land; must I needs bring thy son back unto the land from which thou camest?" And he received this categoric reply: "Beware that thou bring not my son back thither." Then Abraham continued: "The Lord, the God of heaven, who took me from my father's house, and from the land of my nativity, and who swore unto me, saying: 'Unto thy seed will I give this land'; He will send His angel before thee, and thou shalt take a wife for my son from thence. And if the woman be not willing to follow thee, then thou shalt be clear from this my oath."

What troubled Eliezer now was the phrase in the first

part of the instructions: "Unto my country and to my kindred." Was "kindred" an absolute condition? If so, why "unto my country," seeing that Abraham had no kindred outside Mesopotamia? In the second part Abraham had said: "Thou shalt take a wife for my son from thence," as if the country were the absolute condition, and "kindred" only a preference. As far as Eliezer knew, Abraham's family, the people among whom he had done his first missionary work, had shown no susceptibility to his vision. There had been one exception, Lot, and he had come to a bad end. Why the family at all, in fact?

Eliezer prays: "And he said: 'Lord, the God of my master Abraham, send me, I pray Thee, good speed this day. Behold, I stand by the fountain of water; and the daughters of the men of the city come out to draw water So let it come to pass, that the damsel to whom I shall say: "Let down thy pitcher, I pray thee, that I may drink"; and she shall say: "Drink, and I will give thy camels drink also"; let the same be she that Thou hast appointed for Thy servant, even for Isaac; and thereby shall I know that Thou hast shown kindness unto my master.' And it came to pass, before he had done speaking, that, behold, Rebekah came out, who was born to Bethuel the son of Milcah, the wife of Nahor, Abraham's brother, with her pitcher upon her shoulder. And the damsel was very fair to look upon, a virgin, neither had any man known her; and she went down to the fountain, and filled her pitcher, and came up. And the servant ran to meet her, and said: 'Give me to drink, I pray thee, a little water of thy pitcher.' And she said:

'Drink, my lord'; and she hastened and let down her pitcher upon her hand, and gave him drink. And when she had done giving him drink, she said: 'I will draw for thy camels also, until they have done drinking.' And she hastened, and emptied her pitcher into the trough, and ran again unto the well to draw, and drew for all his camels. And the man looked steadfastly on her."

I should think he would. Seldom has a prayer been answered so promptly and with such point-to-point fulfillment. Yet it was not so much what the girl did as the way she did it. She hastened, she ran, and withal she was so deliberate. She let him finish drinking before she offered to water the camels. And she had to do a lot of running back and forth with her pitcher, as anyone knows who has seen camels drink after a long journey. But no hesitations, no questions, no ill-timed courtesies, which would perhaps have been lost on a thirsty man and certainly on thirsty camels; just quick action, thorough, and completed before the conversation was resumed.

I like that girl. So did Eliezer. It does one good to watch her. I can imagine more than one man, especially among such as have found the world a bit too much for them, watching with us and saying, or rather thinking: "That's the kind of girl I should have married."

II

It was the kind of girl Isaac should have married, and did. Whereupon the reader may comment dryly: "Let us rather say the girl he was married off to, no less than

134

she was married off to him." I understand. The reader does not like marriages for the good of without the consent of. Neither do I. Even when they turn out well, yes, even if it could be shown that on the whole the system works better than ours, we should still object. We live in order to grow and develop, and where there is no freedom of choice there is no development. For me too, this view is self-understood, and because its implications are so important, let us pause while Rebekah is running up and down the steps emptying and filling her pitcher —it will take her quite a time—and let us see what bearing our view has on Isaac and Rebekah, and for that matter on the People of the Book generally.

In the instance before us it is undeniable that one of the parties—the man—was disposed of without consultation; and not by the woman, a thing that is liable to happen in the most emancipated societies, but by his father; and even by his father's chief servant. However, it will be seen that Isaac's was a special case; and what really troubles us is the status of Biblical woman. She can be shown by honest quotation to have been a chattel, a serf, a commodity, a sexual plaything, a degraded, disfranchised, second-class human being. One need go no farther than the crushing fiat issued against Eve after the fall: "I will greatly multiply thy pain and thy travail; in pain shalt thou bring forth children; and thy desire shall be to thy husband, and he shall rule over thee." And if today, even in our society, the woman's desire is still toward her husband—in other words, if even today women are more anxious to get married than men— some of the blame attaches to the influence of the Bible.

135

But thank God, or rather, no thanks to God, we have made some progress.

A superficial perusal of the Isaac-Rebekah story strengthens the shocking effect of those words from the third chapter of Genesis. Eliezer comes to Nahor to find a wife for Isaac. The woman he picks will accept the husband sight-unseen. Yes, it is conceded that she might not be willing to follow Eliezer. Let us not make too much of that; the unwillingness might be her family's. And what is Eliezer's criterion? That the woman shall know her place—namely, as the ministrant to a man's needs—and those of his camels. Having found a satisfactory candidate, he puts bracelets on her hands and—how significant!—fastens a ring on her nose. He proceeds to her home, negotiates with the family, settles everything without a word from the young woman, and leads her off—we might say by the nose. What more does one want as proof of women's degradation in the Bible?

Speaking for myself, I want a careful scrutiny of the Text. And now that Rebekah has at last watered all the camels without any assistance from Eliezer or his men, let us resume the reading, and let us go slowly:

"And the man looked steadfastly on her, holding his peace, to know whether the Lord had made his journey prosperous or not. And it came to pass, as the camels had done drinking, that the man took a golden ring of half a shekel weight, and two bracelets for her hands of ten shekels weight of gold. . . ." Later that day, when Eliezer is telling the family about it, he is more detailed. He says: "I put the ring upon her nose and the bracelets upon her hands." Then: "He said: 'Whose daughter art

136

thou? Tell me, I pray thee. Is there room in thy father's house for us to lodge in?' And she said unto him: 'I am the daughter of Bethuel, the son of Milcah, whom she bore unto Nahor.' She said moreover unto him: 'We have both straw and provender enough, and room to lodge in.' "

I insist: mark that pretty chit well. She does not lose her head when the stranger produces the valuable presents. She is still deliberate and systematic. Having given him her parentage, she pauses, then assures him with the right emphasis that his unexpected arrival will not embarrass the household. And when he says: "Blessed be the Lord, the God of my master Abraham, who hath not forsaken His mercy and His truth toward my master; as for me, the Lord hath led me in the way to the house of my master's brethren," when he utters these astounding words, she still does not lose her self-possession, still does not pester him with questions. We read immediately·
—"And the damsel ran, and told her mother's house according to these words."

I hope I have established the image of Rebekah as it rises for me from the Text: lively, intelligent, quick in action even as a girl, a person with—as I have said—"a grasp of things." This is not the submissive and servile Oriental female of popular tradition. And yet—she sits by silently while Eliezer speaks at length with the rest of the family, describing the condition of his master Abraham, the man of wealth, declaring the purpose of his visit, recounting all that has happened at the well, his prayer and the answer. He ends with these words·
"And now if ye will deal truly and kindly with my mas-

137

ter, tell me; if not, tell me; that I may turn to the right hand or to the left." The men of the household, Laban and Bethuel, the brother and father, make answer: "The thing proceedeth from the Lord." As in the case of Balak we cannot tell what "Lord" they mean when they echo Eliezer's word, but they continue piously: "We cannot speak unto thee bad or good. Behold, Rebekah is before thee, take her, and go, and let her be thy master's son's wife, as the Lord hath spoken."

This is really too much. There she is. Take her. Go. And not a word from Rebekah. But why should she speak if she likes what is happening? Just to show us that she has a will of her own?

We read on: "And it came to pass that, when Abraham's servant heard their words, he bowed himself down to the earth unto the Lord. And the servant brought forth jewels of silver, and jewels of gold, and raiment, and gave them to Rebekah; he also gave to her brother and to her mother precious things. And they did eat and drink, he and the men that were with him, and tarried all night; and they rose up in the morning, and he said: 'Send me away unto my master.' And her brother and mother said: 'Let the damsel abide with us a few days, at least ten; after that she shall go.' And he said unto them: 'Delay me not, seeing the Lord hath prospered my way; send me away that I may go to my master.' And they said: 'We will call the damsel, and inquire at her mouth.' And they called Rebekah, and said unto her: 'Wilt thou go with this man?' And she said: 'I will go.' And they sent away Rebekah their sister, and her nurse, and Abraham's servant, and his men."

I turn the phrases this way and that, and I linger over the question to Rebekah, and her answer. The matter has been settled, has it not? "Wilt thou go with this man?" refers not to the sale but only to the time of delivery. If it referred to the sale it would be an empty formality and a mockery. As it is, the question can only mean: "Will you go at once or linger a few days?" And the girl's unfeeling answer means: "At once. This very morning." What are we to make of it?

Was Rebekah so unhappy at home that she could not wait another day if only for her mother's sake, not to mention father and brother? And if that was how she felt, where was filial respect, or the show of it? Or was she so resentful of the highhanded transaction that she said in effect: "I am no longer your property. Deliver me without delay to my purchaser"? These are not idle questions. We are looking for the spirit of the situation.

But we are on the wrong scent. Let us bethink ourselves that Rebekah and her mother—and no doubt the nurse, too—sat up half the night, talking about this fairyland turn in their lives. It is not recorded that they even asked Eliezer what his master's son looked like, or how old he was. They saw the miracle as a whole *à laisser ou à prendre*, and since it was *à prendre*, Rebekah understood that one did not linger over such things, one did not draw them out with increasingly tedious banquetings and farewells. It was all thrashed out in the night. Even the preparations were begun. How else could she have left on such short notice? When Rebekah's mother joined Laban in saying: "Let the damsel abide with us a few days," she did so out of deference to her son, perhaps also her husband, who is very much in the background. And when she joined in the question, it was with foreknowledge of the answer.

Something more, and that of crucial significance. Instinct—by which I mean the totality of her character—told Rebekah that it would be good for her husband to know, and to remember for the rest of his life, that when she was called to him she turned to her family and said: "I will go—at once."

### III

Thus everything falls into place, and it is a willing bride, a ready, capable, clever, and attractive young woman, who goes out to meet her destiny. "And Rebekah arose, and her damsels, and they rode upon the camels, and followed the man. And the servant took Rebekah and went his way. And Isaac came from the way of Beer-lahai-roi; for he dwelt in the land of the South. And Isaac went out to meditate in the field at the eventide; and he lifted up his eyes and saw, and, behold, there were camels coming. And Rebekah lifted up her eyes, and when she saw Isaac, she alighted from the camel. And she said unto the servant: 'What man is this that walketh in the field to meet us?' And the servant said: 'It is my master.' And she took her veil and covered herself."

How this passage expands and unfolds for me, enriched by its enclosing past and future, and enriching them! How fitting it is that when Rebekah first sees Isaac he should be walking in the darkening field, sunk

in meditation! She knows him. She makes her camel
stop and kneel; she dismounts; and only then does she
ask Eliezer: "What man is this that walketh in the field
to meet us?" There are other first meetings of a man
and a woman in the Bible conceived in key, perfect over-
tures. Isaac's son, Jacob, when he meets Rachel, for
whom he will serve fourteen years, begins with an act of
service; exhausted as he is by his long journey across the
desert—the same journey as Eliezer has just made, but
alone, not with a caravan, and not with presents—exhausted as he is, he insists on rolling away the stone from
the well with his own arms, and on watering Rachel's
flock  Moses the Liberator meets Zipporah at a well, too;
and his first act is to defend her and her sisters against
the ruffianly shepherds who are driving them away.
But of all such preludes none reaches so deep as this one
for Rebekah and Isaac, the woman of action and the man
of meditation.

We learn from the Text that Isaac was forty years old
when Rebekah came to him—a man set in his ways. He
did not just happen to go out in the field that evening
for the purpose of meditation; it was a habit with him
—that is to say, a need. We could guess from the preceding account of his life thus far, without drawing on later
confirmation, that he is a man who reacts rather than
acts. His struggles are internal. Things are done for him
and to him, his function is to get at the good in them;
and if anyone confuses this with passivity, let him try it
for a while.

When Isaac was a child he lost his only companion, a
half-brother, Ishmael, not by death, but by unnatural

141

separation. Ishmael, older than Isaac by a few years, was driven out into the desert together with his mother, Hagar; and the one who drove them out was Sarah, Isaac's mother. The cause, it appears, was arrogance on Hagar's side, vindictive jealousy on Sarah's.

If we want to get some idea of what Isaac had to meditate on, we can begin here. And without inventing anything, leaning solely on the Text, we shall discover that though arrogance and vindictiveness were motives and proximate causes in the Ishmael episode, they were irrelevant as far as Isaac was concerned. Seen from within the purpose of his life, the forces were quite different.

We go back to the days when Sarah was still called Sarai, and Abraham Abram; that is, before they were given the new names which declared their destinies, before Ishmael and Isaac were born. We read:

"Now Sarai Abram's wife bore him no children; and she had a handmaid, an Egyptian, whose name was Hagar. And Sarai said unto Abram: 'Behold now, the Lord hath restrained me from bearing; go in, I pray thee, unto my handmaid; it may be that I shall be builded up through her.' "

Such was the custom of the time, and Abraham's grandson, Jacob, was likewise to make use of it, and much more frequently than his grandfather. It is one of the many features of woman's life in the Biblical record which justify the indignation of moderns. On the other hand, it does not seem to have been regarded in this light by Hagar—or by the servants of Jacob's wives. For we read that when Hagar "saw that she had conceived, her mistress was despised in her eyes." Already then

Sarah drove Hagar into the wilderness; but there an angel appeared to Hagar and bade her go back. He also told her that God had great things in store for her offspring: "I will greatly multiply thy seed, that it shall not be numbered for multitude . . . thou shalt bear a son, and thou shalt call his name Ishmael, because the Lord hath heard thy affliction. And he shall be a wild ass of a man, and every man's hand against him. . . ."

Where did this take place? Here, at Beer-lahai-roi, where Isaac is now walking, sunk in meditation.

Hagar returned to her mistress, and some years later, when Sarai had borne Isaac, and her name was Sarah, as Abram's had become Abraham, the second and final expulsion took place. We read: "And Sarah saw the son of Hagar the Egyptian, whom she had borne unto Abraham, making sport. Wherefore she said unto Abraham: 'Cast out this bondwoman and her son; for the son of the bondwoman shall not be heir with my son, even with Isaac.' "

Those words "making sport" have a special meaning, as we might suspect from the "wherefore" which follows them. Let the reader turn a few pages of the Text to the chapter that tells of Isaac as a married man trying to pass off Rebekah as his sister, when they were among the Philistines. There we read: "Abimelech king of the Philistines looked out at the window, and, behold, Isaac was sporting with Rebekah his wife. And Abimelech called Isaac and said: 'Behold, of a surety she is thy wife.' " I may add, once more, that the point is driven home somewhat more sharply in the original, for in the two places the same verb is used in the same tense, gender, number, and mood. But it is clear enough from the English that the wild and precocious son of Hagar was a danger to the child Isaac.

Some thirty-five years have passed since then, and Isaac is walking in these same fields of Beer-lahai-roi. His half-brother is a desert rover, and every man's hand is against him. Between things remembered and things told him Isaac pieces it all together, and understands, as heir to the blessing, the purpose of the loss. For the contemplative man past and future are reversible in meaning; they mold each other; purpose and cause are interchangeable terms; and for two men the same event can have two separate purposes and therefore two separate causes. To each of them the cause that serves the other's purpose is only a pretext. To Ishmael, Sarah's thought for Isaac's well-being was a pretext, her hatred of Hagar the cause. In Isaac's book Sarah's hatred of Hagar was a pretext, her thought for his well-being the cause. He understands, he accepts, he submits.

He also sees why Abraham consented to the expulsion, though only after God had promised him—for the second time—that the boy would live, to become the founder of a great people. But Abraham had suffered, he had found it "very grievous"; and thus, as a cause, had identified himself with the purpose. Abraham had risen before dawn, and had himself sent them away, his concubine and his son, into the desert, with a loaf of bread and a bottle of water, all he could lay his hands on in the darkness, rather than leave the expulsion to Sarah. Whenever Isaac thinks of that parting he stops walking, he is paralyzed for a moment. Yes, he understands, he

144

accepts, he submits; and still the struggle is not over; it never will be, and the pain will never become a mere memory.

When Isaac was twelve years old, or perhaps thirteen —the Text refers to him there as a lad—a terrible thing was done to him. He was offered up as a sacrifice, a burnt offering, on Mount Moriah, by his old and loving father But this was done to him with his wholehearted consent; and let us not call it a near-sacrifice just because at the last moment he was unexpectedly bidden to go on living. He did not anticipate the reprieve, neither did his father; for if they had done, the incident, which left such a mark on him—as it has on the world—would have been childish mummery. He gave up his life; he passed through the valley of the shadow of death; and he came back, and took up his life again. Surely in this alone there was material for a lifetime of meditation.

For me the most interesting role here was played by the mother, who played no role at all. She was not consulted—that is definite. She was never told about it— that is implied. She was excluded from the most significant single event in the life of her son, the event that was her vindication. Isaac must often have pondered this extraordinary fact: she who had guarded him for God was not permitted to know how God claimed him and found him perfect.

The Text informs us that when Isaac was awaiting Rebekah, only two years had passed since Sarah's death, and his heart was still heavy for her. Her tent stood vacant, waiting for her who was to be the wife of the heir to the blessing. And he was not the chooser of his wife any more than he had been the chooser of his mother. Why need he be? The unchosen mother had acted for his good; why should the unchosen wife do less?

Let her come, and let her come quickly; that will be a sign. He reckons the days. Seventeen each way across the desert, and an indeterminate number for the search. Or perhaps, since an angel might have gone before, no search. Thirty-four days, then, for the coming and going, and a week or ten days for preparations and farewells; and only thirty-four days have passed since Eliezer set forth.

But for an unknown reason he has this evening taken the direction from which the caravan will arrive. He has walked a long way, sunk in thought, and suddenly, again for an unknown reason, he raises his eyes from the ground, and against the fading light in the west he sees a line of camels approaching soft-footed over the ridge. Still for an unknown reason he continues his walk instead of turning aside or back, and his heart beats faster. It cannot be. She cannot have come thus, without a moment's delay. And still he continues, and he sees the foremost camel halt, and kneel, and a woman descends. There is an upwelling in his heart, and unspoken words tremble on his lips: "I might have known."

Then we read: "And the servant told Isaac all the things he had done. And Isaac brought Rebekah into his mother Sarah's tent, and she became his wife; and he loved her; and Isaac was comforted for his mother."

IV

Now we may look at Isaac in the light, or the half-
light, of our fuller knowledge. There is something shadowy about him as he stands between the two other patriarchs, between Abraham his father and Jacob his son. It
is written of Jacob that he was "a quiet man, dwelling in
tents." It would be quite wrong, however, to think of
Jacob as being unapt for decisive action. He preferred
quiet and meditation, but he went out to meet events.
He could wrestle with angels and with men, and con-
quer. He worsted an angel in all night combat at the
ford Jabbok; and on his deathbed he could say to his
son Joseph: "I have given thee one portion above thy
brethren, which I took out of the hand of the Amorite
with my sword and with my bow." Abraham, too, medi-
tated much on God; but Abraham too fought with men,
and with God. With his handful of household troops he
pursued and defeated Amraphel king of Shinar and his
allies, and rescued his nephew Lot out of their hands;
and he disputed with God, though unsuccessfully, the
decree against Sodom and Gomorrah. Further, Abraham
and Jacob were travelers, ranging between Mesopotamia
and Egypt. Abraham was born in Mesopotamia, broke
away to found the faith, came to the Promised Land,
descended into Egypt, and returned to the Promised
Land. Jacob, born in the Promised Land, fled to Mesopotamia, lived there for twenty years, returned to the
Promised Land, and descended into Egypt to join Joseph, and died there. Isaac stayed all his life where he
was born, in the Promised Land. His father feared to

let him go to Mesopotamia for a wife. And when there was a famine in the land, God said to him: "Go not down into Egypt. . . ."

Consider also how Abraham the father had Sarah as a principal wife, and Hagar as a concubine, and in his old age, a widower, married again, and begot many sons; and how Jacob had two principal wives, and begot also on their maids, and had twelve sons and a daughter; while Isaac had this one wife, Rebekah, and begot only once, but twins, as if in compensation; but also as if it was not meant that life should be too easy for him.

Isaac is so shadowy that his very existence has been challenged. There are people who insist that he is nothing more than the literal shadow or echo of Abraham. They point to certain striking similarities or repetitions of record. Abraham tries to pass off his wife as his sister, so does Isaac. Abraham has trouble with the Philistines about wells, so does Isaac. Abimelech and Phicol are the Philistine king and general respectively in Abraham's time; they reappear in Isaac's time.

There are of course explanations. We can say that Abimelech was a dynastic name and Phicol an official title; thus one big difficulty is removed. Also, there is no inherent reason why the same situation should not have arisen for father and son. And so on. But these incidents, which some reject without rejecting Isaac's existence, are the ones that make him, in his very shadowiness, so convincing. As to thinking Isaac out of existence—and on the very grounds that make him so convincing—let those do it who can. But let them not forget that when they think away Isaac they must also think away Rebekah.

Such a double feat of destructiveness is surely beyond the power of the human imagination.

v

The quick-witted, energetic, self-assured girl arrives straight out of the world of idol-worshippers to serve a husband she has never met, sole heir to a blessing outside her experience. In Mesopotamia they still talked occasionally of Abraham, or Abram, her grandfather's brother, a queer man who went away many years before her birth, together with her uncle Lot; and stories were still current of some sort of religion he had tried to propagate. At long intervals the families exchanged letters, or messages. It is recorded that Abraham was informed of marriages and births among his kindred. But Abraham's religious influence on his family was nil; Laban, Rebekah's brother, was still a worshipper of images when Jacob came to live with him.

This mysterious blessing or religion that Rebekah suddenly encounters—what is it? The ritual is easy to learn; the ethics are straightforward; but the spirit is elusive, and yet it is all-important. Rebekah gathers that it is a hunger, an aptitude, a dedication, a search, a vision, a penetration, a torment, an ecstasy, and a frightening, desperate responsibility, all in one. It has to do with a knowledge of God. Of God, not of gods; of the One Perfect Maker, not the many brawlers and botchers. It has to do with a people that shall develop under the sign of the hunger, and with a land—this land she has come to—where the hunger shall never cease. Till the end of earthly time the hungerers shall not be without sin, but in sin they shall be without peace. She learns that her father-in-law, her great-uncle Abraham, received or obtained the blessing from the One God, together with promises of worldly values. But she gathers that the blessing is not in those promises. The promises are provisional; the hunger and torment are inherent. She gets glimpses of the truths that Balaam understood so well in vain, and intimations of a costly immortality.

She learns that Abraham has suffered much for the blessing. She sees that her husband, this man of forty with the intense inner life, also suffers. She must, moreover, take account of certain ominous peculiarities in the situation. Why is her husband, who is neither an only son nor the oldest son, nevertheless the heir, the sole heir? Obviously because the other sons are not apt for the blessing. Let the reader note: sons, not son. There were others besides Ishmael. If they are not apt for it, why should they want it? She surmises that they do not want it, they only think they do. They certainly want the worldly promises that they wrongly believe to be inherent in the blessing; but not the blessing itself, which they cannot understand. How much of it does she understand? At least enough to serve her husband, for whom the struggle is so difficult that it has reduced him to a shadow. But that he should give up the struggle does not occur to him. Nor does it occur to her—this is the touch of greatness in her—to ask him to give it up, for either his sake or hers. Of such stuff are the perfect wives of geniuses.

Many sons are born to Abraham; Isaac alone remains

150

within the blessing. We read, immediately after the marriage of Isaac and Rebekah: "And Abraham took another wife, and her name was Keturah. And she bore him Zimran, and Jokshan, and Medan, and Midian, and Ishbak, and Shuah. . . . And Abraham gave all that he had unto Isaac. But unto the sons of the concubines, that Abraham had, Abraham gave gifts; and he sent them away from Isaac his son, while he yet lived, eastward, into the east country."

Abraham had found it "very grievous" to send away Ishmael. Was he indifferent to his sons by Keturah? Why should we think so? He sent them away with gifts, and suffered till the end. They had to go, for besides being unapt for the blessing they were a danger to Isaac in his struggle. But as Rebekah watched these successive expulsions she asked herself, practical woman that she was, a practical question: how did Abraham expect to establish a "people of the blessing" if he set such an example, and if in every generation every son but one was excluded?

This staggering question led to others. Was Isaac, too, going to have many sons, all but one of them unchosen, and therefore given to the desert? But Isaac could not exclude and expel, any more than—ghastly thought!—he could lift the sacrificial knife, though God commanded and the sacrifice consented. Rebekah knew this the moment she met Isaac. How right she was we can at once declare with the complete record of his life before us. It is an astounding fact that Isaac never so much as lifted the sacrificial knife on an animal. His father did; Jacob too. Isaac never went further than the building

151

of an altar. As to lifting the knife on a human being . . . His devotion was not inferior to Abraham's; it was different, and no man is expected to be capable of everything. God would not ask him to do the impossible; Rebekah was sure of that. But suppose certain things would have to be done which were beyond Isaac's strength— was she not there?

The necessity might never arise. She found it reassuring that Abraham's excluded sons were those of concubines. But it still remained to be seen whether sons begotten on a wife of the covenant would all necessarily be fit for the blessing. In her systematic way she canvassed the three possibilities. She could bear Isaac a number of sons, all for the blessing; that would be the highest fulfillment. She could have an only son; that would be a disappointment, but with immense compensation—there could be no exclusions. She could, again, have a number of sons, and one or more would have to be sent "eastward," into the desert. And this third possibility was her nightmare. This was the trial she might have to face, that of playing the stepmother to her own son, of being a Sarah and a Hagar both in one, while she was also, and primarily, a Rebekah, chosen to serve and protect Isaac. I deliberately phrase it thus, putting in second place her forebodings as a mother.

We read: "And Isaac entreated the Lord for his wife, because she was barren." For twenty years he prayed in vain for Rebekah while Keturah kept pouring out sons to old Abraham, for the desert, not the dedication. The quick-witted, loving young girl became the farsighted loving woman in the middle thirties. She even had to entertain a fourth possibility—that she would be driven to the same shift as the mother-in-law she had never known, would have to bestow one of her Mesopotamian bondwomen on Isaac. Here was nightmare upon nightmare. Isaac was not made for more than one wife; and sons by concubines would not ensure him against the killing duty of exclusions and expulsions. The very contrary was far more likely.

These were some of the problems which Rebekah had taken on herself in marrying the unknown kinsman of Canaan; out of this material she had to fashion her service to him. What thoughts they shared during the first twenty years, and how she comforted him for his mother, we must guess. We are only told that he loved her.

VI

Then at last her barrenness was lifted from her. "And the Lord let Himself be entreated, and Rebekah conceived. And the children struggled within her; and she said: 'If it be so, wherefore do I live?' "

What were Rebekah's emotions when she felt inside her the first faint tappings in that miraculous Morse code which no woman has to learn, the message that at once sends quiet, happy tears coursing down her cheeks? They were emotions of purest bliss, of course. The nightmares vanished from her mind. She took it for granted that this was a son—and of course for the blessing. For who would have dared to suggest that this timid little signaller was destined for the desert? In moments of gratitude she made a sacrifice, her utmost concession of the blissful days: that this might be an only son, and thus no expulsions could be exacted. Let the multiplication of the people begin out of this son, rather than out of Isaac; or even out of the son's son. And if there was to be uncertainty for her as long as she could conceive, and there were years before her, let it be only as between the one accepted son and many accepted sons.

She was granted, as we have just seen, no years of hopeful uncertainty. Within a few weeks the gentle tappings became vicious perturbations. "The children struggled together within her; and she said: 'If it be so, wherefore do I live?' "

Is this Rebekah speaking? Rebekah, the self-assured, the valiant? It is the scream of a woman for whom the signals spell out contumely, ostracism, self-reproach, and reproach of another. "Wherefore do I live?" What good am I? What has he done to me? Why was I brought into the world? But such thoughts cannot come to Rebekah; and whatever her thoughts, it cannot be physical pain that has wrung such words from her. What we have just heard is the expression of a shattering spiritual disappointment. Wherefore do I live? What good am I to Isaac? What have I done to him? Why was I brought into his life? That is the meaning. She forefeels evil in the unnatural violence of the motions, and suspects that the nightmare has settled in her life for good. She is right. And her first thought is always for Isaac. Henceforth the best she can offer him is the mitigation of suffering, the

154

two negatives that make such a sad affirmative. And after
the first hammer-blow of disappointment she will reconcile herself to it. She will do her best, and it will be a
wonderful best under the circumstances. She begins her
preparations at once.

We read: "And she went to inquire of the Lord. And
the Lord said unto her:

> 'Two nations are in thy womb,
> And two peoples shall be separated from thy
>     bowels;
> And one people shall be stronger than the other
>     people;
> And the elder shall serve the younger.' "

Two nations! Two peoples! They could not both be
destined for the blessing. But who had said that either
was? God had given His answer in terms of purely
worldly relations, in those material promises which are
not peculiar for a carrier of the blessing, and which are
as revocable for him as for anyone else; more so, in fact,
precisely because his spiritual destiny is irrevocable.
And if neither of the twins was for the blessing, she
would have to bear again, and perhaps again and again.
She might have to become a Keturah before she became
a Hagar and a Sarah. Let us look long and steadily at
Rebekah's forebodings, and understand her courage.

We read: "And when her days to be delivered were
fulfilled, behold, there were twins in her womb. And the
first came forth ruddy, all over like a hairy mantle; and
they called his name Esau. And after that came forth his
brother, and his hand had hold on Esau's heel; and his

name was called Jacob. And Isaac was threescore years old when she bore them."

## VII

Now follows a passage in the most condensed Biblical style:

"And the boys grew; and Esau was a cunning hunter, a man of the field; and Jacob was a quiet man, dwelling in tents. Now Isaac loved Esau, because he did eat of his venison; and Rebekah loved Jacob."

The quiet man who preferred the tent to the open field was no introvert, like his father. Provoked, he fought back. From childhood, from babyhood—what am I saying? the Text records prenatal hostilities!—the twins were at loggerheads. They came out fighting, Esau forcing the passage, Jacob disputing the right of way; and as they were born, so they grew up.

And now the Text, which here compresses twenty years or so into almost the same number of words, pauses to explain why Isaac loves Esau, but leaves it to our common sense to understand why Rebekah loves Jacob. At the same time the explanation is so disconcerting that we too pause, our eyes glued to the Text.

This is no nomad group living hand to mouth, or bow to mouth, on the edge of starvation. We are told: "And Isaac sowed in that land, and found in the same year a hundredfold; and the Lord blessed him. And the man waxed great, and grew more and more until he became very great. And he had possessions of flocks, and possessions of herds, and a great household; and the Philistines envied him." Isaac was the very rich son of a very rich father, and maintained a great household. And this man loved one son more than the other: "because he did eat of his venison"? Come now! Apart from everything else —Isaac the sacrificed one a trencherman, or a gourmet? Isaac sitting down with grateful gusto to his son's kill? Is the chronicler trying to tell us that the way to Isaac's heart was through his stomach?

"Esau," he says, "was a cunning hunter." Then, to make sure of the effect, adds: "a man of the field", that is, one given over completely to the fury of the chase. This was his all, and from this all he brought offerings to his father. Did nobody else in the family like wild game? Was nobody else prepared to make a fuss over Esau for his skill and generosity? Or did he say: "This is for father, nobody else can have any"? These are irrelevant questions. The Text wants us to see that we have only one problem before us, Isaac's preference for his elder son, based on the most improbable of reasons.

Is it not clear by now that Isaac, looking at his elder son, saw in him the potential man of the desert, the possible Ishmael, begotten not of a concubine, but of the covenanted wife? Not to accept the offerings, and not to make a fuss over them, praise them, and praise the bringer, was to begin the expulsion. Let God decree what He would, and Isaac would accept; only let Him not ask Isaac to be the self-activated instrument. Moreover, as long as the decree was not published—and it might never be published—let Esau accumulate memories of his father's love for him as Esau, as himself.

The more obvious it became with the passing of the

years that Jacob was the destined carrier of the blessing, the more Isaac sought to bind Esau to himself; and until the very end, until and including the hour of the blessing, he had nothing to work with but—venison!

In that case should not the Text read: "And Isaac did eat of Esau's venison because he loved Esau"? It is again a question of pretext and cause. We shall indeed be shown before very long that Isaac was indifferent to the taste of food, and only pretended to find in the venison the reason for loving Esau. But it was of the essence of his purpose that Esau should not know it and thus think his only talent rejected. Isaac would have wanted the Text to read exactly as it does, so that the world might say: "Well, at least one pleasure Isaac owed to Esau." Moreover, as much as love, and spiritual distress, and yearning over his son, there was at work in Isaac the contemplative principle of his life, the extraction of good from adverse or difficult circumstance.

And so Isaac loved Esau, and Rebekah loved Jacob. Are we to infer that there was discord between husband and wife, and that each of the sons was unwanted by one of the parents?

There is no hint of discord, and there is no hint that Rebekah ever thought of thrusting Esau out. But she saw what Isaac would not see: that Esau's was a hopeless case, that he would ultimately wind up in the desert of his own accord. With all her managerial skill she could not establish contact with Esau, and this frustration, her one great failure, took on the appearance of relative indifference. It made her unhappy, too, that Isaac should play such a pitiful game with his backward son. But that

she loved Esau is evident enough from the cry she uttered when she learned that he planned to kill Jacob:
"Why should I be bereaved of you both in one day?"

### VIII

It was here that Rebekah and Isaac were in tacit disagreement: Rebekah considered Esau hopeless in respect of the blessing and religion, or anything having to
do with them, and saw his future in the desert. Isaac
thought him thus far redeemable that though he could
not be a bearer of the blessing, he could be persuaded
to remain in its vicinity, as it were, to his spiritual advantage. We know by now that Rebekah was right.
Isaac's faith becomes the more pathetic when we consider the incident known as the sale of the birthright.

I quote the record in full. It is a most curious docu-
ment.

"And Jacob seethed pottage; and Esau came in from
the field, and he was faint. And Esau said to Jacob: 'Let
me swallow, I pray thee, some of this red, red pottage;
for I am faint.' Therefore was his name called Edom
(red). And Jacob said: 'Sell me first thy birthright.'
And Esau said: 'Behold, I am at the point to die; and
what profit shall the birthright do to me?' And Jacob
said: 'Swear to me first'; and he swore to him; and he
sold his birthright unto Jacob. And Jacob gave Esau
bread and pottage of lentils; and he did eat and drink
and rose up, and went his way. So Esau despised his
birthright."

This is one of the most famous incidents in the Bible,

159

and one of the most bewildering. It is commonly visualized as follows:

On a certain day, in the household of the enormously wealthy sheikh Isaac ben Abraham, one of his two sons, Jacob by name, a quiet, studious, stay-at-home young man, is cooking some soup, presumably for himself. To him enters his older twin brother, Esau, the man of the field, faint from a day's hunting, or from several days', perhaps from a week's hunting, for he is practically *in articulo mortis* from hunger. We take it that he staggers in, or reels, or crawls, with the last of his energies.

We are now to suppose that for some mysterious reason the immense establishment is deserted, and there is no one else about to witness the dying man's condition and to bring him succor. He himself is too weak to go in search of food, or may think it futile, being convinced, for another mysterious reason, that everything edible has vanished with the household, and that his only hope of life is the hated brother and his lentil soup. He is certainly too weak to throw himself on the solitary cook and wrest the food from him. So, in the whisper of the dying, he must bargain for it. And it is a hard as well as fantastic bargain that the younger brother drives: nothing less than the birthright, the inheritance. The alternative is death. Solemnly, under oath, almost with his dying breath, the older one delivers the birthright. And the narrator winds up scornfully: "So Esau despised his birthright."

The most astonishing thing here is the narrator's scorn. Surely a man cannot be accused of despising a

160

treasure because he ransoms his life with it. Or are we to infer that Esau was contemptible because, having eaten, he did not there and then try to murder Jacob, or at least force him to cancel the transaction, but instead got up and walked away? I doubt whether the narrator has been building up the recital to that conclusion. Finally, we might suppose that Esau walked away nonchalantly, knowing that the sale was no sale. If so, he had not despised his birthright, except in pretending that he was prepared to sell it. But then again that was under mortal duress. The worst we can then say is that he despised his brother—as who would not?

But let us suppose that the narrator is a moralist of the sternest breed, and thinks it contemptible for a man to save his life by selling, or even by pretending to sell, his birthright: does the incident as here described place Esau in such a life-and-death dilemma? It certainly does not, as I shall show in a moment. And if it did, we should have to answer the most baffling question of all. Was Jacob villain enough to extort the sale? If so he was certainly villain enough to walk away and let his brother die of hunger. Why didn't he? For then the birthright would have reverted to him automatically. No sale would have been necessary, and no seller would have survived to complain.

But all these difficulties are of our own making. We ourselves have unconsciously doctored the story in order to justify our prejudice against Esau, or in our over-anxiety to show that the Bible can't be wrong; and now we are tripped up by our ingenuity. The Bible is not wrong here, and our defense is as unnecessary as it is unconvincing. It all comes out straight if we stick to the Text. Nowhere in it are we told that Esau was on the point of death for lack of a crust and a bowl of soup. It is Esau who makes the statement, and it is implausible. Nowhere are we asked to believe that the house was on that day abandoned by everyone but Jacob, and that there was nothing in it to eat but Jacob's bread and lentil soup. We are told that Esau was faint, and that he said to his brother: "Let me swallow, I pray thee, some of this red, red pottage. . . ." And his brother said: "Sell me first thy birthright." And instead of snarling: "This is no time for stupid jokes," or "Are you mad?" or "You be damned! I'd rather die first," Esau pants: "Behold, I am at the point to die; and what profit shall the birthright do to me?" This from the hunter, the hardy man of the field, who knew what it was to stalk his prey from sunrise to sunset. The offer, made in contempt, is repeated in amazement, and in more urgent form: "Swear." It is not to save his life that Esau surrenders his birthright; it is to satisfy the savage craving of the moment. The tickle of the hot soup in his hairy nostrils crowds out everything else; and it is properly remembered against him in his nickname, Edom, the red.

I call attention to the fact that for the second time in this drama of a high spiritual destiny, evolving in a household of great wealth, food is incongruously made the hinge of crucial developments. On both occasions the incongruity is created by Esau, in his character as huntsman. On the first occasion he makes his father look like a senile glutton; on the second he makes his brother look like a villain and a fool.

Esau was huntsman, nothing but huntsman, delivered up, heart and soul, body and spirit, to the ferocious pursuit of food when that stage of human subjection to nature had been left behind. He was a throwback, a case of arrested development. He despised his birthright as a civilized man, and how much more his birthright as the son of Isaac and the grandson of Abraham! He sold his birthright to Jacob not because Jacob bought it—when a man sells his soul, no purchaser acquires it—but because Jacob was left alone to carry the destiny of the blessing.

The mind of the primitive is elusive. I cannot get a picture of Esau's ideas. He believed the sale of the birthright to be valid—and yet he continued to consider himself entitled to the blessing. We know this because, at the end, when he was "swindled" out of the blessing, he wept that it was the second time Jacob had "supplanted" him. Did he know that the blessing was not a promissory note and therefore not reassignable? Apparently not. Did he know that even though material things, and prospects of material things, are transferable, a sale under duress is not valid? Apparently not. So for him a will and a blessing—or rather *the* blessing—were the same, and he had sold or reassigned his prospects under the will. Nevertheless he seems to have thought that the will or heritage and the blessing were not the same. I give it up. Some of the blame for Esau's confusion belongs to Isaac. He could have done something to straighten Esau out. He could have used the incident of the sale as a starting-point and gradually disillusioned his son about his attitude toward hunting and venison. He preferred to keep up the pretense.

## IX

It went on over the years, from the boyhood of the twins into their manhood, before the death of grandfather Abraham, and after it.

If we take pencil and paper and collate the figures scattered through the narrative, we shall find that Abraham died when the boys were fifteen years old. "He died," we read, "an old man, full of years, and was gathered to his people. And Isaac and Ishmael his sons buried him in the cave of Machpelah."

And then: "It came to pass after the death of Abraham that God blessed Isaac his son."

The terms of the blessing are not given here; they are reserved for a later occasion. Here we read only that God blessed Issac when Abraham died. And suddenly it occurs to us that Abraham himself never bestowed the blessing on his son! We are astounded. We look back carefully through the record. We are not mistaken. There was no farewell ceremonial, no formal charge, no laying on of hands, no statement, no express transmission of the responsibility from Abraham to Isaac. And we realize slowly that the mortal, personal gesture was unnecessary when there was a single heir. The taking over was tacit, and God confirmed it. Ah, if Esau were only to withdraw of his own free will, disinherit himself by his own act, and leave Jacob in sole possession! Then

Isaac would not face on his deathbed the miserable duty of blessing one son and excluding the other.

The longer we contemplate the terms of the blessing which God confirmed for Isaac, the more inescapable that duty is seen to be. These are the words: "Sojourn in this land, and I will be with thee and will bless thee; for unto thee, and unto thy seed, I will give all these lands, and I will establish the oath which I swore unto Abraham thy father; and I will multiply thy seed as the stars of heaven, and will give unto thy seed all these lands; and by thy seed shall all the nations of the earth bless themselves; *because that Abraham hearkened to My voice, and kept My charge, My commandments, My statutes, and My laws.*"

The promises and the blessing are so sharply separated here that we cannot miss their provisional connection. We must always bear in mind that God promised earthly greatness, vast numbers, permanent territories, to others than the carriers of the blessing. Ishmael's progeny would be a numberless multitude. Ammon and Moab are assigned lands in perpetuity. These are promises. The responsibilities, the charges, commandments, statutes, and laws are the blessing of Abraham; they are the principle of man's unfolding; and they were utterly alien to Esau. Isaac knew it no less certainly than Rebekah and Jacob. An attempt to bestow, or impose, this blessing on Esau would have been blasphemous, as well as futile, or blasphemous because futile. It would also have been shockingly cruel, because if done seriously, with demands on the understanding, and on self-discipline, it would—to use modern terms—have split Esau's

165

personality in two without improvement to either half.

Thus, as we approach the climax of the story, let us understand once for all that Isaac never dreamed of bestowing the blessing, or rather of making the attempt to bestow it, on Esau; and Rebekah never suspected him of such a folly. What she foresaw from afar, and what the years taught her increasingly to fear, was the effort it would cost Isaac to do his duty. For do it he most certainly would—and almost as certainly in such a way as to inflict the minimum of pain on Esau: perhaps going so far as to deceive him. From such a deception bitter consequences would follow.

Her fears were justified. The years passed and she watched Isaac deceiving Esau out of love, out of desperate hope pretending to love him for the sake of the venison; this from the day when Esau brought home his first kill to the day Isaac sent him—actually sent him!— out on the hunt as a preliminary to blessing him. Throughout these years Isaac had been growing blind, and by the time of the crisis he was sightless. Rebekah had passed beyond the childbearing years, and the nightmare had ceased to haunt her. There would be no more Jacob-sons, but also no more Esau-sons. Throughout these years Esau, indulged by Isaac, inaccessible to Rebekah, at daggers drawn with Jacob, had followed his own course; and at last he married into the Canaanitish tribes, and, as we might expect, his wives were as unsusceptible to the Abrahamitic code as he. Thus the grandchildren of Rebekah and Isaac by their older son would be as heathen as the sons of Ishmael. We read:

"When Esau was forty years old he took to wife Judith the daughter of Beeri the Hittite, and Basemath the daughter of Elon the Hittite. And they were a bitterness of spirit unto Isaac and to Rebekah."

It must have been a great bitterness indeed to Isaac if he let his feelings be known. Nevertheless he continued to indulge Esau in the pride of the hunt, that symbol and substance of his spiritual disqualification.

## x

I do not know of another episode in the Bible which equals this one of the embezzlement in its combination of vividness, penetration, and inexorability. It is flawless in both logical structure and psychological propriety; and here as nowhere else I am conscious of the Text as the sole source of my information.

Blind old Isaac lay in his tent meditating on the time to come when for him there would be no more meditation. We happen to know that he still had many years of life before him, and that he would go on for a long time meditating in darkness instead of in twilight. But this knowledge was withheld from him. We read:

"And it came to pass, that when Isaac was old, and his eyes were dim, so that he could not see, he called Esau his elder son, and said unto him: 'My son'; and he said unto him: 'Here am I.' And he said: 'Behold now, I am old; I know not the day of my death. Now therefore take, I pray thee, thy weapons, thy quiver and thy bow, and go out into the field, and take me venison; and make me savoury food, such as I love, and bring it to me, that

I may eat, that my soul may bless thee before I die.' And Rebekah heard when Isaac spoke to Esau his son."

The Text implies strongly that Rebekah's presence was unsuspected. Was she eavesdropping? She may have seen Esau entering the tent and stationed herself at the door. It is much more likely, however, that she was within it, and on the other side of the curtain. For she thought Isaac was dying and she hovered about him; and what she heard accorded perfectly with what the years had taught her to expect. Old Isaac, about to die, was going to bless Esau before he blessed Jacob; and he was associating this declaration of priority with Esau as the hunter and the man of the field.

It did not matter that the blessing Isaac would bestow on Esau would not and could not be *the* blessing. What mattered frightfully was that Esau would not know the difference. All he knew was that his father had called him first, and had sent him out to hunt, in preparation. For the rest of his life he would believe himself to be the carrier of *the* blessing, and that on the very grounds which unfitted him for it, or rather constituted his personality and its unfitness. He would pass on to his children, and to his children's children, the legend that Abraham's blessing, transmitted to them through Isaac the son and Esau the grandson, was the blessing of the primitive ones, the wild ones of the desert, and theirs was the fulfillment of man's destiny, and with it would grow the parallel legend of the descendants of Jacob as the rejected ones, the false claimants.

And not Esau alone would propagate this calamitous misconception, but most of those who had been the wit-

168

nesses of the priority, and of the specific preparations for the bestowal.

All this lay implicit in what was about to happen, and all this was what Rebekah had to forestall by turning the solemn occasion into a mockery. There would be a personal deception to prevent a world deception

It is almost impossible to believe that Isaac the thinker did not see as far as Rebekah. But the almost impossible must give way, somehow or other, to the undeniable, and it is undeniable that ever since Esau had taken to the field, his father had deceived him in professing to love him for the sake of venison, and that when he was about to bless him he sent him out to hunt for it.

I harp on this point because it is the crux of the last act: from Isaac's deception of Esau flowed logically Rebekah's deception of Isaac.

Here is what we read next: "And Rebekah spoke unto Jacob her son, saying: 'Behold, I heard thy father speak unto Esau thy brother, saying: "Bring me venison, and make me savoury food, that I may eat, and bless thee before the Lord before my death." Now therefore, my son, hearken to my voice according to that which I command thee. Go now to the flock, and fetch me from thence two good kids of the goats; and I will make them savoury food for thy father, such as he loveth; and thou shalt bring it to thy father, so that he may bless thee before his death.' And Jacob said to Rebekah his mother: 'Behold, Esau my brother is a hairy man, and I am a smooth man. My father peradventure will feel me, and I shall seem to him as a mocker; and I shall bring a curse upon me, not a blessing.' "

169

I must confess that I was staggered when, a few years ago, long convinced that I knew the story through and through, I suddenly realized that I had missed the meaning of this passage. I had until then regarded it as a general but overwhelming improbability that Isaac had any feeling for the pleasures of the table; he was so obviously an absent-minded eater. But here we have such pointed and incontrovertible proof that I can only have missed it because I did not need it. I failed to observe that Jacob passes over the problem of the taste of the food to worry about the smoothness of his hands. He will offer his father a mess of kid's flesh! But who ever heard of an attentive eater mistaking domestic kid's meat for wild game? I have since asked a dozen cooks, fellow countrywomen of Rebekah's, though of course of a more recent generation, whether Rebekah could there and then, in her place and time, and without previous experimentation, have prepared kid in such a way as to make it taste like venison to, I will not say a gourmet, but a person of the most ordinary palatal perceptiveness; and I have never received anything but a compassionate negative. Two of them went so far as to place Isaac's obtuseness on that occasion among the minor miracles.

Rebekah, and Jacob, and I suppose everyone else in the story but Esau, knew that Isaac had no idea whether he was eating vension or kid, or veal, or lamb, or for that matter carob; and while Rebekah was saddened by the pretense, she had to smile at it. "Go now to the flock," she says to Jacob, "and fetch me thence two kids of the goats; and I will make them savoury food for thy father, such as he loveth." And Jacob, understanding the affectionate irony, turns to the serious problem of the smoothness of his skin.

And now we shall see how, throughout all the years, Rebekah has retained undiminished her dexterity, her rapidity of judgment and co-ordination—from the moment when she recognized the thinker in the darkening field to the time when he lay blind in his tent, dying, as she thought. It is an intellectual pleasure to follow her reasoning, or, rather, her intuitive responses.

There were five senses to be tricked, and sight was the most resistant. In every language there is the equivalent of the proverb: "Seeing is believing," but never "tasting is believing," or feeling, or smelling, or hearing; and this strategically central sense God had taken care of. We may also say, perhaps, that He had taken care of Isaac's sense of taste. The other three senses he left to Rebekah, and she disposed of two of them. We read: "And Rebekah took the choicest garments of Esau, her elder son, which were with her in the house, and put them upon Jacob, her younger son. And she put the skins of the kids of the goats upon his hands, and upon the smooth of his neck."

Four of the senses were now accounted for, sight, taste, smell, and touch. There remained Isaac's unimpaired hearing, and nothing could be done about it. With one sense neutralized and three deceived she had to hope that the fifth would be carried along. So it was; to be exact, it was dragged along; for a few moments it was touch and go, and those few moments must have remained in Jacob's memory for the rest of his life.

We read: "And she gave the savoury food and the

171

bread, which she had prepared, into the hand of her son Jacob. And he came unto his father, and said: 'My father'; and he said: 'Here am I; who art thou, my son?' "

How Jacob went through with it is beyond me; to make the incident credible, one has to recall his whole record, and particularly the coolness and tenacity with which he handled Laban, the arch-deceiver, some years later. Even so, he must have been tempted to drop the dishes and run. But we read: "And Jacob said unto his father: 'I am Esau thy first-born; I have done according as thou badest me. Arise, I pray thee, sit and eat of my venison, that thy soul may bless me.' "

It was all or nothing; and he brazened it out, spoke at length, and with great presence of mind referred to the instructions Isaac had given Esau privately.

The next question he must have anticipated. They had had to act with dangerous speed, Rebekah and he, lest Esau return and burst in on the masquerade. "And Isaac said unto his son: 'How is it that thou hast found it so quickly, my son?' And he said: 'Because the Lord thy God sent me good speed.' And Isaac said unto Jacob: 'Come near, I pray thee, that I may feel thee, my son, whether thou be my very son Esau or not.' And Jacob went near unto Isaac his father; and he felt him, and said: 'The voice is the voice of Jacob, but the hands are the hands of Esau.' And he discerned him not, because his hands were hairy, as his brother Esau's hands; so he blessed him. And he said: 'Art thou my very son Esau?' And he said: 'I am.' And he said: 'Bring it near to me, and I will eat of my son's venison, that my soul may bless thee.' And he brought it near to him, and he did

172

eat; and he brought him wine, and he drank. And his father Isaac said unto him: 'Come near now, and kiss me, my son.' And he came near, and kissed him. And he smelled the smell of his raiment, and blessed him, and said . . ."

We must linger over this painful scene, for we are now in the very heart of the case. It is widely held that Isaac saw through the deception, and lent himself to it; or he refused to let himself see through it. It is also said that his blindness was willful; he had developed it for just such an occasion. The Tradition has various hints. Thomas Mann bases his incomparable description of the scene on this assumption. Against them there is the flat statement of the chronicler: "And he discerned him not." If we ignore it, or interpret it away, we shall have to reconsider and re-evaluate the whole massive development of the theme, extending over the lifetime of parents and sons. And we should have to see Rebekah, in her supreme moment, as the silly dupe of her own uncalled-for duplicity. I say it cannot be done, even apart from the character of the blessing. And what are we to say when that is brought into the case?

"*See, the smell of my son*
*Is as the smell of a field which the Lord hath*
    *blessed.*
*So God give thee of the dew of heaven,*
*And of the fat places of the earth,*
*And plenty of corn and wine.*
*Let peoples serve thee,*
*And nations bow down to thee.*

173

*Be lord over thy brethren,*
*And let thy mother's sons bow down to thee.*
*Cursed be every one that curseth thee,*
*And blessed be every one that blesseth thee."*

We start back. This is not the blessing at all! There is not even a remote resemblance. Where is the mention of Abraham, in whose name alone the blessing has meaning? Or even of the land as the place in which the blessing can best be cultivated? All we have here is the material world and its material terms. And it need not startle us that Isaac should give Esau dominion over Jacob. The man who has learned to master circumstance by meditating on God thinks it better that in the quarrel of the brothers Jacob shall suffer subjection at first rather than Esau, who is spiritually resourceless. I emphasize *at first*. The material world does not parallel the moral world, and never did. Its values are transient, for the wicked and the good alike. A material possession "in perpetuity" is understood to be revocable. Here Isaac blesses Jacob, in Esau's guise, with dominion over his brother. A few minutes later, when Esau comes to him, he revokes this "blessing" without effort, he shows it to be provisional; so, for that matter, is everything else in that material blessing.

But one thing was irrevocable: that which had been done. As long as time flows in the same direction, the deed remains as the ebb left it. Esau did not receive the blessing before Jacob. Past and future may be reversible as to their meanings; the fact, the *factum*, the done, stays where it is. Let the case be reopened, and Isaac's intentions cited, a thousand times again; the oftener the facts are cited, the better for Jacob. Embedded with the deed of "firstness," as part of it, is its self-justification, the fact and deed of the exposure. Isaac had no liking for Esau's venison, could not tell it from any other kind of meat; Isaac did not love Esau because he enjoyed the hunter's spoils; Isaac deceived Esau; and Isaac himself was deceived that the world might be undeceived. As for Esau, he was incurable.

We read: "And it came to pass, as soon as Isaac had made an end of blessing Jacob, and Jacob was yet scarce gone out of the presence of Isaac his father, that Esau his brother came in from his hunting. And he also made savoury food, and brought it unto his father; and he said unto his father: 'Let my father arise, and eat of his son's venison, that thy soul may bless me.' And Isaac his father said unto him: 'Who art thou?' And he said: 'I am thy son, thy first-born, Esau.' And Isaac trembled very exceedingly, and said: 'Who then is he that hath taken venison, and brought it me, and I have eaten of all before thou camest, and have blessed him? Yea, and he shall be blessed.' When Esau heard the words of his father, he cried with an exceeding great and bitter cry, and said unto his father: 'Bless me, even me also, O my father.' And he said: 'Thy brother came with guile, and hath taken away thy blessing.' "

In the midst of our sympathy we have to smile like Rebekah at the way the unhappy old man betrays himself. To him it is still venison! And Esau does not, because he dare not, catch him up on this slip of the tongue and ask: "What venison? Whose venison?" And

175

when his father says: "Thy brother came with guile, and hath taken away thy blessing," also: "Yea, and he shall be blessed," Esau does not ask: "How can a blessing be given to the wrong man?" For him the blessing is inseparable from firstness, almost consists in firstness. Merit and fitness have nothing to do with it. Merely by being called first he took over the Abrahamitic blessing.

Esau's blindness to the issue, condoned and encouraged by his blind father, reveals itself here to the full.

We read: "And Esau said: 'Is he not rightly named Jacob? for he hath supplanted me these two times: he took away my birthright; and, behold, now he hath taken away my blessing.' " That there were no two times, that there was not even one time, and that the birthright and the blessing are one—namely, the bitter and ecstatic privilege of the everlasting struggle, for which he is totally unfitted—cannot be explained to him. But he could have been brought to feel, perhaps, that here were matters beyond his reach. His father never made the effort, and shrinks from it now.

We read further: "And Esau said: 'Hast thou not reserved a blessing for me?' And Isaac answered and said unto Esau: 'Behold, I have made him thy lord, and all his brethren have I given to him for servants; and with corn and wine have I sustained him; and what then shall I do for thee, my son?' And Esau said unto his father: 'Hast thou but one blessing, my father? Bless me, even me also, my father.' And Esau lifted up his voice and wept."

Unwittingly poor Esau hit on the truth. Isaac had only one blessing that mattered; but this blessing could

176

have been given equally to ten sons. It could not, therefore, derive a special virtue from the order of its bestowal. How was Isaac to begin now the undoing of a
lifetime of miseducation? He could have said: "I will
give you the same blessing as I gave Jacob," and then
Esau would have gone out of his mind trying to figure
things out. So there had never been a special blessing!
To have been the beloved son carried no advantage!
Thence he might even reach the ghastly conclusion that
he had never been the favorite, and that his father had
never admired his hunting.

Actually the blessing Isaac now gives Esau is not very
different from the one he gave Jacob:

*"Behold, of the fat places of the earth shall be thy
    dwelling,*
*And of the dew of heaven from above.*
*And by thy sword shalt thou live, and thou shalt
    serve thy brother;*
*And it shall come to pass when thou shalt break
    loose,*
*That thou shalt shake his yoke from off thy neck."*

Compare the two blessings. What is there about Esau's
to embitter him? What more would he have got as the
firstcomer except some flourishes and a temporary over-
lordship? He too is given the fat places: corn and wine
are implied. He will live by the sword: but he is not a
quiet man dwelling in tents, and the prospect is not un-
pleasing Suppose he had been given dominion over his
brother, or over brothers (Isaac may have had in mind
his own semi-miraculous birth, and provided for sons

177

still to come) ; see how easily such thing are shown to be revocable. Within a matter of minutes Isaac had put a term to Jacob's dominion. He could even have reversed it if that would not have confused Esau. As for the last two phrases in the first-given blessing, would they have made Esau any happier? He wanted to consider himself the carrier of *the* blessing, which could not be *the* blessing unless it was bestowed first. It was his because he was his father's favorite, and he was the favorite because he was a man of the field. He had remained the favorite after the sale of the birthright, too. Now this had happened. No wonder we read: "And Esau hated Jacob because of the blessing wherewith his father blessed him." All the enmity he had felt till now was as nothing in comparison.

## XI

Before he carried the dishes into his father's tent Jacob was terrified that he might be unmasked and cursed. That would have been horrible. Not that it would have affected the blessing which none but he could carry. He trembled at the thought of his father's anguish, and still more at the impression the curse would make on others. Not only would Esau stand forth as the accepted son who had been blessed first: Jacob, if he ever got a blessing at all, would be pilloried to the ages as the rejected son who had been cursed before the other was blessed. The deception was of course going to be discovered that same day; and Isaac would suffer, and might curse him. That could not be helped, and he would have to endure it. But the situation would have been saved.

Jacob was in a panic. Rebekah thought things out calmly. Certainly it would be a nasty business if Jacob were unmasked in the tent. Nothing would be left for her then but to go in there and, for the first time in her life, make a scene, with Isaac on the point of death. She must have been tempted to eavesdrop, but she cannot have done so. She had to keep a look out for Esau. So she stood at a distance glancing alternately at the tent and at the camp entrance, praying to the God of Abraham, Isaac, and Jacob. Until at last she saw Jacob emerge just as Esau was entering the camp, the buck slung over his shoulders.

As to what Isaac would do later, her mind was at ease. He would be pained for a while, then he would accept; and in his way he would work it out for the good, and understand after the event what she had understood before; or rather he would reconcile himself to it, for no doubt he had seen just as far as she. And so it was. The record tells us of no remonstrances, no reproaches; as for a curse, only Jacob in his panic could have feared that.

Esau was the problem. We read: "And Esau said in his heart: 'Let the days of mourning for my father be at hand; then I will slay my brother Jacob.' And the words of Esau her elder son were told to Rebekah." He went about the camp wild-eyed with fury, muttering his intentions. He too obviously expected Isaac to die soon.

And now as I approach the last recorded episode in Rebekah's life I must prepare the reader for the perfection of the finale. She exits as she entered, in brilliant

action. I am sure that if we were to read of this last incident, with all its details, as occurring in some other
woman's life, we would exclaim: "You know, I can't
help thinking of Rebekah! That neatness, that dovetail-
ing of purposes, that smoothness of calculation. I didn't
think there were two women like that." And of course
there are not, for I am only supposing. But it is not
only the charming repetition, by the grand old lady of
seventy-five, of the graceful movements carried out by
the girl of fifteen It is the beautiful tidying up of her
life's business, the closing of the ring, the completion of
the great theme.

The first thing she did when Esau's words were reported to her was to call in Jacob. "Behold," she said,
"thy brother Esau, as touching thee, doth comfort himself, purposing to kill thee. Now therefore, my son,
hearken to my voice; and arise, and flee thou to Laban
my brother to Haran; and tarry with him a few days,
until thy brother's fury turn away; until thy brother's
anger turn away from thee, and he forget that which
thou hast done to him; then I will send, and fetch thee
from thence, why should I be bereaved of you both in
one day?"

Nothing here about Isaac's imminent death. That she
is convinced of it is implicit in her action. Why send
Jacob away if Esau's revenge would anyhow be delayed
till he forgot about it? But if she breathed a word to
Jacob he would certainly refuse to go. She said: "for a
few days." We know that the journey took seventeen
days each way; we have made it with Balaam, and with
Eliezer and Rebekah She counted on a two-month ab-

sence at least. And she closed with: "Why should I be bereaved of both of you in one day?" She can have meant that the men might kill each other—Jacob not being an Isaac to let himself be sacrificed. She can have meant that whichever son kills the other, he too is lost to her forever. Or that God would destroy him. Whichever of these she meant, the argument was a powerful one when addressed to Jacob.

So much for section one of Operation Rounding Out. We read then:

"And Rebekah said to Isaac: 'I am weary of my life because of the daughters of Heth. If Jacob take a wife of the daughters of Heth, such as these, of the daughters of the land, what good shall my life do me?' "

The daughters of Heth are of course the Hittite women, the wives of Esau, who "were a bitterness of spirit unto Isaac and to Rebekah." She could not have addressed to Isaac a more powerful argument for sending Jacob to Mesopotamia—variously called Aram-naharayim, and Paddan-aram—to find himself a wife. But as she said nothing to Jacob about Isaac's approaching death, she said nothing to Isaac about sending Jacob to Mesopotamia. It is wonderful what opposite purposes silence can serve.

Then we read: "And Isaac called Jacob, and blessed him, and charged him, and said unto him: 'Thou shalt not take a wife of the daughters of Canaan. Arise, go to Paddan-aram, to the house of Bethuel, thy mother's father; and take thee a wife from thence of the daughters of Laban thy mother's brother. . . .' "

There is no Eliezer to send as Jacob's emissary, and

181

Jacob can be trusted to go and come—though with much delay. But Isaac is more explicit than his father was: "Of the daughters of Laban, thy mother's brother," he says. He shared Abraham's abhorrence of the Canaanitish women; and it appears now that although Abraham had made no converts in his family, except for the ill-fated Lot, he had undoubtedly meant "kindred" to be absolute. They had remained heathen, but there was a strain of great promise in their women.

So Jacob is about to depart into safety; the blunder threatened by Isaac's weakness and Esau's ignorance has been averted; this cycle within the great cycle is completed. We lean back satisfied—only to start up again. The blessing! *The* blessing. What happened with that?

It is here. It is the end to which all other ends planned by Rebekah have been the means; for all her means are ends, and by her genius she has placed herself beyond reach of that false ends-and-means division which is the source of so much evil.

We read, immediately after Isaac's instructions, these words: "And God Almighty bless thee, and make thee fruitful, and multiply thee, that thou mayest be a congregation of peoples; and give thee the blessing of Abraham; to thee, and to thy seed with thee; that thou mayest inherit the land of the sojournings, which God gave unto Abraham."

Now there can be no mistake. It is "the blessing of Abraham"—the blessing that Isaac has known all along to be Jacob's inalienable responsibility. He bestows it on him as he has all along known he would, and he learns to be grateful that he has been prevented from marring the bestowal by a miscalculating kindness. Very soon, after Jacob's departure, Esau is not only reconciled to his disappointment; he even shows that he has learned something from it. We read:

"And Isaac sent away Jacob; and he went to Paddan-aram unto Laban, son of Bethuel the Aramean, the brother of Rebekah, Jacob's and Esau's mother. Now Esau saw that Isaac had blessed Jacob and sent him away to Paddan-aram, to take him a wife from thence; and that as he blessed him he gave him a charge, saying: 'Thou shalt not take a wife of the daughters of Canaan'; and that Jacob hearkened to his father and his mother, and was gone to Paddan-aram; and Esau saw that the daughters of Canaan pleased not Isaac his father; so Esau went unto Ishmael, and took unto the wives that he had Mahalath the daughter of Ishmael Abraham's son, the sister of Nebaioth, to be his wife."

I am glad that it ends thus, with a warning to us not to think badly of Esau. I am particularly glad that he came to his senses, and found himself. One meets so many people who are continuously sniveling that they are failures simply because they have not become what they were never intended to be; and it is pleasant to think that Esau in his later years was not of their number. He did his best after he got it out of his head that he was entitled to the blessing. It was not in his power to do what was positive in his father's eyes; so he at least tried this once to avoid what was negative. "He saw that the daughters of Canaan pleased not Isaac his father." He had to lose all hope of the blessing before his eyes were opened to that extent, though the daughters of

Ishmael may not have been much of an improvement on the daughters of Canaan. But as to his essential self Esau at last understood his limitations and where he belonged. He withdrew into the desert, acknowledging Jacob's position. There was everlasting enmity between the descendants of Esau, the Edomites, and the descendants of Jacob, the Israelites; but in so far as Rebekah played a role in its beginnings, she was responsible for a gesture of accommodation.

One detail seems to mar the perfection of Rebekah's last action: Jacob remained in Mesopotamia not two months but twenty years, and when he returned it was with four wives, eleven sons, and a daughter. But the imperfection has nothing to do with the issues Rebekah served. She had been chosen to guard Isaac in the fulfillment of his destiny. We cannot find anywhere a failure by omission or commission, and all the actions recorded sparkle with the peculiar brightness of her spirit.

Her story ends here. She lived on for many years, but nothing more is told or needs to be told about her. The reunion with Jacob is passed over in silence. Even the place and time of her death are omitted. Instead we are given, strangely and significantly, the place and time of the death of another person, mentioned only once before, and in the most casual manner: one who was in the retinue of servants she brought with her as a bride out of Mesopotamia.

Long, long after Rebekah's dismissal from the record, after Jacob's return, after his meeting in reconciliation with Esau, after the sack of the city of Shechem by Simeon and Levi, we read: "And Deborah Rebekah's nurse died, and she was buried below Beth-el under the oak; and the name of it was called Allon-bacuth, that is, the oak of weeping." How much of her character Rebekah owed to her family, how much to her nurse, we shall never know.

# CHAPTER VI

## *Three Wives*

❋

Wᴵᵀʜ all my liking for Rebekah's company, I find her world oppressive. Its individuals are overloaded with responsibility, its single events with consequences. We are standing at the source of things, at the primal watershed, and it depends on a few men and women whether the stream will flow to the Atlantic or the Pacific. Words are portents, and every aside is multiplied into thunder by the megaphone of the millennia.

I originally planned to present these People of the Book in chronological order, for neatness. But I found that in writing as in reading I cannot stay for longer than a chapter at a time with people so portentously conscious of themselves as fateful beginnings, always alert for the "I shall make of thee," and "thy seed shall be," and "unto thy seed," and "multitudes," and "nations." And so, after an hour with Abraham or Jacob, after experiencing the call out of Mesopotamia or witnessing the plunge into Egypt, I go forward to linger with less burdened personalities and among less pregnant events.

My conscience is freer, too. Among the folk of the

prime my responsibilities as portraitist are proportionate to theirs as actors. I am of course just as scrupulous with the People of later ages; with Elijah, or David, or Naomi; or with David's three wives, the theme of this chapter. But if I misdraw them I do not throw all history out of focus. Like us they are immersed in a world set going.

## II

These three principal wives of Israel's most famous king are a group argument against the legend of Biblical woman's "crushed personality." All three were the wives of other men too; Abigail and Bathsheba before, Michal during an intermission. None of the three was a passive acquisition. Michal and Abigail chose their man, and went after him, the first in her father's palace, the second on a mountain road. Bathsheba was "taken" by him, after he saw her bathing, but there is reason to doubt that he saw her by accident.

David had eighteen wives and concubines, and some as unrepressed as Michal, Abigail, and Bathsheba may have dropped out of the record. He is unique in the variety of types with which he intertwined destinies, and is the only man I can think of who has at least three immovable "opposites." We talk of Damon and Pythias, and there's an end of each of them; of Samson and Delilah, of Abélard and Héloïse, of Paolo and Francesca, and so on. But there are David and Goliath, David and Jonathan, David and Bathsheba, three indivisibilities stemming from one name. David and Saul, David and

Absalom are almost if not quite the same kind of folk-
loristic binary. A uniquely multisided personality is indicated here.

### III

Michal fell in love with David when he was brought
to her father's court, a stripling, "ruddy, and withal of
beautiful eyes, and goodly to look upon." An unnamed
friend recommended him as a musician who could exor-
cise the evil spirits that haunted the king, adding, moreover: "A mighty man of valour, and a man of war, and
prudent in affairs, and a comely person, and the Lord
is with him." At most of these irrelevant qualifications
the sponsor must have guessed, because David still had
to prove himself. He had, indeed, been anointed as the
next king by the old prophet priest Samuel: but the ceremony had been performed secretly, within the family
circle, and David's brothers seem to have been more
astonished than impressed. He was courageous; he had
killed wild animals barehanded defending his flock; but
his military talents were latent. As harpist he at once
justified the recommendation. We read: "And it came
to pass, when the evil spirit from God was upon Saul,
that David took the harp, and played with his hand; so
Saul found relief, and it was well with him, and the evil
spirit departed from him."

Saul's condition we may gauge from the following:
"David came to Saul, and stood before him; and he
loved him greatly; and he became his armour-bearer."
Nevertheless there was no full-time appointment. For a
little farther on we read: "David went to and fro from

Saul to feed his father's sheep at Bethlehem." This is significant enough, but there is worse. Saul was subject to devastating fits of amnesia. When David asked his permission to fight Goliath, Saul answered pityingly: "Thou art not able to go against this Philistine to fight with him, for thou art but a youth, and he a man of war from his youth." Persuaded by David against his better judgment, Saul clothed him in his own helmet and coat of mail, and gave him his own sword, all of which David had to cast aside. A few minutes later Saul did not know him. We read: "When Saul saw David go forth against the Philistine, he said unto Abner, the captain of the host: 'Abner, whose son is this youth?'" And Abner answered tactfully: "As thy soul liveth, O king, I cannot tell." Afterwards, when Abner brought in David carrying the head of Goliath, Saul asked wildly: "Whose son art thou, thou young man?" and David answered: "I am the son of thy servant Jesse the Bethlehemite." It is possible that somewhere in the mind of the half-mad king there was a convulsive turning away from his destined successor.

The position of the boy-genius at court was precarious from the beginning. Nor did his brothers, skeptical witnesses of his anointing, have glimpses of his future greatness. They resented his hanging round the camp in the days when Goliath was terrorizing the Israelite army and Saul was offering "great riches" and the hand of one of his daughters to the killer of Goliath. We read of David's oldest brother: "Eliab's anger was kindled against David, and he said: 'Why art thou come down? and with whom hast thou left the few sheep in the wilderness? I know thy presumptuousness and the naughtiness of thy heart.' " They were not impressed either by his part-time employment as court musician and armor-bearer to the king; and if it was told them that Saul "loved David greatly," they put as little stock in it as in the secret anointing, and with better reason.

After the slaying of Goliath, David's appointment was made full-time. "And Saul took him that day, and would let him go no more home to his father's house." For a brief while it might have seemed that David was securely established. A great love sprang up between him and Saul's son Jonathan; in the palace as among the people David's name was becoming a byword. He was entrusted with various missions, and we read: "Whithersoever Saul sent him he had good success; and Saul set him over the men of war; and it was good in the sight of all the people, and also in the sight of Saul's servants."

Then the pendulum swung back. David returned one day with Saul from a slaughtering of the Philistines. "And the women came out of all the cities of Israel, singing and dancing, to meet king Saul, with timbrels, with joy, and with three-stringed instruments. And the women sang to one another in their play, and said:

'Saul hath slain his thousands,
And David his ten thousands.'

And Saul was very wroth, and this saying displeased him; and he said: 'They have ascribed unto David ten thousands, and to me they have ascribed but thousands; and all he lacketh is the kingdom!' " There it was! "And Saul eyed David from that day forward."

He eyed him, and loved him, and hated him, and
feared him, and needed him. He had him play the harp,
and in the midst of the playing suddenly hurled a spear
at him, to pin him to the wall. David, on the alert,
slipped away. Saul brought him back, and made him
play again, and again blacked out and tried to kill him.
Then he sent him away from the palace to a military
command; then he recalled him. And always his fear
grew: "He stood in awe of him. But all Israel and
Judah loved David, for he went out and came in before
them."

In those days, we read: "Michal, Saul's daughter,
loved David."

My feelings about Michal's love for David rise in part
from the setting of those early days and in part from
what happened later; I must remember how she defied
her father and saved David's life; how David abandoned
her, and in what manner he sent for her after many
years; how she became embittered, and her tongue
poisonous. The end throws its light back on the beginning.

David had come to the palace out of nowhere, a
bewilderingly beautiful boy with a magical gift for the
harp. By occupation he was a shepherd. The family,
though descended from the wealthy Boaz, was obscure,
and its flock was small. It must have looked like a great
thing at first, that his unknown lad from the countryside should have the power to calm the nerves of the
distraught king, and to win his love, and be given the
title of armor-bearer. But we have seen how the unpredictable Saul used him at the beginning. David came

and went, a hireling by the hour, one might say, sent for when needed, and alternating as shepherd and court harpist. It is not surprising that his brothers were unimpressed. And what was the effect on Michal, who had fallen in love with David?

Here was the young and radiant genius, a stranger to the ways of courts, apparently indifferent to advancement or divinely ignorant of its techniques; here was the princess who loved him. When we discover later that she was capable of drastic action, and could face danger like a man for the man she loved, when we discover also that she had a mind and tongue of her own, we can go back to reconstruct with confidence the opening scenes. She saw David slighted by her father, whose fitful affections she mistrusted; she saw him needing the protection and guidance of one whose affections were as steady as they were deep. The more successful David showed himself by pure ability, unbacked by cunning, the greater the risks he ran, and therefore the more his need of her.

The wonder-boy of a musician turned out to be a wonder-boy of a warrior. He justified the additional recommendations of his unnamed friend: "Prudent in affairs . . . and the Lord is with him." His star was rising with everyone. "Jonathan loved him as his own soul," and "David had great success in all his ways." His star rose with Saul, too, but the higher it rose with him, the fiercer became his impulse to bring it down. Prudent David might be, and Michal might acknowledge it, but prudence was not enough against the unpredictability of a madman. She might even feel that the Lord was with

David; in that case she was the instrument of the Lord, planted by Him in the palace.

I have described Michal as "romantic." The word is modern, the state of mind old. The Œdipus complex was not invented by Freud, and not even, it is well to note, by Œdipus. If "romantic" means unrealistic, and if David was quite capable of looking after himself, then we could hardly find a better word for Michal's conception of her role in David's life.

Part of our wisdom comes from hindsight. We know the whole of David's career. Michal loved him in its early phase, when her father made repeated attempts on his life, openly in fits of madness, and only half covertly in plots that actually involved his daughters. There had been a promise that the man who slew Goliath would be given the hand of one of them, and "great riches" besides. For a time nothing more was heard of this. Had the slayer of Goliath been another than David, we should have reason for surprise—though not too much, in view of the man we are dealing with. On the other hand it would have surprised us greatly if Saul had kept the promise without further ado when the slayer was David. But he came round to it at last, with a mind clouded by pitiful criminal calculations.

"And Saul said to David: 'Behold my elder daughter Merab, her will I give to thee to wife; only be thou valiant for me, and fight the Lord's battles.' For Saul said: 'Let not my hand be upon him, but let the hand of the Philistines be upon him.' " I am a little sick at these words. What Saul planned so feebly against David, David will one day carry out with savage efficiency against Uriah the Hittite. Saul's calculations were transparent, and the Text does not bother to indicate their secretiveness. They were also pitiful and pointless because David needed no incentive to fight the Philistines, and as Saul's son-in-law he would not be more the marked man than as the slayer of Goliath. These homicidal meanderings of Saul's disappeared and reappeared. For David did not marry Merab. We read: "And David said unto Saul: 'Who am I, and what is my life, or my father's family in Israel, that I should be son-in-law to the king?' But it came to pass at the time when Merab Saul's daughter should have been given to David, that she was given unto Adriel the Meholathite to wife."

We have here a clear indication of a last-minute change. We are free to think that Saul shrank from having to pray for his daughter's widowhood, or that David's reluctance was genuine and sustained, though not at all because of the childish trap, which to him did not look like one; or that Michal worked against the marriage. The last surmise has the best warrant because the next sentence reads: "And Michal Saul's daughter loved David." We are also free to infer that Merab was not in love with David; we are perhaps invited to do so. What happened next is explicit. Michal must have spoken of her love, for her father learned of it; and he fell back once more on the dream of sending David to his death. This time he even concocted the semblance of a plan.

"And Michal Saul's daughter loved David; and they told Saul, and the thing pleased him. And Saul said: 'I will give him her, that she may be a snare to him, and

194

that the hand of the Philistines may be against him.' "
Again David expressed great reluctance. Saul had the
men of the court speak to him, and David's answer to
them was: "Seemeth it to you a light thing to be the
king's son-in-law, seeing that I am a poor man, and
lightly esteemed?"

On the whole, allowing for our hindsight and some
inside information, Michal's attitude was distinctly romantic. David's guilelessness or helplessness, which made
her tremble so for him, is hard to find even in the early
record. He was loved by Michal, by her brother Jonathan, and by the court; he was the slayer of Goliath and
the hammer of the Philistines; and if that was not
enough he had the art of winning popularity: "All
Israel and Judah loved David; for he went out and came
in before them." Also he knew what no one else but
Samuel knew, that he was in truth the anointed one, the
next king. And yet he said to Saul's men that he was
poor, and therefore held in slight esteem. In his case
the sequitur was false, while the premise itself was dubious Saul never gave him the "great riches" due him;
nevertheless David after his marriage to Michal carried
on successfully, did greatly in battle, and was foremost
among "all the servants of Saul." He was not fishing
for riches. He had to talk as he did because this had
been his excuse for refusing Merab. But now Saul, with
the delusion of a genuine plan at work in him, insisted.
The messengers went back and forth, negotiating, and
there was never a mention of the monetary reward.
"And the servants of Saul told him: 'On this manner
spoke David.' And Saul said: 'Thus shall ye say to

David: "The king desireth not any dowry, but a hundred foreskins of the Philistines, to be avenged of the king's enemies." ' For Saul thought to make David fall by the hand of the Philistines. And when his servants told David these words, it pleased David well to be the king's son-in-law."

It pleased him well; so well that he went out at once with his men and killed not one hundred but two hundred Philistines and brought their foreskins and "gave them in full number to the king." And how did the prompt collection of this gruesome and disgusting dowry please the princess? Was she thrilled by David's extravagance, or horrified by his recklessness? I must use the stencil again: we are not told. We are not told what anybody thought about it. And strangely enough I do not remember it as figuring prominently in the popular denunciations of the Bible. To me it is one of the most horrible of the horrible deeds ascribed to its heroes or its villains: this exuberant killing of an extra hundred Philistines, this exuberant mutilation of an extra hundred corpses, as though the first hundred, the condition of the bargain, were unworthy of the esteem in which David held himself, or of his regard for Princess Michal.

For we are speaking here of the lovely shepherd boy, the bewitching harp-player, who advanced on Goliath with a simple sling, exclaiming: "Thou comest to me with a sword, and with a spear, and with a javelin, but I come to thee in the name of the Lord of hosts. . . ." The Tradition, which like the Bible itself rightly makes a tremendous to-do about David's murder of Uriah, is not greatly concerned with the repulsive exploit of the two hundred foreskins. I, who see David as the most passionate of the God-seekers, have never ceased to recoil from it. Almost as much as the murder of Uriah I juxtapose it with the words so often spoken of David: "For the Lord was with him."

What do these words mean? Used by the unnamed friend of David, or by Saul, or by any other contemporary of David's early days, they could mean success and worldly happiness. But how is it when they occur in the Text as the verdict of the chronicler? Much depends on when the chronicler lived. David's career was brilliant in the light of the after ages; to one who wrote shortly after his death it was a mixed thing; and whatever successes he scored were more than offset by failures and by personal wretchedness: the death of Jonathan, the death of Bathsheba's child, sinfully begotten, the rape of his daughter Tamar by his son Amnon, the murder of Amnon by Absalom's command, the rebellion and death of Absalom, and so on to the very end: the thwarting of David's dearest ambition, to build the Temple, and the rebellion of his son Adonijah. It was God Himself who forbade him to build the Temple, on the grounds that he, the anointed, had shed much blood. So he had—but nearly all of it that of the enemies of Israel. In what sense, then, was God with him? In a literal sense that perhaps even the chronicler did not always mean; for the chronicler himself is an evolving figure, and we who interpret him are also chroniclers. God was with David in a terrifically literal sense; for David was possessed, haunted, inhabited, and harassed by God-consciousness. His earthly passions were demonic; equally demonic, if one may so put it, was his anguish over them, and his longing to find himself in God. The heart that could riot in blood-lust, and swell with self-righteousness, could tremble like a child's before the denunciation of the prophet Nathan, accepting punishment without protest; and it could beat to the strains of unearthly music, to give it forth again for our everlasting consolation.

We are going to see how much of this was understood by Michal, whose hand he won with the two hundred Philistine foreskins.

They were married. "And Saul saw and knew that the Lord was with David; and Michal Saul's daughter loved him. And Saul was yet the more afraid of David; and Saul was David's enemy continually."

The recurrent impulse to put David out the way became more urgent. Saul was mad enough to call on Jonathan and the men of the court to murder David; it was no longer a flash or outburst; it was settling into that sustained obsession which was to overshadow the rest of his life. But for the moment Jonathan pleaded successfully for his soul's friend. "And Saul hearkened unto the voice of Jonathan; and Saul swore: 'As the Lord liveth, he shall not be put to death.' And Jonathan brought David to Saul, and he was in his presence as beforetime."

David's self-confidence is astounding. He returns again and again to the center of danger. It may be that side by side with his faith in the anointing there was a deep and troubling concern for Saul. But the limit was reached at last: "And there was war again; and David went out, and fought with the Philistines, and slew them with a great slaughter; and they fled before him  And an evil spirit from the Lord was upon Saul, and he sat in his house with his spear in his hand; and David was playing with his hand. And Saul sought to smite David even to the wall with the spear; but he slipped away out of Saul's presence, and he smote the spear into the wall; and David fled and escaped that night. And Saul sent messengers unto David's house, to watch him, and to slay him in the morning."

This is Michal's hour, and here she is established. Here her romanticism fuses with realism. She was not alone in defying her father's madness against David; Jonathan had done it before and would do it again; but she was a woman, and on that occasion Saul's fury seems to have surpassed all bounds.

"Michal David's wife told him, saying: 'If thou save not thy life tonight, tomorrow thou shalt be slain.' So Michal let David down through the window; and he went, and fled, and escaped. And Michal took the teraphim, and laid it in the bed, and put a quilt of goat's hair at the head thereof, and covered it with a cloth."

I do not like that picture of David escaping into the night and leaving Michal to face the music. He must have been convinced that the situation was desperate; and he was at last beginning to find the king's explosions intolerable—two reasons why he should have hesitated to leave Michal behind, and two grim reflections on his failure to send for her at the first opportunity. Something of a strain between him and Michal is revealed here, almost accidentally. She kept teraphim in her room—

idols; she had neither David's devotion to God, nor the tact to conceal her lack of it. But it is not an excuse.

It is horrifying to learn of the frenzy in which Saul was now raving. "And when Saul sent messengers to take David, Michal said: 'He is sick.' And Saul sent messengers to see David, saying: 'Bring him up to me in the bed, that I may slay him.' " We have never seen him in such a condition before. We must take it that Jonathan was away at the time, and this is another count against David.

"And when the messengers came in, behold, the teraphim was in the bed, with the quilt of goat's hair at the head thereof." What happened, apparently, was this: the first time the messengers came she let them peep in at the door, and that was enough for them. The second time they brushed her aside.

At what exact moment Michal had to face her father, and where and whether she was brought before him, or whether he came to her house, is not recorded. Her answer to his reproaches was both impudent and courageous. "And Saul said unto Michal: 'Why hast thou deceived me thus, and let mine enemy go, that he is escaped?' And Michal answered Saul: 'He said unto me: "Let me go; why should I kill thee?" ' " It did not explain why she had not raised the alarm at once; it did not explain why she had delayed discovery by her ruse, and given David as much time as possible to make good his escape. It explained nothing It was the equivalent of a defiant: "I did it."

And here, in the most astounding way, Michal drops out of the picture. Always when I follow David through the years of his outlawry, there is a nagging at the back of my mind: "Where's Michal? What's happened to Michal? She loves him. She saved his life." David is on the run from Saul, but he is not alone. He takes his parents to him; his brothers join him. We read: "And every one that was in distress, and every one that was in debt, and every one that was discontented, gathered themselves unto him." Then why not Michal? For if anyone was in distress and discontented, it was she.

She was of course not in debt—not to David; he was the debtor. That had much to do with his unforgivable silence. He was managing alone. He fled first to Samuel, and then to Ahimelech the priest; he picked up the sword with which he had cut off Goliath's head, and he became the outlaw. He made his headquarters in the famous cave of Adullam. He deposited his aged parents with the king of Moab. He ranged throughout the country. He smote the Philistines and he smote the Amalekites. "He abode in the wilderness in the strong-holds." And he fled from Saul. Once he had a chance to kill him, and forbore—Saul too was the anointed. They exchanged useless words of reconciliation at a distance: but no mention of Michal. More than once Jonathan came out in secret to visit his beloved friend and renew the bond: not a word about Michal.

So the years pass, and suddenly, when we finish the story of Abigail, and we read how David married her, and took a second wife, Ahinoam the Jezreelitess, we come across these casual words: "Now Saul had given Michal his daughter, David's wife, to Palti the son of Laish, who was of Gallim."

The reader may perhaps remember Palti, or Paltiel, as the weird little man for whom I have such an aversion—Palti the weeper—and may even begin to share my feelings. From what we have seen of Michal, and from what we shall yet see, we know that she was not forced into the marriage. She entered into it contemptuously, and if a sword lay between husband and wife in the night, it was she who put it there.

Then again a long silence. Again the outlaw life, and a meeting with Saul, and a tearful exchange of words of mutual forgiveness, and again nothing about Michal. There were wild adventures. Abigail and Ahinoam were captured by the Amalekites, and David rescued them. That was more like it, he must have thought, the man saving the woman. Then Saul and Jonathan fell on Gilboa, in battle with the Philistines, and David became king, and the secret anointing was vindicated long after the death of Samuel.

And finally David, reigning in Hebron, sent for Michal the princess, addressing these words to Ishbosheth, Saul's son: "Deliver me my wife Michal, whom I betrothed to me for a hundred foreskins of the Philistines."

That was his recollection of her! He was careful to quote the strict terms of the bargain, claiming no credit for the bonus of the extra hundred he had thrown in. He had risked his life to win her, and he had a right to her. I am confused about his motives in sending for her, and I imagine he was, too. It will be suggested that it was a political move; he reclaimed the daughter of Saul in order to strengthen his claim to the throne. To me it seems unlikely that he saw himself beholden to her for any such favor.

She came to Bahurim, we remember, accompanied by the weeping Paltiel, who was sent back by Abner; and she joined David in Hebron. Everything was changed now. David was king of Judah, a man in the middle thirties, with at least two other wives—he married several women in Hebron, and had children by them, before and after sending for Michal. He was no longer the protégé of a romantic princess. The relations were reversed. The house of Saul was all but destroyed, and it was Michal who needed protection. That was not how she had planned it. She came back to David to be one among many.

Seven years David reigned in Hebron, warring on the Philistines and the Amalekites, and preparing the unification of the kingdom. And then he made the decision that has given the world a place-name of unparalleled symbolic sanctity. He moved to Jerusalem; and to signalize his glory and his triumph he had the Ark of the Covenant brought to the new capital, thereafter known, even until this day, as the city of David. During all the centuries since Moses had sealed the Tables of the Law in the Ark, it had been housed "in a tent and a tabernacle." Now David dreamed of erecting for it a fitting habitation. This was to set the visible seal of the divinity on his kingship, and to express in stone what, on the hills of Hebron, in Saul's palace, and in the wilderness and the strongholds, he had expressed nightly on his harp.

What his mood was like, what visions and exaltations

his soul experienced in that time of fulfillment, when he was making his transition from the temporal to the eternal, we can glimpse only in our own highest moments. The recorder hints at it. "He went and brought up the Ark of God from the house of Obed-edom into the city of David with joy. And it was so, that when they that bore the Ark of the Lord had gone six paces, he sacrificed an ox and fatlings. And David danced before the Lord with all his might. . . . So David and all the house of Israel brought up the Ark of the Lord with shouting, and with the sound of the horn."

But a stronger and more helpful hint we find in David's own words, which I take not from the collection of Psalms, some of which are not his, but from the record of his life in the second and supplementary version of the Chronicles. We have here a great cry of jubilant faith, an opening of immense vistas:

> "O ye seed of Israel his servant,
> Ye children of Jacob, his chosen ones,
> He is the Lord our God;
> His judgments are in all the earth.
> Remember His covenant for ever,
> The word which He commanded to a thousand generations;
> Which He made with Abraham,
> And His oath unto Isaac,
> And He established it unto Jacob for a statute,
> To Israel for an everlasting covenant. . . ."

Then he passes from the local and national to the world-wide, and to the universal:

*"Ascribe unto the Lord, ye kindreds of the peoples,*
*Ascribe unto the Lord glory and strength. . . .*
*Tremble before Him all the earth. . . .*
*Let the heavens be glad, and let the earth rejoice . . .*
*Let the sea roar, and the fulness thereof;*
*Let the field exult, and all that is therein;*
*Then shall the trees of the wood sing for joy. . . ."*

Breathless, God-intoxicated, oblivious of everything but the vision, he sang that day, danced and sang, ascending the hill.

And Michal? Where was she? What part had she in the rejoicing, what understanding for the supreme moment in David's life, which was henceforth divided into two parts, that which led up to this glory and that which led from it? Of her who had kept idols in her room we read: "As the Ark of the Lord came into the city of David, Michal the daughter of Saul looked out at the window, and saw king David leaping and dancing before the Ark; and she despised him in her heart. . . ."

It was not the idolatrous strain in her that was revolted. It was the dethroned romantic realizing that she had never been the savior of this man or the source of his strength. When she saw him whirling half-naked before the ark, her possessive soul felt itself disowned. It was more than she could bear. We read: "Then David returned to bless his household. And Michal the daughter of Saul came out to meet David, and said: 'How did the king of Israel get him honour today, who uncovered himself in the eyes of the handmaids of his servants, as one of the vain fellows shamelessly uncovereth himself!' "

There are women who have a marvelous gift for the wounding word, the word that penetrates to the core of a man's honor and kills his love on the spot; or, when love has faded, all prospect of friendship, and even of mutual tolerance. It is a gift that is not necessarily related to intelligence; it resembles rather the unexpected offensive equipment of certain lower species.

As between Michal and David it was he who was in the wrong up to then; now she put herself in the wrong forever, and provided David with the plausible defense: "I knew all along what kind of woman she was." In David's worship of God, his "shameless" self-abasement, his self-surrender, lay his meaning, his excuse for living, and his hope of self-redemption; and if Michal had only known it, her hope of reaching his heart. Instead she struck unerringly at his self-justification.

What a man retorts under such circumstances is forgiven in advance, because the savagery of the thrust has reduced him to reflex action. But there is little to forgive in David's hot reply, or in what followed. We read:

"And David said unto Michal: 'Before the Lord, who chose me above thy father, and above all his house, to appoint me prince over the people of the Lord, over Israel, before the Lord will I make merry. And I will be yet more vile than thus, and will be base in mine own sight; and with the handmaids whom thou hast spoken of, with them will I get me honour.' And Michal the daughter of Saul had no child unto the day of her death."

## IV

On one side stands Michal, the mistake of David's ado-
lescence; on the other, Bathsheba, the crime of his middle age; and between them Abigail, the comrade of his
manhood.

Without putting her in the same class as Rebekah we
may talk of Abigail as the immensely intelligent, loyal,
and wholly admirable helpmeet of a great man. She has
a narrower range of managerial talent; I cannot imagine
her coping with the subtleties of Isaac's character; nor
is hers the finesse which could manipulate the embezzlement of the blessing. But she is not less authentic than
Rebekah, and we watch her with the same satisfaction
applying her abilities to her opportunities.

She is the down-to-earth episode in David's life, and introduces into it a note of humor, not directly, but by
association. For her first husband, Nabal of Maon, is one
of the outstanding comical figures in the Bible. Him we
shall consider at some length, both for the light he sheds
on Abigail and for his own inimitable self.

Among the comics he belongs to the subdivisions of
the dolts and grotesques, and only God knows how Abigail came to marry him. Again I must refer to the old
patter about the enslavement of the Biblical female. Abigail in particular gives it the lie; if ever there was a
woman who made a joke of man's domination it was the
wife of Nabal. It is not beyond conjecture that she married him in the confidence that she could handle any
man under any circumstances; and if she could be a suc-

cessful wife to both a Nabal and a David, she was entitled to that feeling.

"There was a man in Maon, whose possessions were in Carmel; and the man was very great, and he had three thousand sheep, and a thousand goats; and he was shearing his sheep in Carmel. Now the name of the man was Nabal; and the name of his wife Abigail; and the woman was of good understanding, and of a beautiful form; but the man was churlish and evil in his doings; and he was of the house of Caleb."

"The woman was of good understanding." That is excellently put. I have checked it with the original, because it is a key phrase; and the translation is perfect. The learned James Moffat, however, renders it thus: "The woman was shrewd and handsome." I accept the "handsome"; it modernizes without misleading. But "shrewd"! I am afraid that is all wrong; first because as applied to a woman it contains, intentionally or not, the word "shrew"; and second because Abigail was much more than shrewd—we talk of shrewd merchants, politicians, lawyers, real-estate speculators, publishers; she was a woman of good understanding.

David was an outlaw at the time. Years had passed since his escape from Saul's ambush. The last hope of a reconciliation had long since vanished, for Saul knew now beyond the shadow of a doubt that David was to be his successor. Moreover, Saul had ordered a wholesale massacre of the priests who had helped David. It is true that when they met—at a distance, after David had spared Saul's life—they shouted kind words to each other, and shed tears. It meant only that they regretted what had to be. David would go on living as an outlaw until Saul's death; he would go on fighting the Philistines when he could, making alliances with them when he had to, and when he ran short of supplies levying tribute for himself and his band from the Israelites.

"And David heard in the wilderness that Nabal was shearing his sheep. And David sent ten young men, and David said unto the young men: 'Get you up to Carmel, and go to Nabal, and greet him in my name: and thus ye shall say: "All hail! and peace be both unto thee, and peace be to thy house, and peace be unto all that thou hast. And now I have heard that thou hast shearers; thy shepherds have now been with us, and we did them no hurt, neither was there aught missing unto them, all the while they were in Carmel. Ask thy young men, and they will tell thee; wherefore let the young men find favour in thine eyes; give, I pray thee, whatsoever cometh to thy hand, unto thy servants, and to thy son David." ' "

It was a warlord's levy, protection money, and not all the courteous phrasing in the world could change that. If Nabal wanted to say no, he had a case. He could take a stand on prudence, and plead that since the slaughter of the priests it was very dangerous to help the outlaw; though this might not prevent him from paying the tribute secretly. Or he could take a stand on high principle, and disassociate himself from the man who was hunted by the anointed king. Being what he was, he chose to take his stand on his rights as a congenital and irreclaimable fool; and he sent back this message: "Who is David? and who is the son of Jesse? there are many servants now-a-days that break away every man from his master; shall I then take my bread, and my water, and my flesh that I have killed for my shearers, and give it unto men of whom I know not whence they are?"

Nabal was a hotheaded man, or he might have stopped to bethink himself that this David was the slayer of Goliath and a notable slaughterer of Philistines and Amalekites. He might also have conceded that though he might speciously refuse to help the outlaw, he had not scrupled to accept benefits from him. For no sooner were David's men gone than one of Nabal's shepherds ran to Abigail, as might be expected, and poured out the story in these words:

"Behold, David sent messengers out of the wilderness to salute our master; and he flew out upon them. But the men were very good unto us, and we were not hurt, neither missed we anything, as long as we went with them when we were in the fields; they were a wall unto us both by night and by day, all the while we were with them keeping the sheep. Now therefore know and consider what thou wilt do; for evil is determined against our master, and against all his house; for he is such a base fellow that one cannot speak to him."

We have a fair notion of conditions in the establishment if that was the way a shepherd could speak to the mistress about the master; it also makes clear that the men at once looked to Abigail in a time of trouble. The master? "One can't talk to that fellow!" And trouble was brewing in plenty, as the shepherd guessed and Abigail understood. When David's young men came back with Nabal's reply there was not a moment's hesitation: "And

David said unto his men: 'Gird ye on every man his sword.' And they girded on every man his sword; and David also girded on his sword; and there went up after David about four hundred men; and two hundred abode by the baggage."

Nabal's "Who-the-hell-does-he-think-he-is?" reply might tempt us to picture him as one of those mean men who have the courage of their meanness. But there is no supporting evidence that he appreciated the danger he courted; for example, preparation to beat off an assault, or a message to the military. It was, as a matter of fact, inconceivable to him that he, Nabal of Maon, owner of large lands, three thousand sheep, one thousand goats, and Abigail, was the subject of a threat. Every "Who-the-hell-does-he-think-he-is?" carries with it a "Does-he-realize-who-I-am?"

Clever Abigail—and "clever" is as far as I will go toward "shrewd"—wasted neither time nor energy arguing with her besotted husband. Instead, we read: "Then Abigail made haste, and took two hundred loaves, and two bottles of wine, and five sheep ready dressed, and five measures of parched corn, and a hundred clusters of raisins, and two hundred cakes of figs, and laid them on asses. And she said unto her young men: 'Go on before me; behold, I come after you.' But she told not her husband Nabal."

It would really seem to be beneath the dignity of the chronicler to list in such detail the supplies that Abigail packed up for David. It reads like a groceryman's invoice. Surely it would have been enough to say: "And she took provisions, etc." Beware of shrugging and passing on. As with the solemn listing of Ahasuerus's chamberlains, an important effect is being prepared, a psychological mine is being laid. Let us repeat, however absurd it sounds: "Two hundred loaves, and two bottles [meaning skins] of wine, and five sheep ready dressed, and five measures of parched corn, and a hundred clusters of raisins, and two hundred cakes of figs," and with this at the back of our minds let us proceed with the story.

She rode after the young men, Abigail, to meet David; she had to intervene in person; she felt that the most generous tribute could not make amends for the coarse insolence of Nabal. She was right. For as David was leading his band toward Nabal's home he was muttering to himself: "Surely in vain have I kept all that this fellow hath in the wilderness, so that nothing was missed of all that pertained unto him; and he hath returned me evil for good. God do so unto the enemies of David, and more also, if I leave of all that pertain to him by the morning light so much as one male." And there is no mention of his paying attention to the laden asses that preceded Abigail. He went marching on until he came face to face with her.

Now I will ask whether one ought to apply an equivocal word like "shrewd" to a woman like Abigail, and whether "good understanding" is not infinitely more apt. Had she been merely shrewd she would have accompanied the train of provisions. Shrewd people are full of a shallow self-confidence. Abigail had that self-confidence of a deeper kind which contains an element of intelligent modesty. She might after all be wrong; there was the possibility that David, encountering the supplies, would turn back contemptuously. Her intervention would be unnecessary. Also, she would not be exposing herself to the suspicion that she had an interest in making the acquaintance of the famous and fascinating outlaw. Something more: it is not wise to come abruptly on a man in the full flood of his fury, when it is a mad point of honor with him not to be diverted from his purpose. Let David meet the provisions first, and permit himself a smile, even the grimmest and most contemptuous: the interval could only be a gain.

Does this run counter to what I have said about Abigail, that "she went after her man on the highway"? But she did. I never meant to imply that she threw herself publicly at David's head. She did not want it to be suspected that David interested her personally and she took every reasonable precaution against it. She also took the tiny risk of not meeting him, and that was much. It is all that we have a right to expect.

So they met. "And when Abigail saw David, she made haste, and alighted from her ass, and fell before David on her face, and bowed down to the ground. And she fell at his feet and said: 'Upon me, my lord, upon me be the iniquity; and let thy handmaid, I pray thee, speak in thine ears, and hear thou the words of thy handmaid. Let not my lord, I pray thee, regard this base fellow, even Nabal; for as his name is, so is he. Nabal is his name, and churlishness is with him; but I thy handmaid saw not the young men of my lord, whom thou didst send. . . ."

We wonder whether a woman ought to speak like that about her husband under any circumstances. *Nabal* is connected in Hebrew with *nebelah,* a carcass; Abigail hinted, in fact, that her husband was what we would call today a dog's body. *Nabal* also happens to be, both in the original and in transliteration, a palindrome for *Laban,* another miserly lout enshrined in the folklore. Abigail certainly spoke as she did *à contrecœur.* She had no time for circumlocutions; she had to get the disgusting subject out of the way and proceed to her oration. For she had one, and its high qualities of content and form point to careful preparation, which helps to explain why she came on alone. After the panicky preparations of the tribute, she had to be alone for a while, to think things out.

Her central theme, amidst her praises and self-prostrations, is her desire to save David from staining his record with a crime. "As the Lord liveth, and as thy soul liveth, seeing the Lord hath withholden thee from bloodguiltiness, and from finding redress for thyself with thine own hand, now therefore let thine enemies, and them that seek evil to my lord, be as Nabal. . . . The Lord will certainly make my lord a sure house . . . and though man be risen up to pursue thee, and to seek thy soul, yet the soul of my lord shall be bound in the bundle of life with the Lord thy God; and the souls of thine enemies, them shall he sling out, as from the hollow of a sling. . . ."

The reference to Saul's pursuit of David is discreet, the reference to the sling ingenious; and the prophecies of David's ultimate triumph spring from a heartfelt wish. But she returns, in closing, to what she knows will ap-

214

peal most strongly to David. "And it shall come to pass, when the Lord shall have done to my lord according to all the good that He hath spoken concerning thee, and shall have appointed thee prince over Israel; that this shall be no stumblingblock unto thee, nor offence of heart unto my lord, either that thou hast shed blood without cause, or that my lord hath found redress for himself."

There are some who, on the basis of this speech alone, will rank Abigail with Rebekah. They will say: "Look how Abigail, in contrast to Michal, has the perfect gift of the healing word, the word that penetrates to the core of a man's honor to awaken it. And see in what significant and terrible contrast she stands to Bathsheba, holding David back from murder while the other egged him on to it." There are moments when I agree. Still, I am often troubled by the excessive perfection of her oration; and I also watch with some uneasiness her too solidly practical handling of Nabal before and after her meeting with David. I must add, finally, that for me Abigail's closing words detract somewhat from the high effect: "And when the Lord shall have dealt well with my lord, then remember thy handmaid."

David was deeply moved, and he answered on the same high level. "Blessed be the Lord, the God of Israel, who sent thee this day to meet me; and blessed be thy discretion, and blessed be thou, that thou hast kept me this day from bloodguiltiness, and from finding redress for myself with mine own hand. For in very deed, as the Lord, the God of Israel, liveth, who hath withholden

215

me from hurting thee, except thou hadst made haste and come to meet me, surely there had not been left unto Nabal by the morning light so much as one male."

It is a winning and a gallant picture, the warrior and the woman, the noble words, the outlaws, and the wild mountain scenery, to this day as enchanting as any in the world. I was somewhat perturbed at myself for imagining that it was slightly too gallant, especially when I lingered on David's farewell words to her: "Go up in peace to thy house; see, I have hearkened to thy voice, and have accepted thy person." I am not prone to suspicions of that kind, and I was pleased when, in the Tradition, I found that saintlier men than I had pulled their brows together a little when looking on this picture. For the Tradition says that David was as deeply moved by Abigail's beauty as by her wisdom, and she had to call on the latter to temper the effects of the former. She made use, the Tradition reports, both of prophecy and of subtle ritualistic scholarship in holding David off. I had not been as suspicious as that.

She got home safely, and we read next: "And Abigail came to Nabal; and, behold, he held a feast in his house, like the feast of a king; and Nabal's heart was merry within him, for he was very drunken; wherefore she told him nothing, less or more, until the morning light."

This man Nabal gets more and more obnoxious as we go along. One would think that the best time to tell him about the whole business was just then, when he was drunk, and merry, and was giving a feast fit for a king. We must trust Abigail that it was not. So it is obvious that Nabal drunk was as mean as Nabal sober. Probably

216

meaner. His prodigality was that of the gangster; his conviviality was restricted and spiteful. He invited some in order to be able not to invite others, and got the greater pleasure from the second. The Tradition has a proverb that a man betrays himself in three ways: when his money is touched, when he is in a rage, and when he is in his cups. We have observed Nabal in all three areas. Let anyone who considers me malicious ponder what follows:

"And it came to pass in the morning, when the wine was gone out of Nabal, that his wife told him these things, and his heart died within him, and he became as a stone. And it came to pass ten days after, that the Lord smote Nabal, so that he died."

At this point I make a desperate effort to be sorry for the man, but it is no use. I begin to laugh; and I protest I am not to blame. The Text is so sternly and savagely funny. "These things!" Does the reader think the Text is referring to the danger Nabal had brought on himself, and Abigail had averted? Not a bit of it. Why did the Text pause with such solemnity over the "two hundred loaves, and two skins of wine, and five sheep ready dressed, and five measures of parched corn, and a hundred clusters of raisins, and two hundred cakes of figs"? It was "these things" that made Nabal's heart die in him, so that he became as a stone.

For ten days he lay there, uttering no word, twitching no muscle, petrified by the horror of it. What couldn't he have done with the two hundred loaves, and the two skins of wine, and the five—*five!*—ready dressed sheep— but wait! That was what Abigail had told him. How

217

was he to know that it hadn't been ten skins of wine, and twenty sheep? And there was that summer house on the neighboring hill that he could have got for a fraction of what that stupid, terrified woman had . . . or that end of the field which he could have rounded out . . . he could have . . . He contemplated each lost opportunity with a separate pang, then added up all the opportunities and pangs into a single killing paroxysm. "The wine was gone out of Nabal. . . ." The royal feast for his cronies and his hired help—it had been overdone, it had exceeded his original estimates, he did not care to think by how much; and before his wife had given him the unbelievable bill of her insanity he had already been lying awake, dry-tongued, outlining little economies to re-establish his budget. And here, out of the blue, this murderous loss, this wild invasion of his painfully earned capital. He was not a miser, let God witness; look at the banquet; in fact, he had to admit that he was himself on the reckless side, and everybody knew him as Nabal the Hospitable, some even called him Nabal the Spending Fool, and maybe they were right, but at least if he had been wasteful, if he had exceeded by far what anyone expected of a man of his modest means, he had chosen his company among decent folk, whereas she—for who were the recipients of her fancy generosity? Vagabonds, the Adullamites, scum of Israel, the ruin of the country, for whose sake God would surely drive the people of the blessing into exile. And those stories the shepherds had brought back, of David and his men protecting them, and taking nothing for their pains —women believe anything—it was much more likely that those good-for-nothing shepherds were in cahoots with the brigands, and it wasn't the first time David ben Jesse had taken a slice out of Nabal's possessions. And perhaps it wasn't the first time Abigail—oh God, that would not bear thinking of— Help! The woman has killed me!

We must be grateful that the Text states pointedly: "The Lord smote Nabal, so that he died." Not that I, personally, pay the slightest attention to the unuttered ravings of Nabal, except that it makes me uncomfortable to think of Abigail as his wife; and here, possibly, is one of my reasons for the reservations I have voiced in regard to her.

Well, now he is dead; and since it was the Lord who smote him, and since the Text itself treats him with dark derision, let us forget about him. Abigail's emotions are left to our imagination; David's are there, black on white: "And when David heard that Nabal was dead, he said: 'Blessed be the Lord, that hath pleaded the cause of my reproach from the hand of Nabal, and hath kept back His servant from evil; and the evil-doing of Nabal hath the Lord returned upon his own head.' And David sent and spoke concerning Abigail, to take her to him to wife."

She went to him, and married him, of course. I write "of course" and stop to consider. We happen to have known for the last three thousand years that she married him; but if we place ourselves at Abigail's point of time there is no "of course" about it. Here is a woman of discretion and understanding and of handsome person who suddenly finds herself released from an odious marriage

219

the three or four greatest utterances in the Bible. It is, among other things, a landmark in the history of man's struggle for liberation from the absolute authority of the State. But instead of accepting it primarily as a first formulation of the Bill of Rights, we turn it into a case report. Thus we detract from its quality and significance; at the same time we distort the realities of the drama. I shall quote it here, though it occurs in the middle of the story, immediately after David has murdered Uriah the Hittite and taken Bathsheba to wife.

"The thing that David had done displeased the Lord. And the Lord sent Nathan unto David. And he came unto him and said: 'There were two men in one city: the one rich, the other poor. The rich man had exceeding many flocks and herds; but the poor man had nothing, save one little ewe lamb, which he had bought and reared; and it grew up together with him and his children; it did eat of his own morsel, and drank of his own cup, and lay in his bosom, and was unto him as a daughter. And there came a traveller unto the rich man, and he spared to take of his own flock and of his own herd, to dress for the wayfaring man that was come unto him, but took the poor man's lamb, and dressed it for the man that was come to him.' And David's anger was greatly kindled against the man; and he said to Nathan: 'As the Lord liveth, the man that hath done this deserveth to die; and he shall restore the lamb fourfold, because he did this thing, and because he had no pity.' And Nathan said to David: 'Thou art the man.' "

The tender picture of the poor man and his ewe lamb as drawn by Nathan for the greater confusion of David was not meant as a description of the relations between Uriah and Bathsheba. The prophet spoke as he did because such might have been their relations, and were, for all David cared; and nothing could be admitted in mitigation of the crime. Murder is murder whomever it strikes, let it be even a gangster; and David himself blessed Abigail when she prevented him from taking the law into his own hands against a near-gangster. Moreover, David had been king for many years, and it is written of him: "He reigned over all Israel; and he executed righteousness unto all his people." But that which was intended for David's confusion must not lead to ours. Unfortunately it does; the speech is so powerful that it sweeps from our mind the preceding material on which an estimate of the relations between Uriah and Bathsheba can be based. We must therefore go back.

It happened in the spring of the year and the autumn of David's life—a dangerous conjuncture for any man. He was thirty-seven years old when he began to reign over the unified kingdom, and he reigned thirty-three years. There is an unspecified interval between his bringing up of the Ark to Jerusalem, the zenith of his spiritual experience, and the murder of Uriah, the nadir. But it was a considerable one, for he had already begun to entrust his campaigns to generals. He was probably in his middle forties.

We read· "It came to pass, at the return of the year, at the time when kings go out to battle, that David sent

223

Joab, and his servants with him, and all Israel; and they destroyed the children of Ammon, and besieged Rabbah. And David tarried at Jerusalem. And it came to pass at eventide, that David arose from off his bed, and walked upon the roof of the king's house; and from the roof he saw a woman bathing; and the woman was very beautiful to look upon And David sent and inquired after the woman "

That David was in the habit of taking an afternoon nap is further evidence that he was in middle age; and that he saw Bathsheba bathing is good circumstantial evidence that she was in the habit of performing this ritual where he could see her. Otherwise we would have to introduce an unusual coincidence, and there are coincidences and miracles enough in the Bible without unsupported additions of our own That is how I see it, and it makes one's heart sink to imagine the burst of lust which drove David to such shamelessness before his attendants. The prophet Nathan was to say afterwards, when he brought the message of God's punishment: "Thou didst it secretly, but I will do this thing before all Israel and the sun." It was a relative secrecy. The very first step toward the crime, in its way the ugliest, consisted in humiliating disclosure. He called in attendants, he pointed out the roof, he had them make inquiries. It is not even certain that Bathsheba had yet withdrawn into the house!

"And one said· 'Is not this Bathsheba, the daughter of Eliam, the wife of Uriah the Hittite?' And David sent messengers and took her; and she came in unto him, and he lay with her; for she was purified from her uncleanness; and she returned unto her house. And the woman conceived; and she sent and told David: 'I am with child.' "

The narrative moves with breathless speed, even as the events did. That was how it happened: he saw her making her ritual ablutions after menstruation; he sent messengers and "took her"; she was with him once; a little less than a month passed—and then the thunderbolt: "I am with child." (The Latin version is magnificent here. A single word: *"Concepi."*)

I cannot escape from the picture, whatever others may deduce from the Text. They were together only once. More than once would have led to many times; and if many times she would have told him herself. But if only once, it was either a lightning-like flash of lust, leaving behind it loathing, and such hatred as Amnon felt for Tamar, or else a long and mortal complication. We know it was the latter; and he kept her away from him not for lack of inclination but from excess of it. He was afraid.

Reading, farther on, of David's passionate grief when the child of that union died, I marvel at his decision to renounce possession of it if he could manage to plant the paternity on Uriah. It bespeaks the fierceness of the inner struggle that he did not resort at once to the second plan—murder. Of course he thought of it. Saul had suggested the method to him, if suggestion were needed. He also thought of a third way, and rejected it; he did not have to send Uriah to his death in order to get Bathsheba and the child; he could have taken her arbitrarily—a smaller crime than murder, but unfortunately not concealable. So he committed a greater crime to conceal a lesser crime—the geometrical progression of the criminal career—and threw good money after bad, since he was caught anyhow. This is the overtone of meaning in Nathan's words: "For thou didst it secretly; but I will do this thing before Israel, and before the sun."

I sense no moral perturbation in Bathsheba. What did she expect of David when she sent word: "I am with child"? We know that he did not consult her, or he would have learned that his first plan would fail. Did she want Uriah killed? I do not say so. The prophet Nathan ignores her in the denunciation; those who misread his parable will even see her as the innocent, sacrificed ewe lamb. But Nathan was concerned with the criminal abuse of State power, and he focused all his attention on that. And it never even occurred to Bathsheba that David might kill Uriah? I do not say that either. We examine the words "I am with child" in vain: here is the kind of literal, unassailable statement that can be obstinately and interminably repeated in self-defense. We shall meet another like it in Bathsheba's later history—likewise followed by a convenient killing.

Meanwhile we read: "And David sent to Joab, saying: 'Send me Uriah the Hittite.' And Joab sent Uriah to David. And when Uriah was come unto David, David asked him how Joab did, and how the people fared, and how the war prospered. And David said unto Uriah: 'Go down to thy house and wash thy feet.' And Uriah departed out of the king's house, and there followed him a mess of food from the king. But Uriah slept at the door of the king's house with all the servants of his lord, and went not down to his house. And when they had told David, saying: 'Uriah went not down unto his house,' David said unto Uriah: 'Art thou not come from a journey? Wherefore didst thou not go down unto thy house?' And Uriah said unto David: 'The Ark, and Israel, and Judah, abide in booths; and my lord Joab, and the servants of my lord, are encamped in the open field; shall I then go unto my house, to eat and to drink, and to lie with my wife? As thou livest, and as thy soul liveth, I will not do this thing.' "

That speech of Uriah's grates. He did not go to see Bathsheba at all, not even in a daytime visit. This we know because David had to be quite sure his first plan had failed before he proceeded with the second. The speech grates because it is the right and privilege of the soldier on leave from the front to go home to his woman and sleep with her; it is also his duty; custom, and humaneness, and common sense, and national polity concur in this view. To stamp the practice as dishonorable is to treat with superior contempt one of the obvious mitigations of the misery of war, intended for the woman as much as for the man. That is what Uriah did.

In the opinion of the Tradition, Uriah was at fault in disobeying the orders of his king. That is a technical question. The fault was moral. He was either a hypocrite or a brutal pedant; for either he had quarreled with Bathsheba or, loving her, and on good terms with her, he would not even visit her lest he yield to desire; and so he sacrificed her to his superrighteous code. At best he was a brave, stupid, speechifying man, and what he said to the king, who had "tarried in Jerusalem," was pompously tactless. I hear it objected: "One should not talk like that about a man who was murdered." I do not see how getting oneself murdered improves one's character; and God help justice if we must admire a victim of aggression before we undertake to protect him wholeheartedly.

We are beginning to understand Bathsheba. She was an unhappy woman with a tricky streak. She turned her mind away from what she wanted, and took the minimum initiative or none at all, and always remained, as we would say, in the clear. Her one questionable act was to expose herself while bathing; but who can say that she did it deliberately? The only place she could be seen from, probably, was that high-up, projecting corner of the palace, and she did not know of it until David mentioned it—as we may assume he did; and then, we may assume, she offended no more. Suddenly, one night, for no reason she could think of, there were furtive messengers from the king, bidding her come to him secretly. How could she guess what it was for? Would it have been proper to refuse? Then that happened which happened; ought she to have made a scandal in the palace? Who would have believed that she had come with innocent intentions? She returned to her house and went no more. And then she found herself pregnant. She had to let the king know the simple fact, did she not?— and that was all she did.

David made a second attempt to break through Uriah's self-righteousness. "And David said to Uriah: 'Tarry here today also, and tomorrow I will let thee depart.' So Uriah abode in Jerusalem that day, and the morrow. And when David called him, he did eat and drink before him, and he made him drunk; and at even he went out to lie on his bed with the servants of his lord, but went not down to his house. And it came to pass in the morning that David wrote a letter to Joab, and sent it by the hand of Uriah."

A significant contrast between the first and second nights reveals what was happening to David. We read that after the first night the servants told David: "Uriah went not down unto his house." No such report was made—or was needed by David—after the second night. That unnatural abstinence of Uriah's had not entered into David's calculations. He had gone to sleep the first night comfortable in the assurance that the situation was saved. He had seen Uriah leave the palace, he had sent a gift of food after him. It is not written that in the morning he asked about Uriah; he had not set a watch on him; the astonished attendants reported it as an extraordinary fact that Uriah had not gone home. Had they been instructed to watch him, they would have reported before the morning. The second night David did not sleep, and the following morning he did not have to be told. He waited and watched, waited and watched, ground his teeth and waited and watched. "And it came to pass in the morning that David wrote a letter to Joab, and sent it by the hand of Uriah. And he wrote in the letter, saying: 'Set ye Uriah in the forefront of the hottest battle, and retire ye from him, that he may be smitten, and die.' "

An aura of madness and recklessness hangs over the

story, a feverish radiation emanating from David's condition. He was reckless of his own dignity, and of Bathsheba's good name, and of palace morale, when he asked his attendants to identify her, then bring her to him. He was reckless in his instructions to Joab, for he demanded not one man's complicity, but that of a group; a soldier, he undermined the honor and discipline of the army. In one thing he was not reckless—in entrusting Uriah with his own death-warrant.

And Bathsheba? We read: "And when the wife of Uriah heard that Uriah her husband was dead, she made lamentation for her husband. And when the mourning was past, David sent and took her home to his house, and she became his wife, and bore him a son."

There are times when the small mind fascinates us more than the great one; and there are times when the fascination turns into a desperate curiosity. What went on in Bathsheba's? How much did she let herself know? By what devices did she make her peace with herself? Or did she not need to?

She could and should have known everything. Fellow officers of Uriah's could have told her—if she had let them talk—of the circumstances of his death. Let us say she never questioned David, and he never referred to the matter overtly. But there was Nathan's denunciation of David, and what it did to him. It was delivered in private, to be sure; but unless David had superhuman powers of self-control—and self-control was what he lacked—or Bathsheba a subhuman unsusceptibility to his condition, some part of her mind registered the shattering of his spirit and understood what had caused it.

These are Nathan's words: "Thus saith the Lord, the God of Israel: I anointed thee king over Israel, and I delivered thee out of the hand of Saul; and I gave thee thy master's house, and thy master's wives into thy bosom, and gave thee the house of Israel and of Judah; and if that were too little, then would I add unto thee so much more. Wherefore hast thou despised the word of the Lord, to do that which is evil in My sight? Uriah the Hittite thou hast smitten with the sword, and his wife thou hast taken to be thy wife, and him thou hast slain with the sword of the children of Ammon. Now therefore the sword shall never depart from thy house; because thou hast despised Me and hast taken the wife of Uriah the Hittite to be thy wife. Thus saith the Lord: 'Behold I will raise up evil against thee out of thine own house, and I will take thy wives before thine eyes, and give them unto thy neighbour, and he shall lie with thy wives in the sight of this sun. For thou didst it secretly; but I will do this thing before Israel, and before the sun.' "

Of David's horror at what he had done, and of the depth of his repentance, we have the most striking proof in this fact. the man who spoke to him in terms that others would have remembered throughout their lives with hatred remained at court, an honored figure, until David's death. Of David's wild grief when the child lay dying—his attendants feared he would do himself violence—we read soon after the denunciation. And the connection between the crime and the loss of the child stares one in the face. How, then, could Bathsheba not have perceived everything? And perceiving, by what

231

mechanism did she shut out the suggestions of her complicity?

We read, after the death of the child: "And David comforted Bathsheba his wife, and he went in unto her, and lay with her; and she bore a son, and called his name Solomon. And the Lord loved him, and he sent by the hand of Nathan the prophet, and he called his name Jedidiah (Beloved of God), for the Lord's sake."

And now Bathsheba drops out of sight for twenty-five years or so, and when she reappears she is, I judge, a woman in her middle fifties. David is an old man. His age at his death, which took place shortly after, is given as seventy, but he was older than his years, burned out, confined, shivering, to his bed. We read: "Now king David was old and stricken in years; and they covered him with clothes, but he could get no heat. Wherefore his servants said unto him: 'Let there be sought for my lord the king a young virgin; and let her stand before the king, and be a companion unto him; and let her lie in thy bosom, that the lord my king may get heat.' So they sought for a fair damsel throughout all the borders of Israel, and found Abishag the Shunammite, and brought her to the king. And the damsel was very fair; and she became a companion unto the king, and ministered to him; but the king knew her not."

This young nurse-companion of the king becomes an illuminating part of the Bathsheba story. We would pass over her introduction without comment were it not for the surprising information that they searched throughout all the borders of Israel before finding her. It was surely not necessary to ransack the whole kingdom for an attractive young woman of good disposition and normal temperature. One thinks of Ahasuerus's servants in search of a new queen. King David's servants obviously had in mind the possibility that this was what they might actually be choosing. What additional qualities they were looking for I cannot guess, nor what they found, because no picture is suggested; but Abishag's position developed, with or without her contrivance, into something more than a nurse, though less than a queen.

How long did she minister to David? Long enough, it appears, to acquire or establish her peculiar status. She was David's last favorite, his last woman intimate, perhaps as near to him as any had been, and perhaps nearer, because she brought him again the protective and brooding warmth of the first and dearest of relationships. She became a symbol to the people, and she was set apart in its eyes. For her passionless ministration she was rewarded, the people felt, with some transference of David's spirit. Thus any pretender to the throne after David's death would be strengthening his claim greatly by marrying her.

As it happened, the pretender who did come forward for her hand had an original claim of some merit. He was Solomon's half-brother, Adonijah, who was born in the Hebron days, perhaps ten years before Solomon, and of a wife, Haggith, not a concubine. David, ever indulgent toward his sons, had spoiled him, too, for we read: "And his father had not grieved him all his life in saying· 'Why hast thou done so?' " Then the Text adds: "He was also a very goodly man," and leaves us to gather

233

from events that he was definitely not a very intelligent man. His claim to the crown was formal, for David had already promised it to Solomon; but even this claim Adonijah had forfeited by trying to seize the throne while David was still living; and having failed, he forfeited his life after David's death by acting as though Solomon and Bathsheba and their supporters were blind to what he and his supporters saw—Abishag's political value.

There are other indications that for his estimate of himself Adonijah leaned too heavily on his own good looks and his father's good nature. His *Putsch* was a paltry affair, nowhere near as serious as his brother Absalom's had been. "He prepared him chariots and horsemen, and fifty men to run before him. . . . And he conferred with Joab the son of Zeruiah, and with Abiathar the priest; and they, following Adonijah, helped him. But Zadok the priest, and Benaiah, the son of Jehoiada, and Nathan the prophet, and Shimei, and Rei, and the mighty men that belonged to David, were not with Adonijah. And Adonijah slew sheep and oxen and fatlings by the stone of Zoheleth. . . . And he called all his brethren the king's sons, and all the men of Judah the king's servants. . . . And Solomon his brother he called not." In other words, he got the personal backing of the commanding general, but not of the army, and of the high priest, but not of the priesthood. He was convinced of his popularity with the masses, and sought to increase it by cutting a dash with his chariots and his heralds. What he did thereby was to give premature warning of his intentions. When we

compare his careless and conceited lack of preparation
with Absalom's slow, patient, and crafty wooing of the
people, year after year, we understand why David trembled for his throne in the first rebellion, but dispersed
the second by merely ordering a counter-demonstration.

That was all the old man, shivering in his bed, had to
do. Bathsheba and Nathan appeared before him with
the shocking news of Adonijah's rebellion—it is significant that the order of their appearance before the king,
and the words Bathsheba was to speak, were arranged
and dictated by Nathan—and David issued instructions
to Zadok the priest, and Nathan, and Benaiah: "Take
with you the servants of your lord, and cause Solomon
my son to ride upon mine own mule, and bring him
down to Gihon. And let Zadok the priest and Nathan
the prophet anoint him there king over Israel; and blow
ye with the horn, and say: 'Long live king Solomon!' "
So it was done. And the people of course cried "Long
live king Solomon!" instead of "Long live king Adonijah!" That was the end of Adonijah's rebellion. The
noise of the cheering reached him where he sat at a
banquet celebrating—prematurely again—his accession:
"And all the guests of Adonijah were afraid, and rose
up, and went every man his way. And Adonijah feared
because of Solomon; and he arose, and went, and caught
hold on the horns of the altar."

Solomon's behavior was magnanimous. Adonijah,
clinging to the altar, would not come out until he was
promised his life. "Let king Solomon," he cried, "swear
unto me first that he will not slay his servant with the
sword." Solomon gave the promise: "If he shall show

235

himself a worthy man, there shall not fall a hair of him to the earth; but if wickedness be found in him, he shall die." He had only to behave in the future. Some will say that Solomon intended to have him killed later, when David was gone; but if Solomon had a tithe of the wisdom attributed to him, he would not put a brother to death unless compelled to it by genuine considerations of state.

These considerations Adonijah provided as soon as he reasonably could. He seems to have had a talent for doing the foolish thing with the maximum of foolishness, as though anxious not to be misunderstood. A summer fool. Shortly after David's death he appeared before Bathsheba. "And she said: 'Comest thou peaceably?' And he said. 'Peaceably.' He said moreover: 'I have somewhat to say unto thee.' And she said: 'Say on.' And he said: 'Thou knowest that the kingdom was mine, and that all Israel set their faces on me, that I should reign; howbeit the kingship is turned about, and is become my brother's; for it was his from the Lord. And now I ask one petition of thee, deny me not.' "

After long and anxious reflection I have concluded that this was definitely the clumsiest way in which he could have broached the subject, having of course first chosen the most unpropitious person to broach it to. He was entitled to feel that God had imposed Solomon on the people against its wishes, presumably as punishment for its sins, but it was, shall we say, a tactical blunder to air this opinion before Solomon's mother; especially as he was about to ask a great favor of her, and especially as the request proclaimed to anyone but an idiot the renewal of his ambitions, or rather the renewal of his attempt to realize them. But that was Adonijah.

We read: "And she said unto him: 'Say on.' And he said: 'Speak, I pray thee, unto Solomon the king—for he will not say thee nay—that he give me Abishag the Shunammite to wife.' And Bathsheba said: 'Well; I will speak for thee unto the king.' "

If it was Adonijah's misfortune to have fallen in love with Abishag we should pity him for his condition; if he was determined to assert his love in the face of its dangerous implications, we should admire him for his courage. But he makes pity difficult and admiration impossible. If he was driven by love, why did he come up first with his attack on Solomon? But if he was in love and actually did not realize—absurd as this sounds even for Adonijah—that Abishag was the one woman he could not ask for after his attempt to seize the throne, what courage did he display?

What concerns us most, however, is Bathsheba's role. "Very well," she said. "I will speak for thee unto the king." It was a simple and straightforward reply. A stepson comes to ask her for a great favor. She grants it. Can anyone raise objections? It turns out afterwards that the stepson was practically asking to be put to death. Was that her fault? If she had refused him, or tried to argue him out of it, we would have said very nasty things about her. She did the decent and natural thing, did she not? She was an uncomplicated woman; she made the request as she had promised, in her own name. We read:

"Bathsheba therefore went unto king Solomon, to speak unto him for Adonijah. And the king rose up to meet her, and bowed down unto her, and sat down on his throne, and caused a throne to be set for the king's mother; and she sat on his right hand. Then she said: 'I ask one small petition of thee; deny me not.' "

If you want further proof of her innocence, there it is. "One small petition." Her stepson had said: "one petition." She said to Solomon· "one small petition." She even minimized it. On second thought, I take that back; if she minimized it she must have thought it needed minimizing.

We read next: "And the king said unto her: 'Ask on, my mother; for I will not deny thee.' And she said: 'Let Abishag the Shunammite be given to Adonijah thy brother to wife.' "

It would have weakened her case, it would have been unfair to Adonijah, if she had made the request at second hand. To give it weight, in the spirit of her promise, she had to put forward the idea as her own. It is true that we, watching from the side, are at once quite sure that Solomon knows the origin of the request; we also know what followed  But is it fair to judge Bathsheba in this light?

"And king Solomon answered and said unto his mother: 'And why dost thou ask Abishag the Shunammite for Adonijah? ask for him the kingdom also; for he is mine elder brother, even for him, and for Abiathar the priest, and for Joab the son of Zeruiah.' Then king Solomon swore by the Lord, saying: 'God do so to me, and more also, if Adonijah have not spoken this word against his own life.' " We were right. Solomon knows where the request originated. What he thinks of his

238

mother for proferring it is immaterial to him. And whether Adonijah would have found other means of getting himself killed is immaterial to us in our study of Bathsheba; it is even immaterial to us whether Solomon was looking for a pretext. He went on: "Now therefore as the Lord liveth, who hath established me, and set me on the throne of David my father, and who hath made me a house, as He promised, surely Adonijah shall be put to death this day." He was as good as his word: "And king Solomon sent by the hand of Benaiah the son of Jehoiada; and he fell upon him, so that he died."

A Tradition which I find both charming and plausible tells that Bathsheba kept an eye on Solomon's upbringing and, apparently disturbed by his early addiction to women, wrote for his benefit the last chapter of the Book of Proverbs, which is attributed to him. It may have been about the time when Solomon was having his affair with the Sulamite shepherdess, which he sublimated into the Song of Songs. Here, if the Tradition is correct, is Bathsheba's advice to her son on how to choose a wife:

*A woman of valour who can find?*
*For her price is far above rubies.*
*The heart of her husband doth safely trust in her,*
*And he hath no lack of gain. . . .*
*She seeketh wool and flax,*
*And worketh willingly with her hands. . . .*
*She considereth a field, and buyeth it;*
*With the fruit of her hands she buyeth a vine-*
  *yard. . . .*

*She layeth her hands to the distaff. . . .*
*She stretcheth forth her hand to the poor. . . .*
*She maketh garments and selleth them. . . .*
*Strength and dignity are her clothing;*
*And she laugheth at the time to come.*
*She openeth her mouth with wisdom,*
*And the law of kindness is on her tongue. . . .*
*Grace is deceitful, and beauty is vain;*
*But a woman that feareth the Lord, she shall be*
    *praised.*

It is a formidable picture. and Solomon did not find it attractive. What young man would? Or should? And perhaps he understood his mother too well. The advice should have come from another. I have heard it argued that the Tradition ascribes this passage to Bathsheba in order to show that she was aware of guilt, and had repented. I still think it was a mistake on her part to write it. Repentant sinners make poor teachers; their pupils want to go to the same school.

# CHAPTER VII

## *The Hellcat*

❋

O F all the People of the Book, the prophet Elijah alone lives in my mind as a double take; the image brought along out of my childhood refuses to stand apart; it overlaps the image rising from the closely scrutinized Text, often getting the ascendancy over it.

I bring out of childhood the unfading picture of a gentle, playful, compassionate, ubiquitous, and protean friend of the poor and forlorn, a venerable merry-andrew of righteousness, a chuckling incarnation of all the world's benevolent pixies, a prestidigitator of parcels for the poor, a dispenser of free tuition to penniless students, a sneaker-in of keys to the unjustly imprisoned, a milk-warmer and cradle-rocker for neglected babies, a mischievous spoiler of mischief, a finger-on-nose admonisher of the uncharitable rich, a malicious but not murderous marplot among oppressors, usually invisible to them, a knight-errant righter of wrongs armored in prayer-shawl and phylacteries, a graybeard boy-scout performer of odd jobs for the bedridden and arthritic, a kidnapper of cares, a pickpocket of unrighteous mortgages, capable of a thousand forms, human

11

The murder of Naboth, for which Ahab and Jezebel are best remembered, was a mere incidental in their lifelong criminal orgy. It stands out because it was chosen for detailed report, and also because it provides us with remarkable portraits of the two principals, especially if taken in conjunction with other information scattered throughout the narrative. We are told: "Ahab the son of Omri did that which was evil in the sight of the Lord above all that were before him. And it came to pass, as if it had been a light thing for him to walk in the sins of Jeroboam the son of Nebat, that he took to wife Jezebel the daughter of Ethbaal king of the Zidonians, and went and served Baal in the house of Baal, which he had built in Samaria. . . ." And again: "There was none like unto Ahab, who did give himself over to do that which was evil in the sight of the Lord, whom Jezebel his wife stirred up." These two were criminals on what is called the grand scale.

I must warn the reader—and myself too—against twinges of sentimental diabolism. The criminal on the grand scale offends us less than the sordid little scrounger; one even thinks of him as an exponent of human dignity. "A scoundrel, yes! But what a man! There's nothing wrong with him except that he happens to be evil." And we point out that his very bigness safeguards him from mean little crimes, as though it were a virtue in a stock swindler not to snatch purses in his spare time; or that he has done generous things, which is like commending a successful narcotics dealer for being a big tipper.

Jezebel, besides tempting us to diabolism, also bribes us with the counterfeit of a special quality. She "loved" her husband. And therefore men in particular are prone to be magnanimous about her, and to suggest thoughtfully: "A woman who could be so good to her husband can't have been all bad." How she loved· Ahab, and how good she was to him, we shall see in the sequel.

The Naboth incident took place toward the end of Ahab's twenty-two-year reign; that is to say, when he was a mature man. We read:

"Naboth the Jezreelite had a vineyard, which was in Jezreel, hard by the palace of Ahab, king of Samaria. And Ahab spoke unto Naboth saying: 'Give me thy vineyard, that I may have it for a garden of herbs, because it is near unto my house; and I will give thee for it a better vineyard than it; or, if it seem good to thee, I will give thee the worth of it in money.' And Naboth said unto Ahab: 'The Lord forbid it me, that I should give the inheritance of my fathers unto thee.' And Ahab came into his house sullen and displeased because of the word which Naboth the Jezreelite had spoken to him; for he had said: 'I will not give thee the inheritance of my fathers.' And he laid him down upon his bed, and turned away his face, and would eat no bread."

Ahab's behavior suggests a sick petulance rather than rage. The narrator wants us to understand that the king found something particularly offensive in the manner of Naboth's refusal; and whether or not so intended, it certainly was a reflection on Ahab's disdain for his own spiritual inheritance, his inclination toward the Phœnician woman, and her ways, and her gods, and her prophets. We read:

"And Jezebel his wife came to him, and said unto him: 'Why is thy spirit so sullen, that thou eatest no bread?' And he said unto her: 'Because I spoke unto Naboth the Jezreelite, and said unto him: "Give me thy vineyard for money; or else, if it please thee, I will give thee another vineyard for it"; and he answered: "I will not give thee my vineyard." ' "

It argues more than affection, it hints at a fine tactfulness in Ahab that in the midst of his virulent ill-humor he said nothing about the implied insult to his wife. Jezebel was equally tactful. She had reason to believe that Naboth looked with no friendly eye on Ahab's defections from the Israelite tradition. All we read, however, is. "And Jezebel his wife said unto him: 'Dost thou now govern the kingdom of Israel? Arise, and eat bread, and let thy heart be merry; I will give thee the vineyard of Naboth the Jezreelite.' "

And she proceeds to arrange the judicial murder.

### III

Neither Naboth's rebuke to Ahab, nor his defiance of the royal will, explains Ahab's peculiar, one might say pathological behavior. This warrior king—we shall see that he was a fighter—rebuffed in so slight a matter, as it seems to us, lay on his bed, turned his face to the wall, and would not eat. One thinks of a self-indulgent

246

weakling in a fit of the tantrums; and, weakling or not, self-indulgent Ahab certainly was. We read of him that he had seventy sons in Samaria. The number of his wives is not given. The only one mentioned is Jezebel, and it was her son Ahaziah who succeeded to the throne. We read further: "The rest of the acts of Ahab, and all that he did, and the ivory house which he built, and all the cities that he built, are they not written in the book of the chronicles of the kings of Israel?"

It becomes clear that we have to do here with an Oriental monarch who was a superior spirit, a man of tact, a sensuous man, a builder—and an æsthete. His desire to have a garden of herbs, or a vegetable garden, a few yards nearer to his palace obviously had little to do with convenience. It was a question of landscaping, perhaps in connection with the ivory palace mentioned in the text. It made Ahab literally sick not to be able to carry out the perfect designs he had prepared.

And so he lay on his bed, and refused food, until his worried wife asked him for the reason, and, hearing it, laughed at him, and chided him for not acting like a king, and promised him what he wanted, and bade him get up and eat, and be merry-hearted.

She is the type of true and loving wife, for which reason she alone is mentioned among those that bore Ahab seventy sons—and who knows how many daughters. Even if she does not understand, she suffers for him. She does not irritate him with "Oh, you don't really need it, darling," and "What does it matter, after all?" Moreover, she is troubled by her husband's unwillingness or inability to assert his kingly character; she has had occasion to observe in him a certain dangerous vacillation. So she says, in effect: "Leave it to me! I'll show that man who's king here."

Many Bible-readers must have reflected on the resemblance between the Ahab-Jezebel and the Macbeth-Lady Macbeth relationships. The same domination, it would seem, in the woman, the same indecision in the man. He is too infirm of purpose to commit the crime, she has to arrange it for him, or goad him to it ("Give me the dagger!"). The analogy is limited, though it has its uses for a moment. Although Ahab shows a capacity for remorse, and therefore resembles Macbeth, Jezebel in this respect differs greatly from Lady Macbeth. The latter, after the killing of Duncan, was herself killed by the mind diseased to which no doctor could minister; the tough, repulsive old harridan Jezebel survived unrepentant into a third reign. She had to be defenestrated —that is, thrown out of a window—and something about her unceremonious execution, suggestive of garbage disposal in a squalid Oriental alleyway, strikes me as even more fitting than Elijah's fulfilled curse (his only utterance on Jezebel, and made offhand): "The dogs shall eat Jezebel in the moat of Jezreel."

IV

Ahab had fallen foul of Elijah long before the Naboth incident.

On his accession to the throne he is introduced by the narrator in the dark phrases already quoted: "Ahab the son of Omri did that which was evil in the sight of

248

the Lord. . . ." After mention of the Baal, the indictment goes on: "And Ahab made the Asherah; and Ahab did yet more to provoke the Lord, the God of Israel, than all the kings of Israel that were before him." Then, suddenly: "And Elijah the Tishbite, who was of the settlers of Gilead, said unto Ahab: 'As the Lord, the God of Israel, liveth, before whom I stand, there shall not be rain nor dew these years, but according to my word.' And the word of the Lord came to him, saying: 'Get thee hence, and turn thee eastward, and hide thyself by the brook Cherith, that is before Jordan. And it shall be that thou shalt drink of the brook, and I have commanded the ravens to feed thee.' "

Observe how Elijah is introduced. "And Elijah the Tishbite, who was of the settlers of Gilead, said unto Ahab . . ." We do not get the usual: "And the Lord sent Elijah the son of . . ." Indeed, we are never given Elijah's descent. He materializes before us and before Ahab. He was not there, and suddenly he is there, and as suddenly he is again not there. It is appropriate to the wild time and the wild theme, and to the gentle-hearted prophet driven wild by the people he has to deal with. For a great massacre is going on; the prophet teachers of Israel are being hunted down and slaughtered, and by this time only one hundred are left besides Elijah. Jezebel is at the head of the relentless liquidation, and she is assisted by the Baal and Asherah prophets she has brought in, and by the people. Yes, the defender of Jezebel is right in a sense: she is the protagonist of a new religion. Therefore Elijah appears and disappears with cometary swiftness.

Ahab must have taken him for a madman. But the seasons passed, the months of the former rain and those of the latter rain, and once more the months of the former and the latter rains, and the earth was iron and the sky brass. And Ahab, frantic, looked for Elijah everywhere. As Obadiah, the major-domo of Ahab, reported afterwards to Elijah: "There is no nation or kingdom whither my lord hath not sent to seek thee; and when they said: 'He is not here,' he took an oath of the kingdom or nation, that they found thee not." Bear this Obadiah in mind, he is one of the few faithful.

During these two years and more Elijah was in hiding, first under the open sky by the brook Cherith, then in the house of the widow of Zarephath, in Zidon—that is, Phœnicia, the stronghold of Jezebel's religion. His friends and pupils perished, the land lay blasted in drought, fields and orchards were stricken, the cattle died, the Baal priests infested the country, the people collaborated with the killers.

We read: "Elijah went and did according to the word of the Lord . . . and the ravens brought him bread and flesh in the morning, and bread and flesh in the evening; and he drank of the brook. And it came to pass after a while that the brook dried up, because there was no rain in the land. And the word of the Lord came to him, saying: 'Arise, get thee to Zarephath, which belongeth to Zidon, and dwell there; behold, I have commanded a widow there to sustain thee.' "

It would appear on the surface that the story of the widow of Zarephath has nothing to do with the main theme of Elijah's relations with Ahab and Jezebel and

250

the defecting Israelites. But it is not so. Its profound purpose, which popular Tradition has understood so well, is to afford us an insight into Elijah's true nature, and therefore into the cursèd spite of the disjointed time that imposed upon him his bitter role. And it does one good, in the midst of the suffering and the mutual destructions, to dwell on the episode. We read:

"Elijah arose and went to Zarephath; and when he came to the gate of the city, behold, a widow was there gathering sticks; and he called to her, and said: 'Fetch me, I pray thee, a little water in a vessel, that I may drink.' And as she was going to fetch it, he called to her and said: 'Bring me, I pray thee, a morsel of bread in thy hand.' And she said: 'As the Lord thy God liveth, I have not a cake, only a handful of meal in the jar, and a little oil in the cruse; and, behold, I am gathering two sticks, that I may go in and dress it for me and my son, that we may eat it and die.' "

The heart drops, contemplating this vivid picture. The drought which blasted Israel extended into the adjoining territory of Zidon. Such was the widow's extremity that only one wish was left her—that she and her son might at least not die of hunger on an empty stomach. She demurred gently at the thought of parting with this hope, though she did not hesitate to share her precious little stock of water with the strange man. Then Elijah performed for her the famous miracle of multiplication, and kept jar and cruse automatically refilled until the end of the drought; and here, I take it, is the specific origin of his apotheosis into the universal provider for the poor: the symbol of that rescue into security, automatic replenishment—what a sweet thing to dwell on when the last piece of bread is taken from the cupboard!—which is the dream of the hopeless.

We read: "And Elijah said unto her: 'Fear not; go and do as thou hast said; but make me thereof a little cake first, and bring it forth unto me, and afterwards make for thee and thy son. For thus saith the Lord, the God of Israel: 'The jar of meal shall not be spent, neither shall the cruse of oil fail, until the day that the Lord sendeth rain upon the land.' And she went and did according to the saying of Elijah; and she, and he, and her house, did eat many days. The jar of meal was not spent, neither did the cruse of oil fail, according to the word of the Lord, which He spoke by Elijah."

So now Elijah is established as the bringer of food to the hungry; and he is about to be established as the restorer of life. We read:

"And it came to pass after these things, that the son of the woman, the mistress of the house, fell sick; and his sickness was so sore, that there was no breath in him. And she said unto Elijah: 'What have I to do with thee, O thou man of God? Art thou come unto me to bring my sin to remembrance, and to slay my son?' And he said unto her: 'Give me thy son.' And he took him out of her bosom, and carried him up into the upper chamber, where he abode, and laid him upon his own bed. And he cried unto the Lord, and said: 'O Lord my God, hast Thou also brought evil upon the widow with whom I sojourn, by slaying her son?' And he stretched himself upon the child three times, and cried unto the Lord, and said: 'O Lord my God, I pray Thee, let this child's soul come back into him.' And the Lord hearkened unto the voice of Elijah; and the soul of the child came back into him, and he revived. And Elijah took the child, and brought him down out of the upper chamber into the house, and delivered him unto his mother; and Elijah said: 'See, thy son liveth.' And the woman said to Elijah: 'Now I know thou art a man of God, and that the word of the Lord in thy mouth is truth.' "

Immediately on this follows: "And it came to pass after many days, that the word of the Lord came to Elijah, in the third year, saying: 'Go, show thyself unto Ahab, and I will send rain upon the land.' And Elijah went to show himself unto Ahab."

v

We are by this time confronted with a series of questions which must so trouble the reader—that is, if his mind works at all like mine—that it is impossible to continue with the narrative until they have been got out of the way.

What kind of game is going on here? The first thing we learn about Elijah is that he delivers a message from God to Ahab and then has to run for his life because of Jezebel. He is compelled to live in the open, and depend on the ravens and the brook for food and drink. When the brook dries up in the drought he must take refuge with a widow in Zarephath, who has been "commanded" to feed him, but is herself starving to death, with her son, so that it is Elijah who feeds them. One would think that having, for His inscrutable reasons,

253

compelled Elijah to live in discomfort by the brook Cherith, God would thereafter provide him with decent quarters and adequate sustenance. Then, for no reason that we know of—though the poor widow speaks of her past sins—the widow's son dies, and she and Elijah suspect that this is in some way connected with him and his mission. But what is all this about? Why must Elijah flee before Jezebel, when God is on his side? And if God "commanded" the widow to feed Elijah, why is she ignorant of the command? And if the verse merely means that God had "arranged" to have her feed Elijah, why didn't God see to it that she had a perpetual supply before Elijah came? Or, for that matter, even though Elijah had never come. Why could not God have kept the brook Cherith running specially for Elijah? Or have angels deliver the daily ration of water just as He had the ravens bring him a daily ration of bread and meat?

For that is what I would have done if I had been God. Or, better still, I would have taken care of Elijah's safety and comfort to begin with, and not permitted Jezebel to turn him into a starving fugitive. Come to think of it, I would have avoided the whole senseless business. Do not laugh at me. I once intended to write a book about the way I would have arranged things if I had been God. Unfortunately, the only title I could think of, "A World I Never Made," had already been lifted from the poet, and pre-empted by another disgruntled author. So I will only mention one or two more points I had in mind in connection with the Elijah-Ahab-Jezebel situation. What was the drought for? To teach Ahab a lesson? We shall see that he learned nothing from it. Neither did Jezebel, or the Israelites. Thousands of people must have perished, among them innocent men and women and children, for there was a faithful remnant among the Israelites. What about these innocent ones? When the young son of the widow died—presumably from the aftereffects of long malnutrition—Elijah brought him back to life. That was fine; but no provision seems to have been made for the revival of other victims of the famine.

But let us go back still farther. Why, being omnipotent, does God go and create a world that has to be taught lessons? Why did He not—and so on, and so on.

It comes down again to that desperate question of questions which harasses us in all our meditations, and which cannot be answered because it is not a question, but a disguised statement of the limitations of our mental possibilities: Why is the world as it is? Or why is that which is? Why could not that which is have been something else?

At one time or another every man has asked himself: why didn't God make me somebody else? He forgets that to two and a half billion people (to speak only of our contemporaries) he *is* somebody else, and when he thinks otherwise, he is in a hopeless minority of one.

"Why is the world as it is, and not otherwise?" If it were, would we know it?

We are also toying with absurdity when we use the word "omnipotent." We do not know what we are asking for. We can no more conceive omipotence than we can conceive the infinite or the infinitesimal. And when we ask: "Is God omnipotent?" we are really asking:

255

"Can God do that which doesn't make sense to us?" If He can, how can we even start talking about it?

But let us not conclude that because for us there is no infinite and no infinitesimal, therefore there is no bigger and no smaller. And if each of us is not a somebody else to himself, let us not conclude that therefore he cannot change himself into a somebody else to his own past self. Finally, let us not assume that the world is not also otherwise than it is, waiting to be seen as such by the somebody elses into which we shall change.

It is this changing, this dynamism, perceived with the first effort of the human intellect (the conscious will to be better distinguishes us from the animals) , that concerns us; to be aware of it, and to co-operate in the right direction, is the proper destiny of man. In this everlasting dynamism an Elijah tugs with us in the right direction, a Jezebel in the opposite direction.

VI

Now, while Jezebel is perfecting her plot against Naboth, let us continue our study of preceding events. We pick up the thread:

"And Elijah went to show himself unto Ahab. And the famine was sore in Samaria. And Ahab called Obadiah, who was over the household.—Now Obadiah feared the Lord greatly; for it was so, when Jezebel cut off the prophets of the Lord, that Obadiah took a hundred prophets, and hid them by fifty in a cave, and fed them with bread and water.—And Ahab said unto Obadiah: 'Go through the land, unto all the springs of

256

water, and unto all the brooks; peradventure we may find grass and save the horses and mules alive. . . .' And as Obadiah was in the way, behold, Elijah met him."

It was at this point that Obadiah told Elijah how Ahab had searched for him throughout the whole known world, exacting sworn statements from all the governments. And when Elijah said: "Go, tell thy lord: 'Behold, Elijah is here,' " Obadiah pleaded with him not to disappear again the moment his back was turned. "And Elijah said: 'As the Lord of hosts liveth, before whom I stand, I will surely show myself to him today.' "

Was Ahab seeking Elijah so desperately in order to have him put to death? Nowhere in the whole narrative does Ahab express the wish to kill Elijah. Nowhere is he accused directly of having killed any prophets of the Lord. It seems, rather, that he would have liked to reach an accommodation. I think I can follow Ahab's reasoning, and I have just anticipated some of it. He holds Elijah and Elijah's God responsible for the drought and famine, but he cannot conceive this God as omnipotent. He asks himself: "If an All-Powerful God stands behind Elijah, what is the play-acting for? Why does Elijah have to hide from Jezebel? Why has Jezebel been allowed to kill Elijah's fellow prophets and install her own? Why does not the All-Powerful kill Jezebel, and manifest Himself unmistakably?" In other words, why does not God make us all good without our co-operation? Or, to repeat, why is that which is? What Ahab wants is the true God whom one can find without struggling for the truth.

257

From the single remark that Ahab addresses to Elijah when they meet, we see at once that Ahab concedes some powers to God—and so, undoubtedly does Jezebel—but he wants God to exercise His powers somewhere else; in short, go where He is wanted. We read.

"And Ahab went to meet Elijah. And it came to pass, when Ahab saw Elijah, that Ahab said unto him: 'Is it thou, thou troubler of Israel?' "

They are nuisances, God, and Elijah, and the other prophets. By refusing to withdraw at Jezebel's command they are throwing the country into turmoil. Ahab himself has no use for God and His impossible restrictions and injunctions, but he would not go so far as to execute prophets. But neither is he going to break up his happy marriage with Jezebel for their sake. He recognizes that God represents a check on the absolute power of kings, and that is one of the things that infuriate Jezebel. Well then, let them fight it out. He himself will not interfere, the less so as Jezebel has taken over and seems to be doing very well. Let Jezebel imagine—as she no doubt does—that he is a weakling. That rouses her to greater effort in his behalf. Let her imagine, too, that she is the real power in the land. What harm in that, as long as she loves him and works for him? On the other hand, if she gets into trouble . . . But apparently the powers of that God who seeks to limit the power of a king are themselves limited. There is a deadlock between Jezebel and God; so Ahab sees it; and the people see it similarly.

To Ahab's reproachful greeting Elijah answers: "I have not troubled Israel; but thou, and thy father's house, in that ye have forsaken the commandments of the Lord, and thou hast followed the Baalim. Now therefore send, and gather to me all Israel unto Mount Carmel, and the prophets of Baal four hundred and fifty, and the prophets of the Asherah four hundred, that eat at Jezebel's table."

Ahab makes no reply, or none worth recording. We read, simply: "And Ahab sent unto all the children of Israel, and gathered the prophets together unto Mount Carmel."

When we consider all the circumstances, this passage becomes extraordinarily revealing. The calling together of a national assembly even in the limited territory of the Northern Kingdom must have taken several days. Ahab could not have carried it out without Jezebel's knowledge. The Baal prophets could not have attended, or would not, without her consent. So she knew, and she acquiesced. What is more, Ahab knew in advance that she would acquiesce or he would have mentioned the difficulty to Elijah.

One is curious about the divergence of calculations between the husband and wife. They were not told that there was going to be a contest, but they must have guessed it. Jezebel was contemptuously certain of the outcome; nevertheless she made use of the brief interval to root out the remaining prophets of Israel. That is evident from Elijah's later complaint that he alone was left of the faithful. Or perhaps "nevertheless" is irrelevant here; she merely thought it a good occasion for completing the job, with Elijah walking into a trap of his own making as the grand climax. Her gods were with her, and in the ascendant; the people were with her, or definitely not against her. She thought of Elijah, the madman, making his solitary appeal to the vast assembly in the presence of the eight hundred and fifty prophets of Baal and the Asherah, and she could not have arranged a more impressive extinction of Jehovah and His cult. She thought of an old saying: Those whom the gods wish to destroy they first make mad.

Ahab saw it otherwise. He was bound to agree that the odds were hopelessly weighted against Elijah and Jehovah, especially with the last drive against the supporting prophets. He may have thought it unsportsmanlike of Jezebel to change the odds after the announcement, but women are like that and he was not responsible. Strictly speaking, Elijah had posed no conditions. He had issued instructions; Ahab had followed them to the letter. As the technically neutral promoter he had nothing to lose.

What the people expected it is impossible to say, since all sorts of rumors must have been current about the purpose of the emergency assembly. We can only be sure that there was tremendous excitement. After nearly three years of drought and famine they had that desperate feeling of "something has to be done about it," and they came in their thousands and tens of thousands, hungry, haggard, vaguely hopeful, dried-up combustible human material ready for the spark. They gathered in one of the natural amphitheaters that abound in the Carmel range and they stared at the massed ranks of the Baal and Asherah prophets. They speculated until the last moment. And then we read:

"And Elijah came near unto all the people, and said: 'How long halt ye between two opinions? If the Lord be God, follow Him; but if Baal, follow him.' And the people answered him not a word."

It was to Ahab more particularly that Elijah addressed this rhetorical question, and to the people through him. For Ahab represented the people in one of its most debased moments. Debased and yet not wholly lost. For Ahab, let us remember, was the man who was going to prove himself capable of remorse, however transitory. And Elijah's question meant this: "If you are still capable of remorse, you have not thrown out God completely. As long as conscience can trouble you, you are at war with the Baalim of sheer power. Wipe out your consciences if you can, and be done with God. But if you cannot, be done with the Baalim." The people, and Ahab, looked at the solitary wild figure, they looked at the ranks of the prophets; and they answered him not a word.

And Jezebel? She did not attend the contest. She absented herself ostentatiously. She, the supreme support of the Baal and Asherah prophets, would not dignify with her presence their childishly easy victory over Jehovah. She sat in the palace and smiled in anticipation.

I will not dwell on the details of the contest here, though dozens of byplays coruscate from the Text, and I could consume many pages with "Observe this point" and "Notice that particular phrase." The reader is strongly urged to break off, and consult the account; he will need it in order to understand the despair that came over Elijah after his fruitless victory. I will only recall that Elijah arranged two sacrifices, one by himself, one by the Baal prophets. Firewood was heaped under the Baal sacrifice, and the Baal prophets were challenged to kindle it with their incantations. Round his own sacrifice Elijah dug a moat and filled it with water.

All day long the prophets of Baal danced about their sacrifice, and inflicted bloody gashes upon themselves. All day long the people sat and watched. We read: "It came to pass round about noon, that Elijah mocked them, and said: 'Cry aloud, for he is a god; either he is musing, or is gone aside, or he is in a journey, or peradventure he sleepeth, and must be awaked.' " Until the sun began to wester the mad spectacle continued, and the people stared patiently. "But there was neither voice, nor any to answer, nor any that regarded."

The Baal prophets must have performed this piece of magic a thousand times, or they would not have accepted the challenge. It was routine with them, as it was routine with Pharaoh's magicians to change rods into snakes and vice versa. But on that particular day something went wrong. Elijah's miracle did not consist in setting fire by prayer to his own sacrifice after it had been drenched thoroughly with water, but in inhibiting the Baal prophets from setting fire to theirs. This was what he had undertaken to do, one against eight hundred and fifty.

Whether the inspiration for his undertaking came direct from God we do not know. Sometimes a prophet acts with specific directions, sometimes on general faith. What was really proved this day was the futility of miracles as foundations of faith; and those who read the Bible carefully will have observed how, as prophecy developed in Israel, it came to rely less and less on fortuitous demonstration and more and more on the pure relationship to God. This was part of the upward struggle, or we may call it the essential struggle, of the people toward an understanding of the blessing. Elijah, at his stage, called on God to manifest Himself by kindling the drenched sacrifice. We read: "Elijah the prophet drew near, and said: 'O Lord, the God of Abraham, of Isaac, and of Israel, let it be known this day that Thou art God in Israel, and that I am Thy servant, and that I have done all these things at Thy word. Hear me, O Lord, that this people may know that Thou, Lord, art God, for Thou didst turn their heart backward.' Then the fire of the Lord fell, and consumed the burnt offering, and the wood, and the stones, and the dust, and licked up the water that was in the trench. And when all the people saw it, they fell on their faces; and they said: 'The Lord, He is God; the Lord, He is God.' And Elijah said unto them: 'Take the prophets of Baal; let not one of them escape.' And they took them; and Elijah brought them down to the brook Kishon, and slew them there."

Of course he did not slay them all with his own hand. Eight hundred and fifty of them there were, and the mob butchered them at his command, he no doubt wielding the knife too. I close my eyes and ears on the ghastly scene, on the Kishon running red, on the screaming, the stench, on Elijah's unnatural fury multiplied in the mob. The children of Israel had helped the Baal prophets slay the prophets of Israel; now they did execution on the Baal prophets. And they chanted: "The

Lord, He is God! The Lord, He is God!" How long did
it take to finish off the eight hundred and fifty? Was
there a moon to light up the last throat-slitting? However it happened, not a man escaped. And then? Nothing. The people dispersed! They did not rise against
Ahab and Jezebel. They did not storm the palace and
the Baal temple. They had had a wonderful time. They
would remember it to the end of their days. And as far
as the purpose of the miracle was concerned, they were
as blind and as deaf after the revivalist orgy as they had
been before.

## VII

A second and far more beneficent miracle—the breaking of the drought, which Elijah announced that same
night—was just as ineffective as the first. I cannot make
up my mind whether Elijah meant to reward the people
for the butchery, believing that they had thus signalized
their return to the faith, or whether he was offering a
second and more memorable demonstration of the superior powers of God. In either case, I am sure that he
was filled with a mixture of triumph and horror. I cannot account otherwise for his wild behavior. As soon
as the cloud "as small as a man's hand" rose out of the
sea, a furious spirit came over him. We read: "And
Elijah said: 'Go up, say unto Ahab: "Make ready thy
chariot, and get thee down, that the rain stop thee not." '
And it came to pass in a little while, that the heaven
grew black with cloud and wind, and there was a great

rain. And Ahab rode, and went to Jezreel. And the hand of the Lord was on Elijah; and he girded up his loins, and ran before Ahab to the entrance of Jezreel."

He who is to be the forerunner of the Messiah ran that night before one of the vilest human beings, ran through the sheets of water and the dazzle of lightning, to celebrate and to announce simultaneously the salvation of the king and the people. Breathless with exertion and exultation, beside himself with the thought that his mission was ended, he sped through the tangled grasses and thickening mud, and every drumroll of thunder was a shout of triumph in his ears. From the summit of Carmel to the entrance of Jezreel, by winding and descending paths, through gorges that flashed up and disappeared, into the open plain gasping in relief as it expanded its bosom to the cataracts, he ran, unaware of tiredness, crying in his heart: "I bring the redeemed king to the redeemed people"—a ghastly parody and rehearsal of what shall be his reward at the end of days. It did not cross his mind that the man galloping after him was unchanged, or that the people in Jezreel and in the capital was untouched. Only at the end of the furious effort the great doubt came on him, and he slipped away. Then we read:

"And Ahab told Jezebel all that Elijah had done, and withal how he had slain all the prophets with the sword. Then Jezebel sent a messenger unto Elijah, saying: 'So do the gods to me, and more also, if I make not thy life as the life of one of these by tomorrow about this time.'"

If any hope still lived in Elijah, it was killed by that

265

message. If he was waiting for word from Ahab, this one from Jezebel told him to wait no longer. We read: "When he saw that, he arose, and went for his life."

We are not told what passed between Ahab and Jezebel that night. She must have demanded all the details, she must have raged at her idiot prophets who had let themselves be caught napping by the desert maniac—no wonder he had mocked them with: "Peradventure your god sleepeth!"—and perhaps at herself for having in overconfidence let things come to this pass. And yet there was nothing to fear. The mob had slaughtered all her prophets—it served them right; she would have to recruit a new set. The rains had come, apparently at Elijah's bidding, but the city was quiet, there were no crowds before the palace. And the messenger she had sent off to Elijah, partly in defiance, and partly also to test the temper of the populace, returned, his message delivered, without an incident to report—and Elijah in flight after all.

He had failed, and none knew it better than he. And in his failure he asked for death, as Jonah was to ask for it in success. We read: "Elijah came to Beersheba, which belongeth to Judah, and left his servant there. But he himself went a day's journey into the wilderness, and came and sat down under a broom-tree; and he requested for himself that he might die; and said: 'It is enough; now, O Lord, take away my life; for I am not better than my fathers.' "

It was a profoundly self-searching despair, in which Elijah assumed the responsibility that his people had cast off its shoulders. It is the way of the people to say:

"What we are we have been made by circumstance."
And every man blames his father for having brought
him up to be what he is. Whereby he opens the way for
his son to continue the excuse, and in this mechanistic
endlessness no individual exists. But Elijah felt himself
to be guilty because he had not done better than the
prophets that were before him. And so he handed in his
resignation.

It was summarily rejected. He was bidden to go into
the wilderness, and renew himself on the mountain
named Horeb, where the greatest of the prophets had
found inspiration; and there he poured out his plaint:
"I have been very jealous for the Lord, the God of
hosts; for the children of Israel have forsaken Thy covenant, thrown down Thine altars, and slain Thy prophets
with the sword; and I, even I only, am left; and they
seek my life, to take it away."

He was visited by the divine spirit, and renewed, and
he took up his burden again. He was given sundry com-
missions, and instructed to appoint a successor to himself; his ministry, like that of some other prophets of
Israel, was extended to neighboring countries. And he
was given reassurance. There were faithful ones still in
Israel, seven thousand of them, "all the knees which
have not bowed unto Baal, and every mouth which hath
not kissed him."

We ask ourselves at this point: what was the good of
it all? And the answer is clear. In the never-ending internal struggle of Israel, this was one more lesson,
pointed at the people as much as, and more than, at the
rulers. The people had had the power, it had not had

the will, to do good. Let it never thereafter plead: "We are not to blame."

For one benefit the people might, in its frivolity, claim credit though no credit was due. Whether because the recruiting went slowly or because she was for a time disgusted with her Baal—idol-worshippers have their lapses, too, as between one idol and another— Jezebel seems to have relaxed the persecution. In the years that followed the slaughter there were no more liquidations; at least, we read of none. Prophets of Jehovah reappeared here and there, but they were few, while the prophets of Baal, gathering once more under the ægis of Jezebel, gradually became numerous. Prophets of Jehovah even came to Ahab with warnings and messages; but it is recorded that it was difficult to find one of them. It must have seemed to Ahab that the outburst on Mount Carmel had led to an accommodation after all. Also Jezebel may have concluded that she had underrated Elijah's God; He was not ripe yet for destruction. So the years passed, Ahab warred on the Syrians, Jezebel reigned, and Elijah, grim, embittered, performed his tasks, made Elisha the son of Shaphat his heir, anointed Hazael to be king over Syria, and Jehu the son of Nimshi to be king over Israel in days to come. Then he disappeared. The years passed, and we are back now at the murder of Naboth the Jezreelite.

## VIII

We suspended the narrative with the following words: "And Jezebel, Ahab's wife, said unto him: 'Dost thou now govern the kingdom of Israel? Arise, and eat bread, and let thy heart be merry; I will give thee the vineyard of Naboth the Jezreelite.' "

It was simplicity itself. We read next: "So she wrote letters in the king's name, and sealed them with his seal, and sent the letters unto the elders and to the nobles that were in his city, and that dwelt with Naboth. And she wrote in the letters, saying. 'Proclaim a fast, and set Naboth at the head of the people; and set two men, base fellows, before him, and let them bear witness against him, saying: "Thou didst curse God and the king." And then let them carry him out, and stone him, that he die.' "

These few lines are packed with information. We see at once that Naboth was a man of importance in the community, most probably a member of the nobility. The frame-up against him had to be made as impressive as possible, and a public fast, presumably in expiation of an undiscovered sin, would create a mood of awe and expectancy. The "God" meant here by Jezebel, and by the nobles, cannot possibly have been the God of Israel. Everything points to the likelihood that Naboth was one of the "seven thousand in Israel, all the knees which have not bowed unto Baal, and every mouth which hath not kissed him." It is also likely enough that Naboth had been heard to mutter his discontent with the prevailing Baal-worship; and the official accusers, the "base men," did not have to invent their accusations out of whole cloth. But Naboth cannot have been open in his hostility to the foreign prophets; he cannot have protested against the persecution of God's prophets;

269

and herein he felt himself unworthy of the high position he occupied. Jezebel could therefore derive a special pleasure from the contemplation of his sufferings. For his confused conscience robbed him of a clean sense of injustice, and Jezebel could enjoy both the wickedness of her intentions and the moral byplay of the situation. This curious and particularly obscene form of human nastiness is not, as many suspect, a modern invention; it has been standard psychological technique time out of mind, and only its organizational form is modern. The imperfections of the saint have always been a source of genuine moral satisfaction to the villain without moral standards. Do not ask me how this works out, I could more easily explain the splitting of the Red Sea.

The charge against Naboth was both blasphemy and *lèse-majesté*. The two might go together as being in effect inseparable wherever the king had divine status. They might, however, have to be proved separately. The object of Naboth's blasphemy was, of course, Baal. He may or may not have been overheard, at one time or another, muttering against the Baal-worship; he may or may not have been overheard criticizing the king. That he had refused to sell his property to the king was common knowledge. That does not, in itself, seem to have constituted *lèse-majesté*, and this is an interesting sidelight on Israel's constitutional safeguards against royal absolutism. Even a Jezebel did not dare, or did not think it wise, to attack the law frontally, and she did not need to. She could easily have obtained Naboth's garden by means of simple administrative chicanery. She preferred Naboth's death for several reasons, and two of these reasons had to do with the accusation of *lèse-majesté*. Again that happened which, to Jezebel's acute satisfaction, gave an additional twist to Naboth's suffering. His refusal to sell the garden was in itself disrespectful. The reason he gave Ahab—and Jezebel must certainly have learned of it—was a gibe at the king, and at Jezebel too. But instead of being open, Naboth had concealed himself behind an equivocal phrase. Very well, she would make the martyr of him that he did not dare to be of his own free will. She would confer that favor on him. On the other hand, it was a fine touch that, resting his refusal on the law, Naboth should find himself legally condemned. That would certainly teach him who the law was in Israel.

The plot worked with appalling smoothness. We read:

"And the men of the city, even the elders and the nobles who dwelt in his city, did as Jezebel had sent unto them, according as it was written in the letters which she had sent unto them. They proclaimed a fast, and set Naboth at the head of the people. And the two men, the base fellows, came in and sat before him; and the base fellows bore witness against him, even against Naboth, in the presence of the people, saying: 'Naboth did curse God and the king.' Then they carried him forth out of the city, and stoned him with stones, that he died. Then they sent to Jezebel, saying: 'Naboth is stoned, and is dead.' And it came to pass, when Jezebel heard that Naboth was stoned, and was dead, that Jezebel said to Ahab: 'Arise, take possession of the vineyard of Naboth the Jezreelite, which he refused to give thee for money; for Naboth is not alive, but dead.' And it came to pass, when Ahab heard that Naboth was dead, that Ahab arose to go down to the vineyard of Naboth the Jezreelite, to take possession of it."

She had kept her word. She had said to Ahab: "Let thy heart be merry; I will give thee the vineyard of Naboth the Jezreelite!" Here it was, and so much more. She gloated over the gift, and invited him to gloat with her. "Take possession of the vineyard which he refused to give thee for money." Now it would not cost him a prutah, it was the property of an executed state criminal, reverting to the crown. She had kept her word to her dear, foolish, impractical Ahab, she, his one true wife, his chosen one. She had shown him what love could do.

For surely no one will deny that it was love that inspired her. There is only a little difficulty here, an ambiguity, as to the meaning of the word "love." Of a man who loves to eat fish we say, elliptically, that he loves fish. Somehow we do not say of a cannibal that he loves his neighbors. But we all have among our acquaintances moral and psychological cannibals, people who eat up the souls of their "loved" ones; of them we say at worst: "She loves her husband"—or "he loves his wife"—"with a selfish love." Selfish love manifests itself, often with much self-sacrifice, in doing whatever is possible to get oneself loved. If one must do evil for the beloved, if one must teach the beloved how to do evil, it is still for "love." It is a concentrated and focused form of the desire to be popular, and the techniques and philosophy are the same. We take it for granted that to want to be popular shows a love of humanity. We take it for granted that Jezebel's desire to please Ahab was born of her love of him. She could have eaten him up for very love; and she almost did. If she failed, it was for reasons beyond her control.

For one thing, Ahab himself was no mean adept at this kind of love. It touched him and made him smile tenderly when Jezebel, having said: "Dost thou now govern the kingdom of Israel?" at once proceeded, and not for the first time, we suppose, to usurp the royal secretariat and seal. Dear, deluded Jezebel, she was a darling, and he loved her for taking these awkward and ugly chores off his hands; and if it gave her the illusion that she was the real power, if it gave her additional pleasure to pretend that she did not look upon herself as the real power, so much the better. Women are so sensitive; one must know how to handle them.

There were other reasons why Jezebel failed. She could keep her promise to deliver Naboth's garden, but she could not guarantee that Ahab would be merry-hearted in the possession of it. She left out of the reckoning that part of Ahab which she could not reach. She left God out of the reckoning, being ignorant of His promise to the oppressed: "It shall come to pass, when he crieth unto Me, that I will hear; for I am gracious"; or, not ignorant of His promise, she was ignorant of His purpose. As for Elijah, she had almost forgotten his existence during these years.

273

IX

Whenever in my reading of the Text I see approaching the words that God put into Elijah's mouth to repeat to Ahab after the murder of Naboth, a premonitory distress comes over me. It is as though, listening to a familiar piece of music, I saw approaching a climactic phrase too powerful to be endured without preparation, and yet made the more powerful by the preparation. Long before it is on me I feel it in the notes that are its warning outriders. I may have heard it a hundred times, I may know to the last detail the progress of my emotions—the preliminary alarm, the growing helplessness, the tingling at the roots of my hair, the tensing of the flesh for the shock; the moment it breaks on me I forget everything, and I pass again through the undiminished terror of an unforeseen cataclysm.

It is also as though I saw the horizon darkening and my surroundings changing, and I found myself in a primeval world like that suggested by the cavern in da Vinci's *Madonna of the Rocks;* and the light grows more and more thickly somber, till it is unbearably charged; and I long for the terrible flash that will resolve the tension and make the air breathable again.

We have read: "Ahab rose up to go down to the vineyard of Naboth the Jezreelite, to take possession of it." Now we continue, with quickened pulse, with growing apprehension: "And the word of the Lord came to Elijah the Tishbite, saying: 'Arise, go down to meet Ahab king of Israel, who dwelleth in Samaria; behold, he is in the vineyard of Naboth, whither he is gone down, to

274

take possession of it. And thou shalt speak unto him, saying: "Hast thou killed, and also taken possession?" ' "

The face of Elijah, distorted, craglike, towers over Ahab, and a voice, not Elijah's, rolls in from everywhere: "Hast thou killed, and also taken possession?" Everything is speaking in the ghastly light: the convulsed, unmoving lips of Elijah, the knotted, uplifted hands, the thunderclouds above, the veiled, inhabited upper spaces, even Ahab's own cowering, petrified body, his fingertips, and his upstanding hair. Only these few words matter, these words which say nothing and say everything, the rhetorical question to which answer is impossible, because "No" would die in the speaker's throat, and the most wildly screamed "Yes" would be inadequate. Only these words matter, and all the punishments that Elijah enumerates after them are formalities demanded for the occasion by tradition. "Thus saith the Lord: 'In the place where dogs licked the blood of Naboth shall dogs lick thy blood, even thine.' " Of what consequence is it that dogs will lick Ahab's blood when he no longer needs it, and of what consequence that "the dogs shall eat Jezebel in the moat of Jezreel"? Ahab is not thinking of his carcass, which is the same carcass whether gnawed by dogs or swarming with maggots or preserved with unguents. He is not thinking at all; the horror of self-confrontation blots out suddenly the screen on which thoughts usually put up their ingenious performances to divert a man's attention from himself. We read: "And Ahab said unto Elijah: 'Hast thou found me, O mine enemy?' " That is all he can stammer. That man, that disturber, that troubler, had turned up again!

Why? Why? Why couldn't he leave one alone? Then we read: "And Elijah answered: 'I have found thee, because thou hast given thyself over to do that which is evil in the sight of the Lord. Behold, I will bring evil upon thee, and will utterly sweep thee away. . . . And I will make thy house like the house of Jeroboam the son of Nebat, and like the house of Baasa the son of Ahijah, for the provocation wherewith thou hast provoked Me, and hast made Israel to sin. And of Jezebel also spoke the Lord, saying: "The dogs shall eat Jezebel in the moat of Jezreel." ' "

If we analyze calmly the catalogue of punishments that Elijah here announces we are bound to be surprised by its pointlessness. Ahab, we were told, was the worst of all Israel's king's until that time; but he will fare no worse than Jeroboam the son of Nebat, and Baasa the son of Ahijah, though he exceeded them in wickedness; and Jezebel will fare no worse than he, though we are told that it was she "who stirred Ahab up." The fact seems to be that the range of tabulable curses was limited. The phrases were more or less conventional. Nor would it have been different if the prophets had extended themselves in punitive ingenuities: caldrons of boiling pitch, fiery pincers and pitchforks, swollen tongues of everlasting thirst, Dante's *propaginare* and Titus's flea-in-the-brain, they all come down finally to stereotypes; and they have no effect on the sinner. Why should they have had any effect on Ahab, these words, these as yet unfulfilled prophecies, if he had already listened to threats and seen them fulfilled, had witnessed

276

monstrous miracles of testimony and had been un-
shaken? But we read:

"And it came to pass, when Ahab heard those words,
that he rent his clothes, and put sackcloth upon his
flesh, and fasted, and lay in sackcloth, and went softly."

To what words is the narrator referring? To those
with which Elijah opened: "Hast thou killed, and also
taken possession?" In them the prophetic power rises to
a height nowhere surpassed in the entire Biblical record.
For no conventional miracle is performed, no sign is
given, the very name of God is unnecessary. Ahab's so-
phistication, his indifference to the superficially miraculous, his cynical self-mastery, superior to all argument
and inaccessible to threats, collapse in the presence of
the ultimately miraculous, the word brought from the
Source. He rends his clothes, and puts sackcloth on his
flesh, and fasts. . . . He is too rotten to build himself
back, to repent, but not rotten enough, as Jezebel was,
to be unaware of his rottenness, and not to be filled for
a while with loathing of himself.

These words of Elijah's, addressed to Ahab, are the
counterpart of Nathan's words, addressed to David:
"Thou art the man!" Both pronouncements show us the
ultimate purification of the prophet's role. For me the
burning bush, and the splitting of the Red Sea, and
the thunder on Sinai are symbols of miracles, and I do
not care how they are philosophized away. But who
shall philosophize away the two seemingly harmless
phrases: "Thou art the man," and: "Hast thou killed,
and also taken possession?" And who shall explain how

277

the prophetic presence smote two such different men alike, without portents and without apparitions, but with simple, everyday syllables?

We read, at the very beginning of the Bible, how God found pleasure in the successive miracles of the creation: "God saw that it was good." Something similar, something strangely moving, is recorded of the miracle of the breaking through to Ahab's conscience. "And the word of the Lord came to Elijah the Tishbite, saying: 'Seest thou how Ahab humbleth himself before Me? Because he humbleth himself before Me, I will not bring the evil in his days, but in his son's day will I bring the evil upon his house.' "

x

I date from the Naboth murder a deterioration in the relations between Ahab and Jezebel, for the outcome was the greatest disappointment in her life. She had never believed that he could let her down so. In the highly complicated though unformulated gangster treaty which they called mutual love there was no provision for this mad intrusion of the conscience. She had kept her part of the bargain; she had given him the garden of Naboth. Now it was up to Ahab to be merry-hearted.

She had counted on it. She had anticipated his joyful cry of: "Jezebel, you're wonderful." She had approved with little cooings of admiration, his designs—the walks, the arbors, the beds of herbs. It had been such fun to plan the gift; it had been so sweet to come proudly to him and say: "Arise, take possession of the garden of

278

Naboth the Jezreelite, which he refused to give thee for money." What was her reward? Sick looks and incoherent words. He was in worse condition than before, refusing to talk to her, rolling about on the floor, sneaking into corners barefoot, wringing his hands, glaring about him; and whenever she approached him, it was: "Go away! You don't understand! Go away!"

Baal damn and blast it! All this fuss, this fasting and sackcloth and ashes, about a piffling liquidation, an everyday affair which one usually assigned to a minor security officer and then forgot about. And who was the victim? An obstinate, mean-spirited little provincial nobleman who considered the patch of land cultivated by his fathers more important than the king's necessity. To judge by the way Ahab was carrying on—but what sense was there in arguing with a guilt complex? What sense in pointing out to him that for having killed off Jehovah's prophets she had suffered nothing more than the loss of her own. To be sure, she had not expected it. Very well; she had made a mistake, underrating Him. But that had been years ago, and He had not bothered her or Ahab since. And she had not killed one of His prophets since then, either. This Naboth—what business was he of Jehovah's? "You see!" she exclaimed eagerly; "I was the one who did it, but me He leaves alone. There's a fine Jehovah for you! If you only stand up to Him . . ."

There was no sense in arguing with a guilt complex, but she had to talk or burst. She said all these things and more to Ahab, but he did not answer. She blamed herself, however, for having let him go down to the

279

garden alone, for there the horrible Thing had appeared to him, the unwashed, unkempt, skin-girded creature with the piercing voice, and that had ended it. She had followed, and found Ahab lying there, and the servants told her that the mad Jehovah prophet had entered and left, no one knew exactly how or at what particular moment.

It would have been a very different story, she thought, if she had only been there. And indeed it would, though not as she thought. I do not believe for an instant that Elijah could have affected her directly. But looking on Ahab, she would have been made aware of such a repudiation of her, such a loathing, that she would have been frightened for her life. As it was, she found Ahab in the midst of the aftereffects, and they were bad enough. He came out of them, of course, and carried on for another three years, but it was never the same again between them. She did not trust him. He was not fit to be king, and she could not be king for him if this was how he responded to her help. She was perhaps wrong in blaming Elijah. Kill Elijah and Ahab would find himself another bogyman. Naboth, too: he was just a symptom, not a cause. Obviously Ahab was unbalanced; the strain ran through his people, a hereditary debility planted there by their God in the desert days, making them uncivilizable. In vain had Ahab tried to find a cure by marrying into the healthy royal Phœnician stock; in vain had she labored with him and with his people.

She argued the position with shrewd horse-sense. Let us assume that she had heard of God's promise to the

oppressed: "It shall come to pass, when he crieth unto
Me, that I will hear him; for I am gracious." Where had
He been when Naboth died under the stones, his screams
loud enough to be heard by any but the deafest God? Or
when Uriah the Hittite saw himself treacherously abandoned under the walls of Rabbah? For she knew, as
everyone else did, the story of the earlier king. Was *He*
peradventure sleeping, or on a journey, His graciousness
suspended while He took a holiday? So she argued
shrewdly; but to apply coarse common sense to the
promises of God is like applying Euclidean geometry to
astronomical space; the greater the space, the wider the
gap; the larger the purpose, the wider the distortion.

God made of Naboth a reluctant instrument of man's
self-realization. He did, in His infinite purity, that which
Jezebel did in her impurity. He conferred upon Naboth
and Uriah, against their wild protests, roles in which the
futility of their protests was essential; and His graciousness in this instance consisted in endowing their deaths
with a meaning that was beyond their grasp and their
willingness. Sometimes one wonders whether the unwilling sacrifice is not in its way superior—I do not
mean in merit, but in effect—to the willing Isaac-
sacrifice.

XI

I see her waiting for the death of Ahab, which was not
long in coming. Her hopes were now concentrated on
her son Ahaziah, who was at least half Phœnician, and
whom she had brought up carefully. For one thing she
could be grateful to Ahab; he did not disgrace her by

the manner of his death. However, he remained incorrigible to the end, the unpurposeful man halting between two opinions, doing his best to follow the gods of the Phœnicians but subject, on suggestion, to twinges of atavism toward Jehovah.

Some three years after the Naboth incident Ahab made an alliance with Jehoshaphat, king of Judah, to retake Ramoth-gilead from the king of Syria. We read:

"And Jehoshaphat said unto the king of Israel: 'Inquire, I pray thee, at the word of the Lord today.' Then the king of Israel gathered the prophets together, about four hundred men, and said unto them: 'Shall I go up against Ramoth-gilead to battle, or shall I forbear?' And they said. 'Go up; for the Lord will deliver it into the hand of the king.' But Jehoshaphat said: 'Is there not here besides a prophet of the Lord, that we may inquire of him?' And the king of Israel said unto Jehoshaphat: 'There is one man yet by whom we may inquire of the Lord, Micaiah the son of Imlah; but I hate him, for he doth not prophesy good concerning me, but evil.' "

The "four hundred" were false prophets, and we must assume that Ahab used the word "Lord" in alternating senses, as applying to gods and God alike, while Jehoshaphat used it in the proper sense only. Elijah had disappeared, and of the true prophets Micaiah son of Imlah was the only one available to Ahab. He would not have called on Elijah even if he had known his whereabouts; and it must have rankled with Jezebel that her husband let himself be persuaded to call even Micaiah. What had this minor prophet to gain by agreeing with the four hundred false prophets, probably Baal prophets? He seemed, indeed, to be risking his life by foretelling defeat, as he did; but it was doubtful whether Ahab, who had him arrested for this unfavorable prophecy, would have gone so far as to kill him in the event of a victory. Moreover, there was cunning in Micaiah's adverse forecast; for Ahab was courting defeat on both sides—from the God of Israel and the Baal of the Phœnicians—by trusting neither.

Not always had Jehovah's prophets foretold defeat for Ahab. In the early years of his reign an unnamed prophet of Jehovah had appeared to him before he went up to fight the Syrians, and had promised him victory twice: once when he fought in the valley, and once when he fought in the hills; the second time to prove to the Syrians—and perhaps to Ahab too—that God was God everywhere. But those years of favorable prophecy lay in the irrecoverable past, before the murder of Naboth. There was no hope of redeeming Ahab, and his time was come. He suspected it, and once more it galled Jezebel that he should be so susceptible to the prophets of Jehovah. For he went into battle in disguise, while Jehoshaphat wore his royal robes. It was of no avail. We read:

"And a certain man drew a bow at a venture, and smote the king of Israel between the lower armour and breastplate, wherefore he said unto the driver of his chariot: 'Turn thy hand, and carry me out of the host, for I am sore wounded.' And the battle increased that day; and the king was stayed up in his chariot against the Arameans, and died at even; and the blood ran out of the wound into the bottom of the chariot. . . . So the king died, and was brought to Samaria; and they buried the king in Samaria. And they washed the chariot by the pool of Samaria; and the dogs licked up his blood; the harlots also washed themselves there, according to the word of the Lord which he spoke."

The disappearances of Elijah are touched with the same suggestion of dread as his reappearances. Twice we are told where he hid himself; the first time by the brook Cherith and in Zarephath, at the widow's house; the second time in the wilderness, where he communed with God on Horeb. Then for an indeterminate number of years, between his adoption of Elisha and his denunciation of Ahab, his whereabouts are unknown.

Now five years pass between the murder of Naboth and the reappearance of Elijah. But always he is in the background; one feels him, wherever he is, eating his heart out, waiting for the special call, the central spirit of the struggle against the Baalim and Jezebel. He is terrible in the unpredictability of his eruptions. I have likened him to a cometary portent; but he had no fixed periodicity. He was more like a volcano, gathering its fires and exploding at unexpected moments.

We read: "Ahaziah the son of Ahab began to reign over Israel in Samaria in the seventeenth year of Jehoshaphat king of Judah, and he reigned two years over Israel. And he did that which was evil in the sight of the Lord, and walked in the way of his father, and in the way of his mother." In other words, he was a comfort to the widowed Jezebel; for we take it that "in the way of his father" does not refer to the remnant of good in Ahab, but to the massive inheritance of evil. On Ahaziah Jezebel set her hopes. With Ahab she had been a failure, having come into his life too late. Ahaziah might grow into the kind of king she could be proud of, a real king.

That is how I put it, provisionally. A "real" king was what Jezebel thought she wanted in her son, and had wanted in Ahab; that is, a man with a will. But whose will? His own or hers? His own will, she would have said, indignantly—as long as it agreed with hers. We face our original problem in a new phase. We asked: can a bad woman be a good wife? Now we ask: can she be a good mother? More people would give an affirmative answer to the second question than to the first. "But she was a wonderful mother to her children" is a particularly appealing phrase. It echoes a respect for the sanctity of motherhood. And yet, if the phrase must begin with a "but" instead of an "and," it is a pietistic lie. No doubt about it, Jezebel wanted her Ahaziah to be happy, and she was as prepared to sacrifice herself for him as she had been for Ahab. But everything depends on the standards of happiness. An amoralist who loves his son and says, earnestly and unselfishly: "I want his life to be happier than mine," hopes to be consoled in his old age by seeing his thwarted egotisms fulfilled in his offspring.

We are told so little about Ahaziah that I cannot imagine what pattern of mutual cannibalism made up his relationship with his mother, and how it would have developed through the years, what devices they would have found for exploiting each other in the name of love, and how it would have ended. He died young, and therefore one is apt to think that the relationship was a particularly tender one; at least, his mother must have

285

thought so afterwards, since the younger brother who succeeded him, Jehoram, or Joram, was from Jezebel's point of view an even greater disappointment than his father. For of Jehoram it is written: "He did that which was evil in the sight of the Lord; but not like his father, and like his mother." No such unfilial degeneration is mentioned regarding Ahaziah, and we can assume that his mother always remembered him as the great hope which was brutally extinguished.

He died in a strange, stupid, ridiculous, utterly un-called-for fashion: he fell out of a window. It is intimated that he might have survived his fall but for the unexpected intervention of Elijah—and this was Elijah's last intervention in the affairs of the royal house of Israel, his last effort to correct the incorrigible.

No sooner has he been introduced as succeeding to the throne than we read: "And Ahaziah fell down through the lattice in his upper chamber that was in Samaria, and was sick; and he sent messengers, and said unto them: 'Go, inquire of Baal-zebub the god of Ekron whether I shall recover of this sickness.' But an angel of the Lord said to Elijah the Tishbite: 'Arise, go up to meet the messengers of the king of Samaria, and say unto them: "Is it because there is no God in Israel, that ye go to inquire of Baal-zebub the god of Ekron? Now therefore thus saith the Lord: 'Thou shalt not come down from the bed whither thou art gone up, but shalt surely die.' " ' And Elijah departed."

Some will consider it unreasonable that Ahaziah should have had to die for his religious beliefs, rather than for specific crimes. Let us understand what is in play here. Over and over again the Biblical record tells us of high ethical personalities among idol-worshippers. We think of the decency of the sailors toward Jonah, the kindness that Naomi and her children found among the Moabites, the humaneness of Pharaoh's daughter, the wisdom and generosity of Jethro, the father-in-law of Moses, the sweetness that reigned in the household of Naaman the Syrian, the goodness of the Zidonian widow of Zarephath. But nowhere do we learn that the Israelites were ever asked to change their faith for the sake of a superior morality. Nowhere does a pagan proselytizer scourge the Jews—or anyone else—for wickedness. When Israelites were drawn to other faiths it was toward the baser features in them. The change of religion that Jezebel and Ahab and Ahaziah and the rest of them sought to thrust upon the wavering Israelites was not connected with a program of spiritual improvement. The gods they sought to introduce into Israel brought no idealist message. The primary purpose was to spread among the people that contempt for Jehovah and His prophets which the rulers felt, as witness what follows:

"And the messengers returned unto Ahaziah, and he said unto them: 'Why is it that ye are returned?' And they said: 'There came up a man to meet us, and said unto us: "Thus saith the Lord: 'Is it because there is no God in Israel, that thou sendest to inquire of Baal-zebub the god of Ekron? Therefore thou shalt not come down from the bed whither thou art gone up, but shalt surely die.'"' And he said unto them: 'What manner of man was he that came up to meet you, and told you these words?' And they answered him: 'He was a hairy

man, and girt with a girdle of leather about his loins.'
And he said: 'It is Elijah the Tishbite.'

"Then the king sent unto him a captain of fifty with
his fifty. And he went up to him; and, behold, he sat
on the top of the hill. And he spoke unto him: 'O man
of God, the king hath said: "Come down" ' And Elijah
answered and said to the captain of fifty: 'If I be a man
of God, let fire come down from heaven, and consume
thee and thy fifty.' And there came down fire from
heaven, and consumed him and his fifty. And again he
sent unto him another captain of fifty with his fifty. And
he answered and said unto him: 'O man of God, thus
hath the king said: "Come down quickly." ' And Elijah
answered and said unto them: 'If I be a man of God, let
fire come down from heaven and consume thee and thy
fifty.' And the fire of God came down from heaven, and
consumed him and his fifty. And again he sent the
captain of a third fifty with his fifty. And the third
captain of fifty went up, and came and fell on his knees
before Elijah, and besought him, and said unto him:
'O man of God, I pray thee, let my life, and the life of
these fifty thy servants, be precious in thy sight. Behold
there came fire down from heaven, and consumed the
two former captains of fifty with their fifties; but now
let my life be precious in thy sight.' And the angel of
the Lord said unto Elijah: 'Go down with him; be not
afraid of him.' And he arose, and went down with him
unto the king."

Here is cause for wonder! The man who had to run
from Jezebel has but to say the word, and the fires of
heaven wipe out fifty soldiers at a time! And when

Ahaziah and the remaining captains are humbled at last, the angel has to reassure the firewielder, bidding him not to be afraid! It would all be utter nonsense if we did not know that the prophet is given protection or denied it, is defended or bidden to suffer, not according to his wishes, but according to the point that is being made What virtue would there be in prophecy if it were otherwise? And if it seems, again, wildly capricious that a hundred and two men should be burned alive because of their insolence to Elijah, let us look deeper. The attitude of the first two captains, discourteous, peremptory, was in the spirit of their commander-in-chief, the king. They could plead that they were obeying orders. But there are certain orders that may not be carried out, there are limits to the obedience of a soldier. There are certain things that a man, whether as citizen or soldier, ought to be *unable* to do; things which, in attempting to do, he must find himself paralyzed. If Ahaziah said to his captains: "Go, bring me the man of God, quickly," and no shudder of fear went through his subordinates; if they proceeded blithely, unconscious of personal responsibility, complete automata, and cried: "You there, man of God, the king wants you," what befell them was the only possible answer. Twice the king commanded, and twice he let the men be destroyed. The third captain saved himself.

To Ahaziah himself Elijah had nothing more to say than what he had said to the messengers he intercepted on the road. ("So Ahaziah died according to the word which Elijah had spoken.") And Elijah went out from his presence, and his grueling earthly mission was ended.

The burden was lifted from his shoulders, his wanderings as a portent and terror had come to an end, he was about to begin his wanderings as the lord bountiful. He took passage in the element which had played such a big part in his life: fire. The chariot awaited him beyond the Jordan and he was among the few who did not pass through the conventional gates of death. He had only to leave his mantle to Elisha and mount the chariot, and he was off, in his ears ringing Elisha's disconsolate cry: "My father, my father, the chariots of Israel and the horsemen thereof!"

He was all of that, poor man, chariots and horsemen, when he had only wanted to be a pushcart peddler of kindnesses.

XII

Twice when the thunderbolt struck down her men and shattered her hopes, Jezebel was not there. In Naboth's garden, where the lifelong alliance with her husband came to nothing, and in the palace bedroom where she lost her eldest son, the destroyer appeared and vanished, not giving her the chance to battle it out with him. The cowardly assassin darted in and out, leaving ruin behind; and the one chance she had had of crushing him, at the contest on Carmel, she had like a fool despised.

The most nauseating feature about this woman is her fortitude, her dauntless persistence, her invincibility. She had that much longed-for thing, peace of mind; and, if she had a soul, peace of soul, too. She must have taken all the right courses, and read all the right books. Because she had the power of positive thinking she was be-

290

yond the reach of the adversary; disaster could not shake her; the world's intractability made no dent in her heroic devotion to her sinfulness. I am sure that it is to these enviable qualities in a Jezebel that Jeremiah refers in his famous lament: "Wherefore doth the way of the wicked prosper? Wherefore are all they happy that deal very treacherously?" He cannot have meant worldly prosperity, because everyone knows that villainy alone does not ensure success, and that as between the incompetent villain and the competent honest man the former is a very poor bet. But the perfect villain has what the decent man can never have—the happiness that comes from adjustment.

She was, of course, as much of a failure as Elijah, but, not being afflicted with insecurity, she did not suffer as much. To *her* it never occurred that she was not good enough to live. Her guilt complex had been taken care of when she was young; or perhaps they had never developed one in the Zidonian civilization. She was a failure in her public no less than in her private life. She had had to retreat a long way from her first high deals. The liquidation of the Jehovah prophets was a fleeting achievement, for by the time of Elijah's ascent to heaven the prophetic schools had been re-established at Bethel and Gilgal; moreover, Elijah left behind him the pestiferous Elisha, who, not so powerful by himself as his master, had been fortified by a special double injection of the spirit. Also the king he had to deal with, Jehoram, Jezebel's second son, was an even greater weakling than his father, and not a patch on the elder brother he succeeded, the promising and long-lamented Ahaziah. On one occasion this same wretched Jehoram addressed Elisha, the Jehovah prophet, as "my father"! And then there was the scandalous incident during the war with Moab.

This was such a slap at Jezebel, and all that she stood for, that it must be recalled here, though briefly. Jehoram king of Israel, Jehoshaphat king of Judah, and an unnamed king of Edom made a pact to reconquer Moab for Israel. For various reasons the king of Israel lost heart soon after the opening of the campaign, and Jehoshaphat king of Judah proposed that a Jehovah prophet be consulted. An officer of Jehoram revealed that Elisha was in the camp; and the three kings went to him.

Let us mark that. They went to him; they did not send for him. What did Jezebel think of her apostatizing son when she heard that? But it was nothing, compared with what followed. For Elisha spoke to the king of Israel with the utmost insolence, insulting his father and mother; and Jehoram did not strike him down, did not even expostulate. Elisha said to Jehoram: "What have I to do with thee?"—and all the host heard him. "Get thee to the prophets of thy father and thy mother. . . . As the Lord of hosts liveth, before whom I stand, were it not that I regard the presence of Jehoshaphat, the king of Judah, I would not look toward thee, nor see thee." The king of Israel accepted in silence this astounding public insult to his dead father and his living mother. Such a betrayal would have crushed a lesser spirit than Jezebel's. She held her head high until the end, conscious of the rectitude of her cause. She did not live long enough to see the complete obliteration of the Ahab line, for she did not survive by more than a day or two the assassination of Jehoram by Jehu the son of Nimshi. Nor did she die of a broken heart or a broken will. She faced her son's assassin—he was also hers—

*Undaunted mid the crimson conflagration*
*Of the day setting on her baffled prime.*

Jehu, the son (or grandson) of Nimshi, was the scourge appointed by God in those miserable times, and he performed his task against the Ahab-Jezebel sinners with the gusto of the born executioner. He is one of the bloodiest figures in the Biblical record. He reeks. He was a killer in every known style, direct and indirect, retail and wholesale, by assault and by treachery, by command and by hint, in the suddenness of heat and with the relish of calculation. He began with Jehoram his king, like a certain notorious Zimri before him, who fell on Asa, king of Israel, at a drunken feast; he proceeded to Jezebel and to all the remaining offspring of Ahab; and he slaughtered the Baal-worshippers by hundreds and thousands.

Far back, at the end of his sojourn in the Horeb wilderness, Elijah had been bidden to seek out this Jehu, and to anoint him king-to-be in Israel; not for his virtues, nor for his faithfulness to Jehovah. Jehu was even rewarded, though he substituted for the worship of Jezebel's Baalim his worship of golden calves. For one reason or another, this was the man who had to be used, and in the twelfth year of Jehoram's reign Elisha, now wearing the mantle of Elijah, sent one of his disciples to Jehu, to reanoint him, and to start him off on his re-volting career.

It was not given to Jehoram to die a hero's death, like his father. He was convalescing in Jezreel from wounds received in the Syrian wars, and Ahaziah, king of Judah (not to be confused with Jehoram's elder brother), was visiting him, when the messenger of Elisha found Jehu in the midst of his companions. Without loss of a moment Jehu set forth with a band, driving like a madman, as was his wont. Jehoram and Ahaziah, seeing him from afar, went out to meet him in Naboth's garden. Then we read: "It came to pass, when Jehoram saw Jehu, that he said: 'Is it peace, Jehu?' And he answered: 'What peace, so long as the harlotries of thy mother Jezebel and her witchcrafts are so many?'"

"Harlotries" as used here is not a reflection on Jeze-bel's sexual morals. She was a chaste woman, and a har-lot only in the sense that she went "whoring" after false gods. But whatever Jehu meant, Jehoram did not stay to argue the point. He turned to flee, and Ahaziah with him. Jehu shot Jehoram in the back, so that "the arrow went out at his heart," and for good measure he sent killers after the fleeing Ahaziah too, though this was not strictly in the line of his mission. And that day, or the day after, he went after Jezebel, who already had word of the death of Jehoram.

This is the moment for which Jezebel is remembered in the popular phrase, a wholly misleading one, used indignantly; whereas if her conduct were understood, "painted Jezebel" would be a high tribute wherever courage in moral monsters is admired for itself—which means practically everywhere. We read:

"And when Jehu was come to Jezreel, Jezebel heard of it; and she painted her eyes, and attired her head, and looked out at the window. And as Jehu entered in at the gate, she said: 'Is it peace, thou Zimri, thy master's murderer?' And he lifted up his face to the window, and said: 'Who is on my side, who?' And there looked out to him two or three officers. And he said: 'Throw her down.' So they threw her down; and some of her blood was sprinkled on the wall, and on the horses; and she was trodden under foot. And when he was come in, he did eat and drink; and he said: 'Look now after this cursed woman, and bury her; for she is a king's daughter.' And they went to bury her; but they found no more of her than the skull, and the feet, and the palms of her hands. Wherefore they came back and told him. And he said: 'This is the word of the Lord, which He spoke by His servant Elijah the Tishbite, saying: "In the portion of Jezreel shall the dogs eat the flesh of Jezebel; and the carcass of Jezebel shall be as dung upon the face of the field in the portion of Jezreel; so that they shall not say: 'This is Jezebel.' " ' "

## XIII

It would not help much toward an understanding of Jezebel to know what was in her mind when she was primping herself and putting on her regalia for the reception of Jehu. As a matter of fact, we can be pretty

295

certain about her thoughts—and they were, in the good colloquial word, corny. She was thinking: "I will meet my son's murderer like a great lady. He will not see on my face what no man has ever seen there—fear. For I am a king's daughter; and if I must die, I shall die like one." And so on, and so on. This was how she felt, with all the sincerity of which she was capable.

Yes, but what about her "real" thoughts, as we would say, the thoughts behind the thoughts? The question is; had she any? Thus, for instance, she confronts Jehu scornfully with the reproachful phrase: "Thou Zimri, thy master's murderer." That too was how she felt. Zimri was a murderer. So was she, of course. Ah, yes, but she had never murdered her king, had she? She had murdered only Naboth and a few hundred prophets. And there were no thoughts behind that thought. She was filled with genuine moral indignation against this murderer of his master, particularly as he had committed the crime not in open rebellion, but by a ruse, a cowardly ambush. Of course one would say that she had killed Naboth by a ruse, and not in a particularly heroic fashion. "What are you talking about?" she would have answered, her queenly eyes flashing more brightly than her tiara. "What one does with a dog like Naboth, who defied my husband, is of no consequence! How dare you make the comparison? . . ." There is, as you see, nothing interesting or instructive to be got out of her.

And yet one persists. "Surely, somewhere, behind four, five, or six successive façades, certain perceptions lurked, certain susceptibilities, half-thoughts. . . ." That is what I doubt. Jezebel was, among other things, a bore, though

296

this is a rather odd statement in connection with a woman who rouses such an intense feeling of loathing. And if there was something behind the fifth or sixth façade it could no longer be called a thought, and neither she nor anyone else had access to it.

When she had seated herself at the window, her officers standing behind her, impressed by her regal bearing, she had given her all. Tragic queenliness shone from her as she looked down into the courtyard, and queenly scorn was in her voice when she cried to Jehu, standing below in his chariot: "Is it peace, thou Zimri, thy master's murderer?" Unfortunately Zimri was not in an impressionable mood, and he spoiled the theatrical effect by shouting up: "Chuck her out of the window"— and all of a sudden the officers saw, instead of a queen, a bundle of garbage. It will be objected that a good person, yes, a Naomi even, would also have looked like a bundle of garbage in these circumstances, and defenestration has been practiced on decent people, too. That is so; but what a good person looks like does not matter; his essence is not connected with the show he puts up, and his impressiveness—to use a rather dubious word— has no element of the dramatic in it.

By the show which a person puts up I mean not only the physical and æsthetic trappings, but those qualities called "the virtues" as distinguished from "virtue." I sometimes suspect that my detestation of Jezebel has a particular edge for reasons I have already indicated—because she compels me to believe in something that is always getting me into trouble, both with myself and with others. She makes me see the meaninglessness of "the virtues"; and in a manner I can never satisfactorily express she had convinced me that courage, loyalty, endurance, and all the other admired qualities are no more moral in themselves than a sound digestion, or a well-planned behavior pattern, which is only a system of conditioned reflexes. These things have nothing to do with goodness. They are good only as possessed by a good person, and they are horrible when possessed by a bad person. Such views get me into trouble with other people because I deprive them of the common refuge from moral emptiness; they get me into trouble with myself for the same reason.

This is a really extraordinary mix-up, is it not? I detest Jezebel on moral grounds because she exposes my immorality to me. But if I am on moral ground, should I not be *grateful* to her for exposing my immorality to me? Ah well! A Tradition tells us that certain problems which are insoluble at our present stage of knowledge and self-knowledge will have to wait for the day when Elijah announces the Messiah; for besides serving as the Messianic herald, he will finally resolve all riddles of ritual and behavior. It would be most fitting that this particular riddle should be left to him too.

## CHAPTER VIII

## *The Brilliant Failure*

❀

I STAND awestruck before Thomas Mann's monumental *Joseph and His Brothers.* So does the author, and why should he not? "Pyramidlike" he calls it, and it is. Contemplating it with a touch of stupefaction, he reflects that it "differs from its brother monsters at the edge of the Lybian Desert only in the fact that no hecatombs of scourged and panting slaves fell victim to its erection but that it is the product of years of patient labour on the part of one man. . . ." He does himself less than justice. *Joseph and His Brothers* is assuredly one of the greatest achievements of the human imagination. I know of longer books, and have heard of more diligent writers; but no other work of modern times, and no other personality behind it, have cast such an enduring spell on me. It is only of late that I have been able to assert myself against it and find the courage to insist that the Joseph who wanders through the enchanting sixteen hundred pages of Thomas Mann's evocation is not the Joseph intended by the Biblical text. *C'est magnifique, mais ce n'est pas Joseph.*

There are, I think, two originating causes for Mann's

misconstruction. One of them is connected with the heritage of "the blessing." Mann understands its nature thoroughly. We have seen that it is no blessing in the vulgar sense, no compulsive formula for the ensurement of prosperity. It is, instead, the gift of a dangerous and disturbing insight into God, or rather of an obsessive longing and striving for such an insight. This blessing is the primary significance of the people Abraham founded. It is its *raison d'être*. Abraham of Ur was first chosen to carry it. He in turn had to choose the next carrier from among his sons, because only one of them was fit to receive it; so Ishmael and the sons of Keturah were rejected, and Isaac became the elected one. But Isaac too had to choose between his sons, and Jacob was the next carrier, while Esau relapsed into the man of the desert. And we have also seen that this process of elimination, this rejection of all but one in each generation, could not go on indefinitely, or no people would ever have been founded. It had to stop somewhere, and it stopped with Jacob's sons, all twelve of whom remained within the people; that is to say, within the orbit of the blessing.

But Thomas Mann, while acknowledging that the blessing is the heart of significance in the people and its history, continues the process of elimination into the sons of Jacob! He makes it appear that Joseph and his brothers were at war for the possession of *the* blessing, even as Jacob and Esau had been, and Isaac and Ishmael before them. As he sees it, Judah becomes the next carrier of *the* blessing, and the others receive ordinary blessings. Then why not keep up the elimination until the end of time, with only one man in each generation chosen and all the rest extruded? Actually Jacob blesses all his sons; unevenly, to be sure; but not to a single one of them, as we shall see, does he transmit the exclusive Abrahamitic blessing as such. And the reason is that all of them have their share in it; it has become by now the tacit possession of the whole folk. Judah is, indeed, singled out to be the progenitor of the Messiah; a great distinction certainly; but it does not exclude a single brother from the people of the blessing, from a full share in its torments, ecstasies, lapses, punishments, and recoveries.

Thus the nature of the struggle between Joseph and his brothers is put in false perspective, and confused with the struggle of the patriarchs. But within that erroneous perspective itself there is a secondary distortion. Let us for a moment grant that the Abrahamitic blessing is the prize for which the sons of Jacob contend. Joseph is the hero of the epic. He not only outshines everyone within range; he is obviously the one son suited by his insights (that is, according to Thomas Mann's vision of him) to be the recipient. But when the reader reluctantly closes the enormous book, he realizes to his chagrin that he has, in the English phrase, been led up the garden path. The blessing is not going to the hero, but to the peripheral Judah. And what is worse, this blessing, for the sake of which Tamar plays the whore to her father-in-law Judah, is somehow disposed of in an anticlimax. The centricity of the folk theme does not coincide with the centricity of the hero. Joseph, the genius with the unbelievable career, is a side-show; the "necessary busi-

301

ness" has been proceeding elsewhere; and the necessary business — the blessing — is played down at the end so that Joseph's failure might be obscured. Joseph himself is hardly disappointed.

Now as it happens the Joseph I see, whom I take the liberty of calling the real Joseph, was in fact a brilliant failure, as I shall show. He cannot have taken as easily as Thomas Mann believes his loss of the Messianic line, secondary though it was by then. But his failure goes deeper, and his loss of the Messianic line is its symbol. An enormous task had been assigned to Joseph: to save the folk from extinction by famine. Great as this privilege was, it did not in itself rank with the privilege of Abraham, Isaac, and Jacob as sole carriers and conservers of the blessing. Noah was chosen to save the whole human species from extinction, and yet he was not chosen to be the founder of the faith. No one will deny the service rendered by Noah to all of us—where would we be without him?—but no one places him on a level with Abraham. We are beholden to Joseph for the survival of the folk, and therefore of the means of continuing the blessing; but he is not ranked with the patriarchs. I think he could have been. Moses, for instance, ranks at least with the patriarchs, though he was not a sole custodian and transmitter of the blessing. What happened with Joseph was this: he carried out his assignment to the letter; he conserved the people, but he did nothing more; he rescued it, but did not grace the rescue with a spiritual achievement.

A second distortion is one that flows from Mann's relationship to Joseph. He shares Jacob's sinful preference

302

for the beloved first son of "the lovely, too-soon-departed Rachel." Preference in itself is not sinful; we cannot have the same love for everyone. It is sinful when it leads to injustice, or to more than a certain degree of injustice. I gladly admit that Mann does his best to expose Joseph's faults, and he makes it clear that he is doing his best. That is perhaps the trouble. His admissions of Joseph's misdemeanors are at once overfrank and understated. He makes them so elaborate and fascinating that in our delighted appreciation of the writing we forget that certain grim and ugly truths are involved. He throws the weight of his personality into the exoneration. No, not exoneration, either, that is too sharp. He does not plead for Joseph in so many words; it is only that he loves Joseph so much that we are reluctant to hurt his father feelings, and we hasten to reassure him: "It wasn't too bad." We go along with him in his fascinating and affectionate discourse; and before we know it we are committed to his emotions; before we know it the insincere pardon has slipped out of us. When, at a distance, we recover our balance, we are alarmed at the seduction.

II

Let me illustrate. Mann introduces us to the fabulously attractive and almost unnaturally gifted young Joseph at great length before he takes up his story. The description is permissible and acceptable, as well as entrancing. But once he gets down—after the long and unforgettable digression on Jacob's early life—to the irrefutable bedrock facts about Joseph's actions, he automatically betrays his unwillingness or his inability to face them. He uses a technique of evasion which concedes only to retract; and he does it with so much wit, so much bribery of style, that we do not want to renounce the pleasure of surrender.

He begins, as he should, at the beginning, and refers to the actual Text, reproducing it without shading or mitigation. I quote Thomas Mann: "The story goes on to tell how Joseph, being seventeen years old, was feeding the flock with his brethren; and the lad was with the sons of Bilhah and with the sons of Zilpah, his father's wives." Here Thomas Mann interpolates: "that is correct," and we are of course pleased to have his corroboration; it makes us sure of our ground. He continues: "We have instances of the fact which the saga further states: namely, that Joseph brought unto his father their evil report."

Nothing, so far, to make us suspicious of Thomas Mann. The instances of Joseph's talebearing he refers to are found in the Tradition. Joseph told his father that his brothers were in the habit of eating the flesh which they cut from living animals; and that they were carrying on with the women of the countryside. Whether they actually did these things is doubtful, and for our purpose does not matter. We are concerned with Joseph's talebearing, which Mann honestly sets forth, as indeed he must. But he adds immediately: "It would not be hard to find a point of view from which Joseph could be regarded as an unlicked cub. It was the brothers' point of view. I do not share it; or, rather, I might entertain it for a moment, but I would give it up. For Joseph was more."

Certainly Joseph was more; sagas are not written round unlicked cubs who have not in them the seeds of greatness. But that ingenious and disingenuous, smiling understatement: "It would not be hard to find a point of view . . ." We glide along with it, out of politeness, out of respect and liking for the author, out of tenderness for his feelings. And the playful phrase: "an unlicked cub"! It was at the fifth or sixth reading of the entire work, when I was looking for the causes of my dissatisfaction, that I thought of consulting Mann's German text. The phrase in the original is: *"ein unausstehlicher Bengel."* "An insufferable brat" comes nearer, I think, to the intention. Even so it is a softening, a kind of tongue-clucking and headshaking of minor condemnation. The brothers did *not* think of Joseph as an unlicked cub or as an insufferable brat; not at all. They saw him, correctly, as a poisonous infection in their relations with their father. They forefelt lifelong consequences in his sneaking, underhand habits; and they did that to Joseph which one does not do to an unlicked cub or even an insufferable brat.

Let it be noted that Mann himself is not quite satisfied with his first description of Joseph's behavior. After he has softened us up he goes back for more admissions. He does not spare us the effects of Joseph's "innocent prattle"; he does not avoid the picture of the anguish inflicted on the brothers. He takes up in detail the following Biblical passage:

305

"And Joseph dreamed a dream; and he told it to his brethren; and they hated him yet the more. And he said unto them: 'Hear, I pray you, this dream which I have dreamed: for, behold, we were binding sheaves in the field, and, lo, my sheaf arose, and also stood upright; and, behold, your sheaves came round about, and bowed down to my sheaf.' And his brethren said to him: 'Shalt thou indeed reign over us? Or shalt thou indeed have dominion over us?' And they hated him yet the more for his dreams, and for his words. And he dreamed yet another dream, and told it to his brethren, and said: 'Behold, I have dreamed yet another dream: and, behold, the sun and the moon and the eleven stars bowed down to me.' And he told it to his father, and to his brethren; and his father rebuked him, and said unto him: 'What is this dream that thou hast dreamed? Shall I and thy mother and thy brethren indeed come to bow down to thee to the earth?' And his brethren envied him; but the father kept his saying in mind."

Mann carefully separates and fills in the two occasions. The first dream Joseph tells only to his brothers, to their alarm, and rage, and partial incredulity. To the telling of the second dream he inveigles his father, so that by his presence and acquiescence he may compel the brothers to believe wholly the unbelievable, to accept the inacceptable. The scene, as Thomas Mann powerfully depicts it, is in the open field, the time a rest period in the harvesting. And when Joseph blurts out his second and more terrific dream, about the thirteen celestial bodies, Mann tells us: "Nobody stirred. Jacob, the father, kept his eyes severely cast down. It was very still; but in the stillness came an evil, mysterious, and yet distinct sound. It was the gnashing of the brethren's teeth. Most of them kept their lips closed, but Simeon and Levi showed their teeth as they gnashed. . . . It is hard to say whether Joseph grasped its significance. He was smiling quietly and dreamily to himself, with his head on one side. . . . Jacob looked timidly round the circle. It was as he expected: ten pairs of eyes were fixed wildly and importunately on him. He summoned up his powers. And sitting at the boy's back he addressed him, as harshly as he could: 'Yehosiph! What sort of dream is this thou hast dreamed, and how couldst thou dream so unsavoury a thing and tell it unto us? . . .' "

This, Mann tells us, is how it happened, and we are sure that he is right. He is also right when he interprets at some length that significant sentence in the Text: "But the father kept his saying in mind." For after rebuking Joseph "as harshly as he could," Jacob, we are told by Mann, gave free rein to quite other thoughts as he walked home alone: "The reproof had cost him much to utter; he only hoped that it had satisfied the brethren. If any real anger had spoken in it, that could be only on the score that the lad had not told the dream to him alone, instead of being so mad as to make the brethren witness of the telling. . . . Probably he [Jacob] understood how shrewdly Joseph had used the brothers as protection against himself, and himself as protection against the brothers. For he even suppressed a smile in his beard, as he went homewards, over the cleverness of this double-dealing. . . . Quite absurdly, he prayed God that the dream might have come from Him—which

307

was utter nonsense, seeing how unlikely it was that He had had anything to do with it. And tears of sheer tenderness came into his eyes at the thought that his son's innocent prattle might represent, though vaguely and uncomprehendingly, actual premonitions of future greatness. Ah, poor weak father-heart! He might well have been angry to hear that he and the brethren would come to bow down before the good-for-nothing—that was perplexing for him to hear, for did he not adore him?"

Thomas Mann does at least deal more justly with Joseph's brothers than their father did. He does at least confront us sternly with their suffering, not only here but, even more powerfully, when he describes their ghastly, tormented condition at Dothan, whither they have removed themselves with the flock to be away from the little sneak and the doting father. It is there, at Dothan, that Joseph visits them, flaunting his coat of many colors; and it is there that they throw themselves on him, bash him into unconsciousness, rip his coat to pieces, and throw him into the pit. By that relentless portrayal of the intolerable provocation Mann honorably vindicates the brothers, in so far as they can be vindicated. Yes, he even enlists Joseph himself in the vindication. For when Joseph is lying in the pit, starving, smeared in his own filth, hopeless of rescue, reconciled to death, he realizes what he has done to the brothers. And to the old merchant who finally rescues him and takes him down to Egypt to sell him, he describes his own transgression (Mann tells us) in these words: "It was culpable, and is named confidence. Criminal con-

308

fidence and blind, unreasoning presumption, that is its name. For it is blind and deadly to test men beyond their strength and require of them what they neither will hear nor can. Before such love and respect their gall runneth over and they become like ravening beasts. . . . But I did not know or I flung it to the winds, so that I did not hold my tongue and told them my dreams, in order that they might marvel at me. . . ."

### III

What remains now of my complaint that Thomas Mann is as sinful as Jacob in his preference for Joseph? Does it not appear—and did I not in fact admit—that Mann deals more justly with the brothers than Jacob did? More justly only in one sense. In another sense, no; for Thomas Mann has subtler instruments of analysis at his disposal than Jacob had. I have more to say about the phrase "innocent prattle," with which Jacob described Joseph's wild boasting without drawing a comment from Thomas Mann. "Unlicked cub" and "innocent prattle"—they go together, they link Mann to Jacob; and they also linked the brothers in bitterness and hatred. To get the full weight of my charge against Mann we must go to the end of the story, pausing first for a brief, partial comment on Joseph's character as I see it.

To Joseph had been granted, side by side with stupendous practical abilities, the unanalyzable and fatal gift of personal magnetism. He had that mysterious power to bewitch or to wound, which in contact with others gave him that advantage in the psychic field which a Samson has in the physical. The possession of either kind of strength is of course accompanied by the overwhelming need to make use of it. When not absorbed in a task, a strong man likes to throw people around, in playful exhibitionistic roughhousing or in brutal bullying, according to his character. Joseph had to do things with individuals; in the excess of his magnetic energy he could not leave them alone, he could not let a relationship spring up tacitly and naturally. He had to dictate it. If he could not force liking, he would force dislike.

He played with individuals. Individuals were to him material for psychic exercise, therefore material for dramatic exploitation and the enhancement of his personality. He was an actor who always had to "upstage" his fellow actors, and he expected them to like it.

This side of him was offset by an equally great endowment as a manipulator of public affairs. But there the exercise of his powers was directed not primarily at personal aggrandizement and self-inflation, but at the satisfaction of his craftsmanship. He was farsighted and responsible in public service, blind and reckless in private relations. Unfortunately his private relations had some bearing on his public service where his own people was concerned. There the two could not be kept apart, for we must remember that we are again standing very close to the sources of the folk, and individuals carried enormous loads of historic responsibility.

When a man plays with people he becomes a "player" in the old sense of the word, an actor and actor-manager.

Assigned a destiny, he tries to make "good theater" out of it, squeeze from it the maximum of histrionic effect. And he does it "harmlessly." He does not mean to slight the others, that is what we say; and that is what "innocent prattle" implies here.

But is that true? Does any man ever boast without the intention to make his listeners feel inferior? Or make an insulting remark without intention to wound? Of course if he is a "goodhearted" person he will want them to *like* the feeling of inferiority, and to smile away the pain of the wound. He will, in fact, want it both ways, for that surely is the maximum of power over others.

Had Joseph been seven years old instead of seventeen when he goaded his brothers into madness we still would be disturbed by that phrase "innocent prattle." I have known people to laugh at Saint Augustine because as a grown man he wept bitterly over the recollection of a childish sin. Once at the age of seven or so he had stolen some pears from an orchard, and in later years, analyzing himself, he discovered that he.had not stolen the pears because he wanted to eat them; that would have troubled him little. He had stolen them because he had wanted to steal. And he recognized in that early aberration the true willfulness and—fundamentally—the incomprehensibility of sin. The child that seeks to wound, by boasting or by insult, is, to put it mildly, in a bad way. It is already grown up in wickedness. It has the technique upon which the grown-up will improve only superficially. Its prattle is no more innocent than the drive of the power-maniac who must wring his applause from his fellow men at any cost in oppression and blood-

311

shed. And Joseph is not seven years old when the story opens; he is seventeen.

## IV

We leap over for a while to the closing acts of the Joseph drama. Many years have gone by. Joseph has become governor of Egypt, and his brothers come before him out of famine-stricken Canaan to buy corn. They do not recognize him, for the boy of seventeen is now in his fortieth year, and he is in Egyptian garb; he is, moreover, surrounded by the pomp in which important people conceal themselves.

And how does Joseph behave toward his brothers? He responds at once to the obvious, irresistible dramatic suggestiveness of the situation. You can almost hear him say to himself: "This is too good to pass up!" And: "This was tailor-made for me." And he enacts those famous scenes which even orthodox Jewish children, as unfamiliar with the stage as their teachers, have found to be a "natural" and have been re-enacting for hundreds of years. Joseph's treatment of his brothers at the reunion is perhaps the key to the meaning of the Joseph story; but though Mann has much to say, in his most fascinating vein, about the reunion, its bearing on the deeper meaning of Joseph's life is not hinted at.

Let us turn to the Text. We read that when the brothers appeared before Joseph in Egypt: "He made himself strange to them, and spoke roughly with them. . . ." Not because he harbored any resentment. He had never hated them; and he knew by now that everything had been for the best. Everything: the bashing he got at their hands, the tearing up of his beloved coat of many colors, the selling of him to the wandering merchants who had pulled him out of the pit—everything had served his destiny. But he makes this explanation to the brothers only after he has had his "innocent" little bit of fun at their expense, has tormented and frightened them, and reduced them more than once to utter despair; after he has jeopardized the life of Benjamin, the youngest of the brothers, and even of old Jacob in Canaan.

Yes, it is quite fantastic. Mann invents a plausible scene earlier in the story. He tells us how, on the day of the brothers' revenge, Joseph overhears them plotting to report his death to their father. They will dip the torn coat of many colors in the blood of a kid and present it to Jacob, to make him believe that Joseph has been eaten by a wild beast. And Joseph, though he is himself done for, as he thinks, though he has no chance to live, pleads with his brothers for the old man. They must not do this thing. It will kill Jacob. And this thoughtfulness for his father is, under the circumstances, most creditable to young Joseph. But twenty-two years later, when he is thirty-nine, and the brothers, aging and troubled men, stand before him, or rather lie prostrate before him in their need and their father's need, he holds up relief twice, and twice subjects old Jacob in far-off Canaan to cruel strains which might easily have killed him. All in order that he might play out the irresistible game to the end. And all this Thomas Mann recounts with his own Joseph-like charm as if it were again nothing but innocent prattle, whereas to the serious observer it is a frightful instance of destructive infantilism destined to bear tragic fruit.

This is such a serious matter that we must go over the ground most carefully.

"He made himself strange unto them, and spoke roughly with them." So the Text reads. He accused them of being spies. He watched their consternation and he toyed with it, while they, poor devils, stammered their protests at this unbelievable turn of events, and argued and argued with him, to no effect of course. It was like arguing with a lunatic—an omnipotent lunatic. They thought of their families at home, their wives and their little ones, and old Jacob—very old by now—waiting for bread. And here was this mad governor of Egypt.

They said: "Nay, my lord, but to buy food are thy servants come. . . . We are upright men. . . . We thy servants are twelve brethren, the sons of one man in Canaan; and, behold, the youngest is this day with our father, and one is not." How deep their perplexity was, what kind of terror they were sweating out, we gauge from the fact that they brought up everything before this governor—including the memory of the brother they had sold into slavery twenty-two years before. "As Pharaoh liveth, surely ye are spies," repeated the governor—forswearing himself. And he had them locked up for three days.

The Text does not tell us what he, and they, were thinking about during those three days, but it is not hard to guess from the subsequent conversation. Joseph, as Mann sees it—and I with him—was working on "the play"; he was mulling over various ideas for the maxi-

mum of good theater, the most effective way of prolong-
ing and heightening the suspense. And the brothers, having once brought up at the audience the subject of the
long-forgotten Joseph, were pondering their far-off miserable crime. For my part, I believe with the Tradition
that they had talked about Joseph even on their way
down into Egypt. The Tradition tells that they had
meant to look for him, knowing the direction taken by
the merchant to whom they had sold him. They were
prepared to find him in want and misery; they intended
to seek him even in brothels, say the rabbis. Once more
the Tradition is psychologically sound. The brothers remembered Joseph's beauty, and they had believed him
to have been fundamentally little more than a vicious
good-for-nothing. Put the two together and where would
they lead you? Nevertheless they wanted to find him
and rescue him, at whatever risk to their relations with
their father, who would thus learn the truth about Joseph's "death." Let us make the worst of it and assume
that they were also pleased by the thought that they
would be his saviors instead of he theirs, that they would
pick up out of the gutter him who had once thought to
lord it over them. Even so, how much better they come
off than Joseph, holding up as he was, for his histrionic
pleasure, the supplies for the starving families in Canaan!

On the fourth day he admitted them again to audience, and said: "This do, and live; for I fear God: if ye
be upright men, let one of your brethren be bound in
your prisonhouse; but go ye, carry corn for the famine
of your houses; and bring your youngest brother unto

315

me; so shall your words be verified, and ye shall not die."

He spoke through an interpreter, pretending not to know their language; but he overheard them as they muttered frantically among themselves. They were still carrying on the fierce argument of the last three days. They said to each other: "We are verily guilty concerning our brother, in that we saw the distress of his soul, when he besought us, and we would not hear." And Reuben, who had been the least vengeful of the brothers, and who had prevented the others from murdering Joseph on that fateful day in Dothan; Reuben, who, according to the Text, had said: "Shed no blood, cast him into the pit which is in the wilderness, but lay no hand upon him"; Reuben now kept reiterating his past innocence, or comparative innocence, as though appealing on his merit to God Himself. "Spoke I not," he interposed in the hurried conference, with Joseph an unsuspected eavesdropper, "spoke I not unto you saying: 'Do not sin against the child'?" It was a terrific scene of course, in the magnificent Egyptian hall. Joseph himself could not stand it. He broke down in the middle; he had to run off stage—that is, out of the hall—to weep in the wings. But he wiped his eyes, returned, and took up the role with renewed zest.

He, for his part, had put the three-day interval to excellent use and now had the dramatic development under control, with many ingenious turns and twists. He would release the brothers—all except one—and send them back with provisions for the starving families. Then they were to return to Egypt later for the hostage,

316

who happened to be Simeon, the eldest, and they would bring with them Benjamin, the youngest, to whom old Jacob had transferred some of the blind love he had felt for Joseph. But just to make things more interesting Joseph instructed his steward to return each man's purchase money, not openly, but by concealing it in the sacks. Was not that a clever touch? The brothers would be utterly bewildered. And so we read how the brothers discovered the money in the sacks when they were already on the road: "And their heart failed them, and they turned trembling to one another, saying: 'What is this that God hath done unto us?' And they came unto Jacob their father unto the land of Canaan, and told him all that had befallen them."

It hurts us to think of Jacob's consternation and terror. He was a very old man. He said of himself, perhaps with a little exaggeration, that he had reached his hundred and thirtieth year. "Few and evil have been the days of the years of my life," he told Pharaoh shortly afterwards, "and they have not attained unto the days of the years of the life of my fathers in the days of their sojournings." For the moment he is in Canaan, the land smitten with famine, hungering with his children and grandchildren and great-grandchildren; and the nine brothers return, with food, but without Simeon the eldest, and with a demand for Benjamin the youngest.

A cry of despair bursts from Jacob's lips: "Me ye have bereaved of my children: Joseph is not, and Simeon is not, and ye will take Benjamin away; upon me are all these things come." These are strange as well as bitter words. "Me have ye bereaved of my children. . . ." I

find everyone, including Mann, surmising that somewhere, in an obscure, self-concealing part of him, Jacob
knew that the brothers were responsible for Joseph's dis-
appearance; and he did not quite grasp the terrible
thing he was saying. But the words are strange only in
the sense that the ways of the mind are strange, even
when known. What Jacob really meant to say, or would
have said he meant, if he had been challenged, was this:
"You're always coming back one short. I sent Joseph to
you in Dothan, you came back without him. I sent
Simeon with you to Egypt, you have come back without
him." Twice is not always, we know; but when two out
of twelve children in a family die of the same disease,
what do the parents begin to think?

Then Reuben made an utterly ridiculous suggestion.
He would guarantee, he said, Benjamin's safety. How?
"Thou shalt slay my two sons if I bring him [Benjamin]
not to thee; deliver him into my hand, and I will bring
him back to thee." Utterly ridiculous, were it not that
we catch a glimpse of the desperate straits of the clan—
while Joseph is rubbing his hands in artistic satisfaction
in Egypt. We read on:

"And the famine was sore in the land. And it came to
pass, when they had eaten up the corn which they had
brought out of Egypt, that their father said unto them:
'Go again, buy us a little food.' " He had waited perhaps
for a miracle. He had been remembering God's promises, and particularly the one at Luz: "Thy seed shall be
as the dust of the earth. . . . And I am with thee and
will keep thee whithersoever thou goest; for I will not
leave thee until I have done that which I have spoken

318

to thee of." He waited while the supplies dwindled, and the daily ration was cut down, and the cries of the children rang through the settlement: "Mummy, I'm hungry," mingled with the wilder, more inarticulate but less bearable crying of the tiny ones who clung desperately to deceptive breasts. He could not understand. No doubt salvation would come in the end, but if his seed was to be as the dust of the earth, why was he losing his sons one by one? Was that how God intended to do it, through his agony, for the greater display of His miraculous powers? Was the old story of the rejection of the many to be repeated, but in lingering form? How could he bear it?

In the end he had to say: "Go again, buy us a little food." He knew what the answer would be. It came from Judah: "The man did earnestly forewarn us, saying: 'Ye shall not see my face except your brother be with you.'" And Jacob had his own futile, heartbreaking response ready: "Wherefore dealt ye so ill with me, as to tell the man whether ye yet had a brother?" And Judah answered miserably that there had been no reason not to tell. How could they have suspected it would turn out thus? "The man asked straitly concerning ourselves, and concerning our kindred. . . ." It had all been simple and aboveboard. Thus it is that we stand around confronting a calamity, and go over the details of the irreparable past—if we hadn't done this, or said that, as if it would have helped in the slightest! As if the implacably playful Joseph, for instance, would have been deflected from his game by this or that remark, this or that omission, on the part of the brothers.

The argument between Jacob and his sons became acrimonious. Judah offered a personal guarantee for Benjamin's safe return, as Reuben had done, and added the nasty, unnecessary comment, so obvious as to be infuriating: "Except we had lingered, surely we had returned a second time. . . ." We could have been back by now, and the children would not be wailing for bread, and it's all because of your obstinacy, and so on, and so on.

And they went away again, the nine, taking with them Benjamin, the tenth; and Jacob was left there without a single son, not one out of the twelve—the loneliest and most tragic figure imaginable. They took with them such presents as the time afforded, and double money, to return the original amounts and to pay for the new supplies. And they set forth across the southern desert, a two- or three-week journey. They pressed forward, calculating, measuring out the supplies among themselves, thinking anxiously of the rations at home. They could be back, with luck, in four or five weeks; God grant that no one died of starvation in between. And they came at last into Joseph's presence.

If you have forgotten some details of the story, if you think that Joseph is now satisfied, that having had his innocent little revenge, he calls the shocking comedy off, then you do not know your man. The actor has an insatiable appetite for encores, especially if he is acting out himself. Joseph practically repeats the first act, with Benjamin now in the cast. The details vary a little, the spirit and technique are the same; and Joseph weeps again, and again enjoys his tears.

They stand before him, and their first thought is of course to return the money they had found in their sacks. They could not explain it; they could only offer it again, together with money for the new purchases. Not at all, says the governor of Egypt: "Peace be to you, fear not; your God, and the God of your father, hath given you treasure in your sacks; I had your money." And forthwith he produces Simeon, all unharmed, gives orders to have their beasts looked after, and invites them to a noon banquet in his residence. It is wonderful!

So they came to Government House, with their presents in their hands, and they bowed as low as the ground before Joseph. We read: "And he asked them of their welfare, and said: 'Is your father well, the old man of whom you spoke?' " Well might he ask! And what a mess it would have made of his ingeniously planned performance if Jacob had died, of hunger and heartbreak. But they reassure him: "Thy servant our father is well, he is yet alive." These are striking words: "He is yet alive." But Joseph is too intent on himself to get more than their literal meaning. "And he lifted up his eyes, and saw Benjamin, his mother's son, and said: 'Is this your youngest brother of whom ye spoke to me?' And he said: 'God be gracious unto thee, my son.' And Joseph made haste; for his heart yearned toward his brother; and he sought where to weep; and he entered into his chamber, and wept there. And he washed his face, and came out; and he refrained himself, and said: 'Set on bread.' "

"Refrained himself" is very good. He did not send out Egypt's swiftest camels with orders to ride relays day and night on the Imperial roads to bring provisions to his father. He did not reveal himself to his brothers. He refrained himself. The brothers feasted with him, "and they drank, and were merry with him." I take it that "merry" is ironical; or half ironical. It is not likely that they enjoyed stuffing themselves, and guzzling Egyptian wine, at that particular moment. But it was an immense relief to be received with such friendship, astonished though they must have been. Joseph certainly wanted them to be merry, to believe that all their troubles were over. That was what made his next trick so frightfully amusing. It was the first trick, with a new twist. Once more the brothers' sacks were filled to bursting, and once more their purchase money was surreptitiously returned, hidden among the provisions, by the steward; but for variation Joseph's silver goblet, his "divining cup," was shoved into Benjamin's sack.

They left at dawn, eager to get back with the good news and the good food. One can imagine their joy, their gratitude, and their impatience. Not a bad fellow, that governor, even if a little *meshugga*. (Do not start, dear reader; the word has good Biblical warrant.) It had all been a stupid mistake, probably the work of an over-zealous member of the Egyptian Intelligence. The governor had made decent amends, he had entertained them at a great if—for them—somewhat untimely banquet. And now . . . but as they talked thus, urging their beasts forward, the steward and his posse overtook them.

This is another part of the Text which I always read hurriedly: how the steward accuses the brothers of having stolen Joseph's silver cup; how they deny it, with

the suspicious vehemence of the innocent, and declare
that if it be found with one of them, that one shall be
put to death, while the remainder of them shall become
slaves; how the goblet is found in the last sack examined,
Benjamin's; and how they rend their clothes and are led
back to the city. I read hastily out of shame for Joseph
as well as out of distress for the brothers. Still, I read. It
is not permissible to avert one's eyes from the unpleasant; but this wantonness of Joseph's, this frivolity, this
cruelty, is particularly embarrassing.

It is no use asking me not to be stuffy, and to have a
sense of humor. I just do not like this kind of fun. Nor
do I like to see audiences at Joseph plays having a good
time identifying themselves with Joseph, and shrugging
it off afterwards, saying that the brothers didn't really
mind, and weren't really suffering. I may have something of a complex on the subject. I remember that at
my high school there was a big, redheaded boy who, for
reasons never made clear to me, found much pleasure in
bullying me "good-humoredly," but with considerable
vigor, and making two of my boyhood years miserable.
We met afterwards when we were young men, and to my
astonishment he shook my hand with genuine affection,
slapped me on the back, and referred sentimentally
to our happy innocent school-days together. It dumb-
founded me to realize that I was one of his pleasantest
boyhood memories; and it would have been impossible
to explain that he was far from that to me without making myself out to be a humorless idiot. If I have a complex on the subject it is a useful one.

No, I cannot share Joseph's "good-humored kidding"

323

of his brothers. I keep thinking of them as real persons, as men and fathers. I think of their despair at this moment, and wonder that they did not turn on Benjamin and do worse to him than they had done to Joseph at Dothan; and perhaps only the presence of the Egyptian police held them back. They returned to the city, their hearts dead within them, to play their parts in the last tremendous scene which Joseph had prepared, so that he might wring the last delicious drops out of the situation.

Once again they lie before him on the ground, this time in the garments they have torn in their lamentation, symbols of the ripped-up coat of many colors. "What deed is this ye have done?" he asks. And now the brothers know definitely that they are expiating their crime against Joseph, and they believe all is lost. Judah says: "God hath found out the iniquity of thy servants; behold, we are my lord's bondmen, both we, and he also in whose hand the cup is found." Then Joseph magnanimously offers them the impossible, namely, that he keep the thief, Benjamin, but release the others: "As for you, get you up in peace unto your father"—the very condition that would most certainly mean the death of Jacob, as Judah explains in his magnificent speech.

And at last it all comes out. Joseph cannot "refrain himself" any longer. He orders all the Egyptians from the hall and declares himself to his brothers. He says: "Be not grieved, nor angry with yourselves, that ye sold me hither; for God did send me before you to preserve life. . . . Hasten ye, and go up to my father, and say to him: 'Thus saith thy son Joseph: "God hath made me lord of all Egypt; come down unto me, tarry not."' . . .

And ye shall tell my father of all my glory in Egypt."
And with that: "He fell upon his brother Benjamin's
neck. And he kissed all his brethren, and wept upon
them; and after that his brethren talked with him."

"Come down unto me," is his message to his father.
"Tarry not!" All of a sudden he is in a tremendous
hurry. The old man might die after all, and he would be
robbed of the climax to the climax. To the brothers, too,
he says: "Hasten ye!" And his last instruction to them is:
"See that ye fall not out by the way." That is just a face-
tious touch—they have nothing more to quarrel about.
They have only to move fast.

I cannot see eye to eye with Thomas Mann when he
describes in beautifully embroidered detail how the sons
broke the news to Jacob, with cautious hint, and delay-
ing parable, and the music of the little singing maid. It
is great writing but, I fear, misleading invention. For,
to begin with, Mann seems to have forgotten that everyone was frightfully hungry; the encampment was in a
half stupor of starvation. "The famine was sore in the
land," and: "They had eaten up all the corn which they
had brought out of Egypt"—even before the brothers
set out on their long second journey. Moreover, the
eleven brothers were not diplomats and psychologists,
and the pressure, from within and from Joseph, was too
much even for ordinary common sense. Here is how the
Text reads: "And they went up out of Egypt, and came
into the land of Canaan unto Jacob their father. And
they told him, saying: 'Joseph is yet alive, and he is ruler
over the land of Egypt.' And his heart fainted, for he believed them not." What does the narrator mean to tell us

here? Thomas Mann assumes, as everyone else seems to do, that Jacob fainted with the pain of his joy. But "if he believed them not" why should he have fainted with joy? The narrator is driving at something else. *Jacob did not believe that Joseph could have behaved with such savagery toward himself and toward his brothers.* That is the shocking point, and I insist that we have here the most damning comment in the story.

Then we read: "And they told him all the words of Joseph, which he had said unto them; and when he saw the wagons which Joseph had sent to carry him, the spirit of Jacob their father revived. And Jacob said: 'It is enough; Joseph my son is yet alive; I will go down and see him before I die.'"

"It is enough." The wagons convince him that the "ruler over the land of Egypt," the cold jester who had said: "Ye shall not see my face except your brother be with you," has decided to end the cat-and-mouse game, and the Joseph of old, the Joseph the father believed in, is yet alive. It is enough, and more than enough. Nothing matters but that Joseph is alive; and the old man prepares for the last journey of his long life.

v

I have given the beginning and the end of the Joseph story, in order to set up what I think is the right moral perspective: not quite the end, however, for there is an epilogue which, morally and psychologically, is perhaps the most instructive part of all. But now we must turn

326

to Joseph in Potiphar's house, and his public career after his imprisonment.

The affair with Potiphar's wife, Mut-em-enet, as Thomas Mann names her, is another instance of Joseph's irrepressible need to play up to a situation. Mann has expanded the brief record into a love tragedy of unparalleled insight and power. Once again Mann dilates frankly on Joseph's culpability, which is indeed shockingly manifest. But he traces it to a more respectable source than I will allow. He finds adventure there, and a genuine emotion, whereas I find only irresponsible exploitation of suffering for dramatic effect.

Joseph began in Lord Potiphar's house as an obscure, foreign-born slave-boy of seventeen, and ended up, at twenty-eight, as the solidly established overseer of the great feudal estate. His descent, however, was much faster than his rise: he was accused by his mistress, the Lady Mut-em-enet, of attempting to rape her; and he was cast into prison; the truth being, however, that it was she who had attempted the rape, and had failed.

That the business was not so simple the Text itself intimates, for it begins the Mut-em-enet story with these words: "And it came to pass after these things, that his master's wife cast her eyes upon Joseph; and she said: 'Lie with me.'" We must remain forever grateful to Thomas Mann for his masterly expansion of the Bible's brusque "after these things" into the full scroll of the woman's fall and Joseph's complicity. Mut-em-enet was no wanton, and no nymphomaniac driven helplessly to snatch at every man within reach. She was a great lady.

327

She was a dedicated person, even as her husband, the eunuch, was. Her passion for Joseph was not a sudden and furious flare-up of lust, already sated a hundred times indiscriminately and still insatiable. It grew slowly, and it came into the open only "after these things"—these developments which Mann exhumes with the painstaking scrupulousness of a psychologist-archæologist. And long before it came into the open Joseph was aware of it, and went through the gesture of discouraging it.

Yes, we agree that Joseph tried to dissuade Mut-em-enet from loving him; and we also agree that his efforts—except at the very end, when the avalanche had already been set in motion—were hypocritical. He saw what was coming, and he refused to see it; he knew what the result would be, and he refused to know it. It is the replica of the attitude toward his brothers; and his first confession would have done just as well for his second sin: "I did not know, or flung it to the winds." In Potiphar's house there was only one thing for him to do: get out, whatever the consequences to his career. It would have meant disaster, but nothing worse than what he courted by remaining, and what he actually got. The trouble was that he could not resist the role.

And what was the role that Joseph was now working for all it was worth? It was that of the little immigrant boy who had made good, and with whom the wife of his employer was falling in love. It would make us feel better if we thought that a true emotional response, even though soaked in gratified vanity, was forthcoming in Joseph, and that he had to struggle against it, struggle,

328

that is to say, with the very demon who was assailing Mut-em-enet. The Text, however, does not warrant such a deduction, and Mann himself does not make it, except at the very end, and fleetingly, when Mut-em-enet threw herself on Joseph and his flesh "stood up against him." Concerning Mut-em-enet's growing passion, and her struggle against it, Mann writes: "To delude oneself up to the point where it is too late to turn back—that one must do at all costs. To be awakened, warned, called back to oneself before it is too late; there lies the danger which is at all costs to be avoided." He makes it seem that the words apply to Joseph, too, except that in Joseph it was not lust but a spirit of adventure. This is the implication which I will not allow.

Joseph was neither the lover nor the adventurer. He was, in this matter, the actor. He saw, with his perfect flair for the dramatic, that if he yielded to Mut-em-enet, he would be reducing himself to the commonplace; the play would become run of the mill And of course he felt no desire for the woman. She was material for the exercise of his gifts.

Let us ponder the Text. We read, after Mut-em-enet's desperate demand: "But he refused and said unto his master's wife: 'Behold, my master, having me, knoweth not what is in the house; he is not greater in this house than I; neither hath he kept anything back from me but thee, because thou art his wife. How then can I do this great wickedness, and sin against God?' "

It is a self-righteous and a provocative speech. He dwells on his master's helplessness and unsuspiciousness. Does he have to emphasize the fact that he could assuage

329

her need safely if he wanted to? "He knoweth not what is in the house. . . ." He made this speech not once, but many times, for we read: "And it came to pass, as she spoke to Joseph day by day, that he hearkened not unto her, to lie by her, or to be with her." Day by day, then, he flaunted his success, his control of the situation, his mastery of himself—so easy when there was no desire to master—until the maddened woman actually assaulted him, and came as near success as it was possible for her to come; that is to say, she forced the issue, to her undoing, and Joseph's. She committed the crime, and it was Joseph who was cast into prison.

Thus on the surface. In reality it was Joseph who forced the issue, as he had done in his boyhood with his brothers, forced it steadily day by day, until the explosion came. In those days he had played with his brothers' hatred; now he toyed with a woman's love. In both instances he was the active agent, and set the pattern; and to make this clear, in both instances he had his coat torn off him—in a kind of unmasking—and was thrown into the pit.

## VI

Now, armed against Joseph's wiles—and Thomas Mann's—we turn to the most outstanding worldly career in the Bible.

How worldly it was, despite the divine planning that went into it, is at once evident from the curious fact— nowhere pointed out as far as I know—that God never once appears to Joseph, not even in a dream, and he *the* man of dreams. No one else in the Bible takes up so much space, and plays so important a part, without direct communication from God. Certainly Joseph is very conscious of God, and speaks of Him the way all successful men do. They feel the need to propitiate Him; also to warn off competitors: "God is with me." Joseph has every right to say that. We read of him in Potiphar's house: "And the Lord was with Joseph, and he was a prosperous man. . . . And his master saw that the Lord was with him." Also in prison: "The Lord was with Joseph, and showed kindness unto him, and gave him favour in the eyes of the keeper of the prison." Joseph makes frequent acknowledgment of God. He says to Mut-em-enet: "How can I sin against God?" When Pharaoh's butler and baker, in prison, ask him to interpret their dreams, he answers: "Do not interpretations belong to God? Tell it me, I pray you." When his sons are born during the years of plenty in Egypt he names them Manasseh and Ephraim: "For God hath made me forget all my toil and all my father's house"; and: "For God hath made me fruitful in the land of my affliction." To his brothers, as we have seen, when he bids them bring Benjamin to him: "This do, and live; for I fear God"; and again, when he reassures them of his goodwill: "Be not grieved, nor angry with yourselves, that ye sold me hither; for God did send me before you to preserve life." He is always talking about God, and yet never receives from Him a single direct communication.

As if to emphasize this unique reticence, God addresses Himself to old Jacob-Israel on his way down to Egypt, to meet Joseph. "And Israel took his journey with all that he had, and came to Beersheba, and offered sacri-

fice unto the God of his father Isaac. And God spoke to
Israel in the vision of the night, and said: 'I am God, the
God of thy father; fear not to go down into Egypt, for I
will there make of thee a great nation. . . .' " The last
time God had spoken to a human being was far back at
the beginning of the Joseph story; and then it was also
to Jacob, when he returned from Laban's country. The
immense gap arrests our attention, as it was meant to do.

Worldly, again, is the proper description of the man
who never once in his tumultuous career addresses himself to God in prayer or meditation. Joseph, the son of
Jacob, the grandson of Isaac, the great-grandson of Abraham, does not open his heart to God from the pit, or
in prison. His humblest supplication and his saddest
plaint is addressed to—of all persons—a butler, Pharaoh's disgraced butler, whom he meets in prison and
whose dream he interprets favorably, foretelling his pardon. "Have me in thy remembrance when it shall be
well with thee," he pleads, "and show kindness, I pray
thee, and make mention of me unto Pharaoh, and bring
me out of this house. For indeed I was stolen away out
of the land of the Hebrews; and here also have I done
nothing that they should put me into prison."

A sad speech, with its total denial of guilt, regarding
both his brothers and Mut-em-enet. It is the time of
Joseph's greatest adversity, for he has by now known
worldly power, and has lost it. It makes us uncomfortable to think of him paying court to a butler in such
lachrymose phrases. No ordinary butler, to be sure, as
Mann reminds us, but the Pharaoh's Cup-Bearer, a distinguished official, and a former power in the land. But

these, the humblest and most nearly broken-spirited
words Joseph ever uttered, should have been addressed
to a Higher Power, and with more honesty. I say
"should" from the point of view of Joseph's ultimate
fatal defect, and not from the point of view of his
character, with its worldly greatness and its poverty in
other-worldly elements. Joseph was a God-helps-those-
who-help-themselves man. Here was the butler, a provi-
dential opportunity to enlist the goodwill of a member
of the Imperial household. It was in Joseph's nature to
petition the man direct, rather than via God; and the
move was of course successful. Not that the reinstated
Chief Cup-Bearer had him in remembrance out of gratitude. That is not the way worldly relations work. He forgot all about Joseph, and all about that unpleasant time.
But God having sent the perplexing and oppressive
dreams to Pharaoh, the Cup-Bearer did himself a good
turn in recommending to Pharaoh's attention Joseph's
uncanny skill as an interpreter of dreams

Thomas Mann admonishes us against thinking of Joseph as a schemer and timeserver, with an eye always on
the main chance. That is well said. Joseph schemed for
the exercise of his compulsions, which on the private
side were disastrous, and on the public side beneficent.
But on his Egyptian side too there was close interplay
between his virtues and his deficiencies. Joseph was a
great and faithful servant of the high-placed He had a
singular capacity for relieving his employers of the burdens of responsibility. But he never tried to displace
them He was always a steward; he never operated as the
titular master. And this must have been a frustration for

which he compensated by an increase of secret pride. We read that "Potiphar left all that he had in Joseph's hand, and, having him, he knew not aught save the bread which he did eat." Also: "And the keeper of the prison looked not to anything that was under his hand, because the Lord was with Joseph; and that which he did, the Lord made it to prosper." Further: "And Pharaoh said unto Joseph: 'Forasmuch as God hath shown thee all this . . . thou shalt be over my house, according to thy word shall all my people be ruled; only in the throne will I be greater than thou.' " This circumstance has its deeper meaning, too; Joseph could not aspire to that foremost place to which his abilities entitled him; and the reason is, perhaps, that he served God's purpose strictly according to the letter, and his worldly masters according to the spirit.

Two qualities were needed by this predestined right-hand man: outstanding practical ability and a responsive sense of loyalty toward those who trusted him. He was very proud of his loyalty; he dramatized it; he made speeches about it to Mut-em-enet; but it was there. He never thought of supplanting Potiphar, or the warden, or Pharaoh. I have dwelt at great length on his play-acting; we must give equal weight to his industriousness, his managerial craftsmanship, his grasp of realities, and his integrity in service. A third quality was interwoven with these by his beauty and his charm—the knack of inspiring. He could not otherwise have been the successful administrator of a vast estate, a prison, and an empire, in turn. He must have been a wonderful superior to work for. When he turned his charm on for his employers—and I do not mean that he did it craftily and cynically, he was charmed by himself, too—he was irresistible. What must have been its effect on his underlings?

He was thirty years old when he was called out of prison to take charge of Egypt. He had by then known a lifetime fullness of experience and adventure. He had touched the extremes. He had been the spoilt darling of a rich sheikh in Canaan; he had been a slave; he had managed a princely estate; he had been wooed by a lady of the nobility; he had been a convict; and he had administered a prison. His new and sudden elevation found him ready for great action.

VII

To get the measure of Joseph's statesmanship we must examine in some detail the profound and lasting changes that he brought into the social structure of Egypt. On this side—but on this side only—he was not content to discharge his life's assignment, which was simply to prevent his clan from perishing in one of those frightful famines which were—and are—the periodic scourges of the East. The fact is, as we shall have reason to note more than once, that he discharged the divine assignment formally, and so to speak dryly, adding no contribution of his own. But on his self-appointed task he expended a wealth of creative imaginativeness and a staggering industriousness. Had he applied the same prehensile insights into his relations with his brothers he might have ranked with the patriarchs. In short, he revolutionized

335

the Egyptian system of land tenure and the basis of personal law; he did not revolutionize his relations with his brothers.

For if he had been as niggardly with Egypt as he was with his family he would have stopped after making the agricultural forecast for the next fourteen years after Pharaoh's dreams, leaving the execution of the necessary measures to others; or, even taking over the direction of affairs, he would merely have made sure that the excess production of the first seven years was properly spread over the second seven years. He went, as we know, much farther.

It is for social theorists to determine whether Joseph's policy, which he carried out with ruthless determination, represented in that time and place progress or reaction I examine it only to draw certain conclusions as to Joseph's character It bespeaks, first, loyalty to the crown and no doubt to the person of Pharaoh; and second, a powerful imagination linked to extraordinary willpower. We must think of certain outstanding historical figures, men who had daring, the executive ability, and the single-mindedness to revolutionize lands and empires; a Diocletian, a Peter the Great, a Kemal Atatürk. We must also take it for granted that during the seven fat years Joseph was laying the groundwork for the systematic exploitation of the seven lean years. It is unthinkable that he improvised such a transformation; unthinkable also that he left to chance the personnel with which he carried it out. Everything points to calculation, to a weighing of forces and forms and personalities, an ability to enlist the services of the right men and to put them in the right places, and therefore, of course, the parallel ability to get rid of the inefficient and the obstructive.

We read: "In the seven years of plenty the earth brought forth in heaps. And Joseph gathered up all the food of the seven years which were in the land of Egypt, and laid up the food in the cities; the food of the field, which was round about every city, laid he up in the same. And Joseph laid up corn as the sand of the sea, very much, until they left off numbering; for it was without number."

We are left to guess whether the overproduction was confiscated or paid for. It is a strong presumption that there was some compensation, over and above a high taxation; it did not have to be much in a time of excessive glut, and it was a brilliant investment in goodwill. Whatever the farmers got was in their eyes money for nothing, found money. I draw attention to Joseph's far-sightedness and long-range planning: "The food of the field, which was round about every city, laid he up in the same." We are asked to note that he did not concentrate the country's supplies in the storehouses of the capital; and at first it looks merely like a common-sense avoidance of double transportation. It was that, and it was much more. The deeper purpose of the measure is concealed for six chapters while the narrator reverts to Joseph's family history. But then we read: "As for the people, Joseph removed them city by city, from one end of the border of Egypt even to the other end thereof." Now we understand.

In order to break up the hold of the local barons and

moneylenders on the mass of the population, it was necessary to break up ancient associations rooted in local soil. It was immensely helpful, too, that when the grain was being doled out in the famine days, the applicants should not be getting back at a high price the very produce which they had been glad to sell for a trifle in the fat days. A central treasury, besides being wasteful of transportation, would not have had the same psychological effect; the people would have remembered that their grain had gone into the general supply. And so, since Joseph intended to redistribute the people later, it was a brilliant idea to leave the supplies where they were.

The breakup of the old associations and the new centralization of power went on by planned and logical stages during the famine years. "And Joseph gathered up all the money that was in the land of Egypt, and in the land of Canaan, for the corn which they bought; and Joseph brought the money into Pharaoh's house." In the second stage the Canaanites dropped out of the picture; they were not part of the larger plan. "When all the money was spent in the land of Egypt and the land of Canaan, all the Egyptians came unto Joseph, and said: 'Give us bread; for why should we die in thy presence? For our money faileth.' And Joseph said: 'Give your cattle, and I will give you money for your cattle, if money fail . . .' and he fed them with bread in exchange for all their cattle for that year." The following year they came again: "We will not hide from my lord, how that our money is all spent; and the herds of cattle are my lord's; there is nought left in the sight of my lord but our bodies and our lands. Wherefore should we die

338

before thine eyes, both we and the land? Buy us and our land for bread, and we and our land will be bondmen unto Pharaoh; and give us seed that we may live, and not die, and that the land be not desolate." The livestock had become crown property; it does not mean, it cannot mean, that the herds were driven off into government enclosures. That would have been a senseless act. They remained where they were, but the title had passed to the crown. And then we read: "So Joseph bought all the land for Pharaoh . . . and the land became Pharaoh's."

It was at this stage, when he had changed the basis of property relations and of civic status, when he had made the Egyptians aware that they owed their lives to the foresight and efficiency of the central government, that Joseph began the mass transfers of the population. "Joseph said unto the people: 'Behold, I have bought you this day and your land for Pharaoh. Lo, here is seed for you, and ye shall sow the land. And it shall come to pass at the ingathering, that ye shall give a fifth unto Pharaoh, and four parts of it shall be your own, for seed of the field, and for your food, and for them of your households, and for food for your little ones.' And they said: 'Thou hast saved our lives. Let us find favour in the sight of my lord, and we will be Pharaoh's bondmen.' And Joseph made it a statute concerning the land of Egypt unto this day, that Pharaoh should have the fifth; only the land of the priests became not Pharaoh's."

The system that Joseph instituted lasted until the time of the Bible chronicler, who lived many centuries later. Whatever the economists and sociologists will have to say about the system, they will have to take into account the topography of Egypt, a country that could not exist without a strongly centralized government. It lives by the bounty of the Nile, it is in fact the creation of the Nile. The annual overflow of the river is the only source of irrigation in that almost rainless territory; the management of the waters, the reapportionment of the land after the landmarks were washed away annually, had to be carried out by a strong government. Some centralization there must already have been before Joseph's time; it may have disintegrated, perhaps it was never very strong. It is certain that the seven-year famine, caused by light rainfall and snowfall at the sources of the Nile, would not have been so severe if large dams had been in operation; but large dams would indicate a strong central government, which precisely was lacking.

All this Joseph had in mind when he was put, overnight as it were, in charge of the country. He had been in Egypt thirteen years. On Potiphar's estate he had come to understand the workings of the agrarian system. He had become absorbed in the life of Egypt, and his awareness of his original task—the salvation of his family—grew dim for long periods. It might be argued that he never really understood that task until the brothers appeared before him begging for bread; but we must reject this view because it runs counter to Joseph's character. He *had* to believe that some day he would vindicate himself against his brothers. The dreams of his boyhood make that clear. Also, on the other assumption, we would never be able to explain why, having become an important figure on Lord Potiphar's estate, he never

340

communicated with his family; or why, later, knowing that his brothers would have to come to him in the famine years, he did not forestall their misery by taking action during the fat years. He was waiting for them, but intermittently, with long stretches of indifference. Let us now recall the strange names he gave his two sons, born in the prosperous years. One meant: "God hath made me forget all my toil and all my father's house"; the other: "God hath made me fruitful in the land of my affliction." His mission from God lived in the interstices of his attention, which was concentrated on the welfare of his adopted country. This was what he saw predominantly as the purpose of all his experiences, and this grand panorama, now opening before him, was the fulfillment of his life. For this he had been thrown into the pit, and brought to Egypt; for this he had been thrown into prison, and brought before Pharaoh. I think of him, on the day when he was invested with the supreme power, in the terms that Winston Churchill uses of himself describing his assumption of the Prime Ministership in the Second World War: "I cannot conceal from the reader of this truthful account that as I went to bed about 3 a.m. I was conscious of a profound sense of relief. At last I had the authority to give directions over the whole scene. I felt as if I were walking with destiny, and that all my past life had been a preparation for this hour and this trial."

## VIII

Joseph came to his high and fateful position with clean hands. Whatever his errors and misdemeanors at home, and in Potiphar's house, they had nothing to do with his present elevation. He had correctly interpreted the dreams of the butler and baker in prison; he had convinced Pharaoh that the double dream of the cows and ears of corn was a message from God; he had deciphered the message and prescribed the course of action, adding: "Now let Pharaoh look out a man discreet and wise, and set him over the land of Egypt. . . ." And Pharaoh was not frightened off by the boldness of the suggestion. The history of Oriental monarchies abounds in instances of viziers deposing their masters, and here Pharaoh was being advised by a stranger, a foreigner, a jailbird, to set "someone" over the land of Egypt. We read: "And Pharaoh said unto his servants: 'Can we find such a one as this, a man in whom the spirit of God is?' " Certainly there must have been panic in the heart of Pharaoh; the forebodings of which the intense and enigmatic dreams had been a part did not disappear at once; but this fascinating stranger had lifted the weight from Pharaoh's heart by his clear interpretation. He had, in fact, already taken over. Willingly, with a vast sense of relief on his part, Pharaoh relinquished his formal powers to Joseph: "You do everything. I am in your hands."

There was no intrigue, no shouldering aside of rivals, no patient building up of connections, no manipulation of cliques, no planting of suspicions, no balancing of group against group. At a single bound Joseph rose to supreme authority. The envy of the nobility was lost in stupefaction, perhaps also in genuine admiration. A miracle!

So it was at first. But afterwards? All sorts of miracles

342

have happened in human affairs—all sorts but one: namely, the permanent miracle. "Naturally," says the reader, "the permanent miracle would be the Messianic era," and one must agree. Within a month, perhaps within a week, courtiers were rubbing their eyes, and in corners they muttered something like: "By Thoth! He certainly pulled a fast one!" The sad truth is that miracles don't wear well; they need endless patching with unmiraculous material. And perhaps as long as man is man and not his Messianic sublimation, this is as it should be. God says to man: "Here's a miracle. See what you can do with it." Man has never done much. The writer and the artist know all about miracles. Every inspiration is a miracle, and inspirations, good ideas, are not infrequent; it is the execution that is the test of the recipient; and it is a common observation that when God wants to show up a mediocrity He sends him a good idea.

Within a month, or two, or three, they were saying at court: "Yes, he's got the idea, but he's going about it the wrong way. It's ridiculous to leave the corn where it's grown, as he plans to do, instead of bringing it to the capital where we can keep an eye on it. There'll be riots in the provinces round those supplies, if the lean years come—which isn't at all certain. But even if he guessed right, he's not practical, he's not the executive type. His bookkeeping system, if you can call it that, is all wrong; it's breaking down; he hasn't the foggiest notion of the principles of accountancy. Has he ever heard of such a thing as political economy? What's his record, apart from his lucky way with dreams? All he did was man-

343

age old Potiphar's estate, and if it hadn't been for Potiphar's wife—you know her—he'd never have got that far either. At that it turned his head, and he tried to throw her over; but it didn't work. You see what I mean? He's a brilliant starter, but a poor finisher."

It was for Joseph to prove that he, no mediocrity, was worthy of the miracle; and he had to do it without any more miracles. What some courtiers meant by "keeping an eye" on the supplies we all know: graft is the only great feature of the ancient Eastern civilization which has resisted the corrosion of the centuries. But deeper than the tradition of public thievery, and crossing with it, is the struggle for power. It would have been a second miracle if Joseph, in counterplot and counterintrigue, was not compelled to hurt the innocent with the guilty; or if he could avoid lying, pretense, and betrayal. There were of course honest men who were horrified by his enactments; there were arguments of great weight against his policy of centralization; local traditions of immense antiquity, appealing to genuine pieties, were threatened with extinction by the transfers of population. Even in our own day there is division of opinion as to Joseph's policy. He is spoken of as a ruthless monopolist; he is accused of cornering the grain market; he is described as a tool of Oriental despotism, and a lackey of imperialism.

He has been called the Disraeli of the ancient world. The comparison goes much further than is usually perceived, and if it has not yet been done, someone should write two Plutarchian parallel lives of Victoria's Prime Minister and Pharaoh's vizier. There are many differences between the two men, but the similarities are astonishing. Both were brilliant, and brilliant alike in their ability to irritate and to charm. Both were "foreigners," though Disraeli was second-generation English-born. Both were democratic conservatives, concerned with the welfare of the masses as much as with the retention of the traditional authority. The two men even had, across an interval of more than three thousand years, a common bond in Egypt; Disraeli bought up the Khedive's shares in the Suez Canal in a bold and irregular maneuver and thereby determined England's Egyptian policy forever after. The two men had a peripheral interest in the people of their origin, though in different degrees—and here again I touch on Joseph's deviation from his mission; again I point out that though he was far more deeply involved than Disraeli in the fate of his people, Joseph gave his best to the country of his adoption. I emphasize "his best" as applying both to his abilities and to the proportion of his energies. I would also add that while he brought his dubious personal complexes heavily into his efforts for his people, he applied a relatively objective craftsmanship to the welfare of Egypt.

He was objective to the extent that this worldly career of his was dominated by his carefully thought-out plan for the improvement of Egypt's condition; the love of power, though of course indestructible, was subordinate to it. "All great men are bad," says Lord Acton flatly. We certainly do not know of anyone who has achieved and maintained worldly greatness without dishonesty, without letting down friends, without hitting rivals below the belt; and, above all, without instinctively weighing most persons, as and when met, for usefulness in the cause. No matter how noble the cause, this automatic reduction of human beings to functional units is of the essence of badness. No matter, too, how well subordinated the *love* of power, the *need* of it for effective worldly action is a corrupting reality which will not disappear from the human scene until the Messianic era.

We do not know in detail how Joseph managed Egyptian affairs during the seven fat years, and the seven lean years, and all the years thereafter as long as he lived. We have to assume that he schemed, manipulated, inspired, fixed, labored, in a great mixture of effective statesmanship. But this much we must say: if he let the end justify the means, the end was Egypt's welfare, and not the satisfaction of a destructive quirk in his psyche: Egypt's welfare as he saw it, to be sure, but if we disagree with his policy it is a technical, not a moral judgment.

I X

The difference between Joseph the Egyptian and Joseph the son of Israel may then be summed up thus: As an Egyptian he served the nation wholeheartedly, as a son of Israel he served his people negligently; as an Egyptian he displayed only the degree of badness which cannot be disassociated from the exercise of power; as a son of Israel he was superfluously bad; in his Egyptian dealings the bad was subordinated to the good; in his family dealings the good was subordinated to the bad. His attitude toward his family inflicted permanent damage on the psyche of the folk. That he did not understand it seems to surprise no one but me; for his lack of understanding is shared by all with whom I have discussed the matter.

I speak particularly of the reunion in Egypt, which was Joseph's great historic opportunity; for, side by side with the physical rescue, the redemption of reconciliation offered itself, only to be spurned with what I would call frivolity if the roots were not so deep and the consequences so far-reaching.

I can imagine that he said something like the following to himself: "I am entitled to this bit of fun at my brothers' expense. In justice to myself . . ." That last is the dangerous phrase. I have never heard a man say: "In justice to myself I ought to be sent to prison." It is always a mealy-mouthed phrase; as an excuse for mischief it has only one equal, perhaps its twin: "I meant no harm."

Well, what harm was there in the little comedy? *That* we shall see in a moment. Meanwhile the reader is astonished. Look what Joseph did for his people! He not only brought them down to Egypt; he exerted himself for them in every imaginable way. The Text spreads itself on his benefactions. Though his brothers were shepherds, and "every shepherd is an abomination to the Egyptians," he interceded for them, and presented five of them to Pharaoh himself. We read: "And Pharaoh spoke unto Joseph saying: 'Thy father and thy brethren are come unto thee; the land of Egypt is before them; in the best of the land make thy father and thy brethren to dwell. . . . And if thou knowest any able men among

347

them, make them rulers over my cattle.' " Further: "And Joseph placed his father and his brethren, and gave them a possession in the land of Egypt, in the land of Rameses, as Pharaoh commanded. And Joseph sustained his father, and all his father's household, with bread, according to their little ones." What more could he have done?

Nothing. There was only much that he could have left undone. As witness:

Seventeen years later, when old Jacob died, the rescued brothers drew together in fear. We read: "And when Joseph's brethren saw that their father was dead, they said: 'It may be that Joseph will hate us, and will fully requite us all the evil which we did unto him.' And they sent a message unto Joseph, saying: 'Thy father did command before he died, saying: "So shall ye say unto Joseph. 'Forgive, I pray thee now, the transgression of thy brethren, and their sin, for they did unto thee evil.' " And now, we pray thee, forgive the transgression of the servants of the God of thy father.' And Joseph wept when they spoke unto him. And his brethren also went and fell down before his feet; and they said: 'Behold, we are thy bondmen.' And Joseph said unto them: 'Fear not, for am I in the place of God? And as for you, you meant evil against me; but God meant it for good, to bring to pass, as it is in this day, to save much people alive. Now therefore fear me not, I will sustain you and your little ones.' And he comforted them, and spoke kindly unto them "

For seventeen years they lived in dread of their father's death, secure only in the thought of his presence. The reader will object: "That was not Joseph's fault;

they could not get rid of their guilt complex." Did Joseph ever try to help them? It was not a good start, even the most biased reader will admit, to have staged for the reunion in Egypt those dramatic scenes with which half the world is familiar, and in which all who know them take such delight. If their effect has persisted on a hundred generations, what must it have been on the brothers, participant-victims? Think how, through the seventeen years before their father's death—and afterwards too, in spite of Joseph's reassurance—they woke in night-sweats, reliving the accusation that they were spies, the days of imprisonment, the discovery of the money in their sacks, the horror of their return without Simeon, old Jacob's anguish, the long wait in Canaan with the dwindling rations, the return to Egypt with Benjamin, the "theft" of the goblet: reliving the sick, bewildered memory of the hungering ones at home, and the fantastic behavior of the governor of Egypt. This was what Joseph had rubbed into them, and to wash it out was now impossible. We may say, literally, that he had rubbed it into them with a vengeance.

And as for Joseph, he rid himself easily enough of *his* guilt complex. Indeed, if we examine the speech he made to the brothers after the father's death, we perceive that he no longer acknowledged—if he ever did—his responsibility in the family tragedy. "As for you," he says, "you meant evil against me; but God meant it for good." And had *he* meant it for good when he had goaded them into their murderous outbreak at Dothan, in his boyhood? Had he meant for good his histrionics in Egypt? Not a word from him to equalize their foot-

349

ing. He was the rescuer, the forgiver, the blameless one, the generous one. He wept. The way of the benefactor is hard, he reflected; beneficiaries are so touchy, especially when their consciences are not clean. "And he comforted them, and spoke kindly to them."

We are dealing here with matters which go far beyond the errors and sufferings of certain individuals, far beyond, into the past and the future of Joseph's people. He was play-acting not only with his brothers, but with the destiny of the folk of the blessing. A tradition of fratricidal strife had dominated the seed of Abraham since the time of the bond with God, an inheritance from primitive times. Here was the opportunity to bring the tradition to an end, to bury the hereditary hatchet in a magnificent act of family statesmanship. But Joseph gave all his understanding and statesmanship to Egypt; he ignored the opportunity nearer home, and confirmed the tradition of the folk division which, centuries later, under another form, led to the splitting of the kingdom.

With astonishing pointedness the great story ends where it began. So much has happened—and nothing has happened! The sheaves are bowing to Joseph, the stars are saluting him. But he and his brothers still stand apart, mistrust between them; old men, terrified, lying in the dust before the fortunate one, himself no longer young. And the father's last act—if the brothers did not in their terror make up his instructions—one of mediation after the wrong he had himself committed.

I am disturbed by the absence, in the Text, of a report of Jacob's admonition to Joseph. In so important a matter, surely the father's final warning to Joseph should have been given direct, instead of being left to the brothers to transmit. In suggesting that the brothers made it up I do not mean they invented it. They only put into words what they knew their father had wanted. They must have spoken with him more than once about the future; and perhaps Jacob even promised them that he would speak with Joseph, but could not bring himself to do it. Perhaps the subject was too painful to him because of his own share in the disastrous complex.

And since we are now closing the circle, let me once more try to justify the seriousness of my disagreement with Thomas Mann's light dismissal of Joseph's early misdemeanors. Let me recall the opening again: "Joseph, being seventeen years old, was feeding the flock with his brethren, being still a lad, even with the sons of Bilhah, and with the sons of Zilpah, his father's wives; and Joseph brought evil report of them unto their father." We may read: "being a lad" in two ways. First· "He was only a lad, after all"; that is to say, an unlicked cub, an insufferable brat, which is the way Thomas Mann prefers, though even that only for a moment. Second: "Though still only a lad he was already showing that perveisity which was to keep the family permanently divided"; which Thomas Mann will not entertain even for a moment, but which the course of events justifies.

x

When death stood at the head of Jacob's couch he called in his sons to bless them. We read: "All these are the twelve tribes of Israel, and this it is that their father

351

spoke unto them and blessed them; every one according to his blessing he blessed them." The twelve tribes of Israel; no son was to be excluded from the folkhood; and therefore it was not the Abrahamitic blessing that was involved here. As Abraham did not bless Isaac before his death because the distinguishing heritage was not in dispute, so Jacob did not have to transmit the Abrahamitic blessing. The ordinances and laws and judgments are not mentioned; the name of Abraham does not come up; the folk is already established under the sign of the founder. Only one spiritual privilege is at stake: the progenitorship of the Messiah, and on this alone Jacob must make a fundamental decision.

Thomas Mann has equated the progenitorship of the Messiah with the Abrahamitic destiny. I have tried to show that this is a basic error, the more so as in the far-off future the distinction of the tribes will be lost, and if the promise to Judah holds good we have not by now the genealogical proof. Any descendant of Israel may now hope to be in the line. Nevertheless Jacob's decision was important enough, and chiefly as his form of confession.

A confession is a decision; it is the decision to see one's past life under the aspect of truth rather than of self-serving prejudice. For more than half a century Jacob had fixed his affections preponderantly on Joseph, to the injury of his other sons. On this day of decision he renounced and denounced his weakness. Joseph would not be given the Messianic lineage. Once this was clear in Jacob's mind, the blessing of the lineage went by law to the eldest of the undisqualified sons. But the three

eldest, Reuben, Simeon, and Levi, had disqualified
themselves, and Judah was next in line.

Jacob's case bears some resemblance to his father's.
Isaac too had been forced by the thought of death to
make acknowledgment of a lifelong weakness, and to
deny the last expression to his inclination. But he had
Rebekah to help him. Jacob had no skillful and courageous wife at his side to help him carry out his decision.
He had to make the announcement, with its startling rejection of Joseph, alone and openly, in the full presence
of the twelve. If the issue was not as fateful as the primary blessing, the situation was none the less a difficult
one. The struggle of Jacob's soul is reflected in the testa-
ment.

Apart from the Messiahship the blessings were earthly
ones, part blessing, part characterization, part prophecy,
part repudiation and admonition. He called up his sons
in the order of their birth, as evidence of his objectivity;
but in the substance of the blessings he showed parti-
ality, out of confusion and distraction. To Joseph and to
Judah he gave practically as much space as to all the
other ten combined. Reuben received six pronouncements; Simeon and Levi, lumped together, ten between
them; Zebulun three; Issachar six, Dan seven; Gad,
Asher, and Naphtali, two each; Benjamin, the youngest,
three. This is a total of thirty-eight as against seventeen
to Judah and nineteen to Joseph, a total of thirty-six.
So much for the wordage—that is, for the volume of attention. The quality varied even more.

His mind was fixed on the Messianic heritage; and so
with the seven sons who were younger than Judah and

353

did not come into the problem (Joseph, the eighth in that group, stands apart, of course) he was partly perfunctory, partly absent-minded.

> *"Gad, a troop shall troop upon him,*
> *But he shall troop upon them";*

and:

> *"As for Asher, his bread shall be fat,*
> *And he shall yield royal dainties";*

and:

> *"Naphtali is a hind let loose,*
> *He giveth goodly words."*

That is all! Zebulun he merely describes in prophecy, without the show of benediction:

> *"Zebulun shall dwell at the shore of the sea,*
> *And he shall be a shore for ships,*
> *And his flank shall be upon Zidon."*

He got rid of Benjamin with a conventional Esau offering:

> *"Benjamin is a wolf that raveneth;*
> *In the morning he devoureth the prey,*
> *And at even he divideth the spoil."*

Issachar receives longer mention, but tired and sad, though kindly:

> *"Issachar is a large-boned ass,*
> *Couching down between the sheepfolds.*
> *For he saw a resting-place that it was good,*

*And the land that it was pleasant;*
*And he bowed his shoulder to bear,*
*And became a servant under task-work."*

Dan comes off best among the seven outsiders:

*"Dan shall be judge of his people,*
*As one of the tribes of Israel.*
*Dan shall be a serpent in the way,*
*A horned snake in the path,*
*That biteth the horse's heels,*
*So that his rider falleth backward."*

But this effort on Dan's behalf seems to have exhausted
Jacob, for an interpolated phrase, a gasp, occurs here:

*"I wait for Thy salvation, O Lord."*

And thus the seven outsiders are disposed of, each in
his turn, with Jacob's mind obviously elsewhere. It was
with the five insiders, the three who were rejected, the
one that was chosen, and the one that the father loved
more than all the others.

Reuben's claim as the eldest had been the strongest,
but he had forfeited it long ago. Shortly after Rachel's
death "Reuben went and lay with Bilhah, his father's
concubine; and Israel heard of it." It is safe to assume
that this was one of Joseph's "reports." After these many
years Jacob refers to the incident, without bitterness,
almost mitigating it, but indicating and explaining its
consequences:

*"Reuben, thou art my first-born,*
*My might, and the first-fruits of my strength;*

355

*The excellency of dignity, and the excellency of*
  *power.*
*Unstable as water, have not thou the excellency;*
*Because thou wentest up to thy father's bed;*
*Then defiledst thou it—he went up to my couch."*

We have here a note of plaintiveness rather than of indignation. Perhaps if Reuben had not sinned with Bilhah, thereby forfeiting the heritage and opening up the question of the succession, Jacob would never have entertained the hope that he would be allowed to bestow it on Joseph, and he would have been spared much heartache. "Have not thou the excellency." It is an explanation as much as a command. Very different is the furious outbreak against the next in line, the second and third brothers. Their disqualifying sin was older even than Reuben's, but in Jacob's eyes it was a much more terrible one. Treacherously, after a wrong to their sister Dinah had been righted by an agreement, these two, Simeon and Levi, fell on the city of Shechem, and sacked it; they slew all the males, and led away captive the women and children. An "odious" deed Jacob had called it then, and on his deathbed he roused himself to fury over it:

*"Simeon and Levi are brethren;*
*Weapons of violence their kinship.*
*Let my soul not come into their council;*
*Unto their assembly let my glory not be united;*
*For in their anger they slew men,*
*And in their self-will they houghed oxen.*
*Cursed be their anger, for it was fierce,*

356

*And their wrath, for it was cruel;*
*I will divide them in Jacob,*
*And scatter them in Israel."*

So we have accounted for ten of the sons: seven who
were never under consideration for the blessing, three
who lost their rights, and there remain only two contestants. Actually there is only one, and Jacob knows it;
the contest is not between the men, but between his feelings. Over Judah and Joseph their father pours, in brilliant pronouncement after pronouncement, all the
strength of his spirit. To one not familiar with the ultimate issue it is difficult to choose between the two benedictions—for these were benedictions in the full though
only the earthly sense of the word. But on reflection it
would seem—I am still speaking of the uninformed bystander—that Joseph's was the better. He has nineteen
pronouncements against Judah's seventeen; and the language is richer, the imagery more urgently abundant:

*"Joseph is a fruitful vine,*
*A fruitful vine by a fountain.*
*Its branches run over the wall.*
*The archers have dealt bitterly with him,*
*And shot at him, and hated him;*
*But his bow stood firm,*
*And the arms of his hands were made supple,*
*By the hands of the Mighty One of Jacob,*
*From thence, from the Shepherd, the Stone of*
    *Israel,*
*Even by the God of thy father, who shall help thee,*
*And by the Almighty, who shall bless thee,*

357

*With blessings of heaven above,*
*Blessings of the deep that coucheth beneath,*
*Blessings of the breasts, and of the womb.*
*The blessings of thy father*
*Are mighty beyond the blessings of my progenitors*
*Unto the utmost bound of the everlasting hills;*
*They shall be on the head of Joseph,*
*And on the crown of the head of the prince among*
*    his brethren."*

It is magnificent, and only the initiate will perceive at once that the distinguishing phrase is not there. Excepting for that it is superior to the benediction of Judah:

*"Judah, thee shall thy brethren praise;*
*Thy hand shall be on the neck of thine enemies;*
*Thy father's sons shall bow down before thee.*
*Judah is a lion's whelp;*
*From the prey, my son, thou art gone up.*
*He stooped down, he couched as a lion,*
*And as a lioness; who shall rouse him up?*
*The sceptre shall not depart from Judah,*
*Nor the ruler's staff from between his feet,*
*As long as men come to Shiloh:*
*And unto him shall the obedience of the peoples be.*
*Binding his foal unto the vine,*
*And his ass's colt unto the choice vine;*
*He washeth his garments in wine,*
*And his vesture in the blood of grapes;*
*His eyes shall be red with wine,*
*And his teeth white with milk."*

There are contradictions in the two benedictions. To Judah, Jacob says: "Thy father's sons shall bow down before thee," while he calls Joseph "the prince among his brethren." But we have already seen that the worldly side of the patriarchal benedictions was not absolute; we remember that Isaac had given Jacob dominion over his brother Esau, and then had retracted it, promising Esau: "Thou shalt shake his yoke from off thy neck." Only one thing mattered here in the absolute sense, and that was the Messiah heritage. There it was in the three pronouncements:

> *"The sceptre shall not depart from Judah,*
> *Nor the ruler's staff from between his feet,*
> *As long as men come to Shiloh. . . ."*

For Shiloh is the place of the sanctuary, the earthly symbol of the divine spirit. As long as men come to Shiloh, as long as men turn to the spirit, a descendant of Judah's shall be pre-eminent; therefore in the supreme moment of the universal turning, the Messiah's moment, it shall be proclaimed that its central figure must be credited to Jacob's fourth son.

The millennia have diffused the distinction. Anyone who could trace his lineage back to Judah could also trace it back to another son of Jacob, and likewise, no doubt, to convert progenitors; and therefore the choice of Judah is far more important as a last-moment act of restitution on the part of Jacob than as a Last Day proclamation of genealogical fulfillment.

But till the last moment Jacob's heart was with his

best-beloved son, to whom he tried to make up, when he denied him the Messiah-lineage, with a dazzling abundance of the worldly. He had known for a long time, perhaps he had known all along, like Isaac, that this would be the situation in the final accounting. Shortly before the deathbed announcement he had done an astounding thing for Joseph, conferring on him a privilege withheld from all the others. He had blessed, separately and specially, Joseph's two boys, Ephraim and Manasseh, singling them out from scores of grandchildren. He had said then to Joseph: "Behold, I die; but God will be with you, and bring you back to the land of your fathers." Thereby he meant, of course, the entire folk. And he added: "Moreover I have given thee one portion above thy brethren." It may be that Joseph understood then; he may have accepted the consolation prize, and it may have helped him to withstand the shock of the rejection. And on the other hand it may have added to the fear of the brothers, who came to him shortly thereafter, reporting his father's command that he forgive them their ancient sin against him.

### XI

Of all the Traditions the one I find it hardest to swallow is Joseph's accepted title, unique among the People of the Book, of *ha-Tzaddik*, which is an amalgam of the Just One, the Righteous One, and the Saintly One. The Rescuer, the Philanthropist, or, in Mann's word, the Provider, yes. But how the *Tzaddik*? And yet the Tradition neither ignores nor condones Joseph's defects, even

360

in the matters I have discussed. Not, either, that a *Tzaddik* must be without defects, but, as I see it, they cannot be the kind that abounded in Joseph. I am afraid he has earned the title by a single act of self-abnegation, his refusal of Potiphar's wife. Ignoring all the dubious circumstances, and assuming that it was the decent thing to do, what was there about it to overshadow the rest of his life? And how much temptation was there for him to overcome? It is not told or implied of him that he was greatly drawn to women. Abraham his great-grandfather voiced his admiration of Sarah's beauty; we are explicitly informed that his grandfather Isaac loved Rebekah, and his father's love for Rachel has become a byword. Joseph the vizier married the daughter of the Egyptian priest Poti-Phera and had two sons by her, and that is all we know. We are left with the impression of a *mariage de convenance.*

In all these thing I have said about Joseph I invite the charge of belittlement and ingratitude. It may be true that I labor under the discomfort of the beneficiary, but let us consider whether that discomfort is not, in its way, a just protest against the outrageous rewards collected by the worldly benefactor. He saves lives with a minimum of sacrifice, and accumulates public credit in huge and disproportionate quantities—not to mention his own pleasing private suspicion that his example shames that of the impractical saint. The protest goes deeper: why should one man be in a position to save a life for a dime, and another at death's door for lack of it? What an ironical saying that is: "It is more blessed to give than to receive"! Really! I have yet to meet a panhandler who needs moral suasion to change places with a philanthropic millionaire.

"Ah yes," I hear. "The real meaning is that it is more blessed to sacrifice than to acquire." That is profoundly true. But what sacrifice, exactly, does the philanthropist millionaire make? What did Joseph sacrifice in the rescue of his brothers and his intervention for them in Egypt? Did he not, in fact, acquire great public credit with no loss of capital, and exact from his brothers the gratification of his ancient, deep-rooted passion for demonstrative dominion? If he had only sacrificed this passion, if philanthropists would only sacrifice their publicity, we should have a different world.

I do not wish to close on an unseemly note of censoriousness. If I had not felt myself compelled to protest against the general misunderstanding, the Tradition's as well as Thomas Mann's, of the meaning of Joseph, I should have sounded another note. There is so much to marvel at in his career, and I have tried to do justice, though briefly, to his masterly reorganization of the Egyptian Empire. The Egyptians forgot about it. We read how, in the course of time: "There arose a new king over Egypt who knew not Joseph." This too must be understood. It is inconceivable that within two centuries after these tremendous reconstructions an Egyptian prince should not have heard of the man who brought them about. The meaning is double: first as refusal to acknowledge, as when a father says to a son: "I no longer know you"; second as trained ignorance: "He knew him not as Joseph." The name and identity were "suppressed." It was as impossible for the Egyptians of

362

that time to acknowledge their indebtedness to Joseph the son of Israel as it was for the Germans of Nazi days to acknowledge theirs to Walther Rathenau the Jew. An even better example is Heine. In Nazi days young Germans sailing past the Lorelei rock on the Rhine could not help singing Heine's song, which had become an irremovable part of their country's folklore; so the song was credited to Anonymous. The Egyptian king who knew not Joseph is now known only for that fact, and stands immortalized by his purposive ignorance, eternal symbol of a nation's ingratitude. If the descendants of Israel have exaggerated the merit of Joseph, it may also have been in protest, and it is at least the defect of a virtue. They may have erred on the one side, I on the other. But that Joseph is one of God's most wondrous works is not matter for debate.

## Acknowledgments

*The translation of the Bible which I have used through-out, with very minor changes, is that of the Jewish Publication Society of America. Nearly all the references to the Tradition will be found in Ginzberg's monumental The Legends of the Jews, more particularly in the magnificent volumes five and six of Notes. I would perhaps never have got down to this long-contemplated, frequently deferred labor of love if I had not been invited by The Eternal Light program to participate in two series of broadcasts, in the summers of 1953 and 1954, and if I had not on both occasions been placed "opposite" Mark Van Doren, whose gentle and penetrating insights into some of the Bible characters here discussed moved me to my own definite formulations.*

MAURICE SAMUEL

A NOTE ON THE TYPE

The text of this book was set on the Linotype in a type face called Baskerville. The face is a facsimile reproduction of types cast from molds made for John Baskerville (1706–75) from his designs. The punches for the revived Linotype Baskerville were cut under the supervision of the English printer George W. Jones.

John Baskerville's original face was one of the forerunners of the type style known as "modern face" to printers—a "modern" of the period A.D. 1800.

The book was composed, printed, and bound by The Plimpton Press, Norwood, Massachusetts. Paper manufactured by S. D. Warren Co., Boston. Typography and binding based on designs by W. A. Dwiggins.